Ninigret, Sachem of the Niantics and Narragansetts

D1500647

Ninigret, Sachem of the Niantics and Narragansetts

Diplomacy, War, and the Balance of Power
in Seventeenth-Century
New England and Indian Country

JULIE A. FISHER AND DAVID J. SILVERMAN

CORNELL UNIVERSITY PRESS

ITHACA AND LONDON

First published 2014 by Cornell University Press
First Printing, Cornell Paperbacks, 2017

Library of Congress Cataloging-in-Publication Data

Fisher, Julie A., 1979– author.
    Ninigret, sachem of the Niantics and Narragansetts : diplomacy, war, and the balance of power in seventeenth-century New England and Indian country / Julie A. Fisher and David J. Silverman.
        pages cm
    Includes bibliographical references and index.
    ISBN 978-0-8014-5000-6 (cloth : alk. paper)
    ISBN 978-1-5017-1361-3 (pbk. : alk. paper)
    1. Ninigret, approximately 1610–1677. 2. Niantic Indians—Kings and rulers—Biography. 3. Narragansett Indians—Politics and government—17th century. 4. New England—History—Colonial period, ca. 1600–1775.
    I. Silverman, David J., 1971– author. II. Title.

    E99.N6F57 2014
    974'.00497092—dc23
    [B]
                                        2013040957

Cornell University Press strives to use environmentally responsible suppliers and materials to the fullest extent possible in the publishing of its books. Such materials include vegetable-based, low-VOC inks and acid-free papers that are recycled, totally chlorine-free, or partly composed of nonwood fibers. For further information, visit our website at www.cornellpress.cornell.edu.

Contents

Preface

Picturing Ninigret

Historians who study New England Indians of the seventeenth century rarely know what their subjects looked like. To be sure, sometimes the historical record contains brief descriptions of prominent Indian men or ethnographic surveys of entire Indian populations, but that's about it. Not only had photography yet to be developed, but there is also a remarkable absence of drawings and paintings of individual Indians. One's imagination is left to fill in the blanks, which for historians can be a temptation to drift into fiction.

The only possible exception to this trend is the subject of this book—Ninigret, the sachem (or chief) of the Niantics and closely affiliated Narragansetts of what is now southwestern Rhode Island. For the better part of two hundred years, the only known portrait of a seventeenth-century New England Indian has been identified as Ninigret. But recently some art historians have questioned that judgment. The issue remains a puzzle, like so much of Ninigret's actual life.

The painting contains numerous contextual clues about the life and times of its subject— an earring, headband, and necklace interlaced with white and purple shellbeads; a deerskin or wool mantle draped over the subject's shoulder; a knife in hand, pointed downward; a background rich with images of the natural world. Certainly, one must be careful not to read this evidence too literally. After all, the original painter or those who restored the painting in future years might have tailored the appearance of the subject to appeal to a particular audience, which is to say, a paying one. Still, comparing the features of the portrait against what we know about coastal Indian life during the colonial period from the historical and archaeological records can be telling. Such

FIG. 1 American, Native American Sachem, ca. 1700. Oil on canvas, 84.1×76.5 cm. (33 ⅛×30 ⅛ in.). Gift of Mr. Robert Winthrop 48.246. Photography by Erik Gould, courtesy of the Museum of Art, Rhode Island School of Design, Providence.

cross-checking suggests, but only suggests, where the subject was from, when he lived, the nationality of his painter, and even who the subject might be. In other words, to identify this portrait is to deal in likelihoods, in probabilities, rather than in either absolute facts or flights of fancy.

Attempting to unravel the mystery of this portrait is analogous to re-searching and writing Ninigret's biography. Unlike the subjects of most biographies, Ninigret did not leave his own written records, as neither he nor any of his people practiced alphabetic literacy.[1] Most of the colonists who dealt with him and wrote about it were concerned with just a narrow slice of his affairs, mostly diplomacy and war, and even then lacked a dynamic understanding of how Indians conducted those activities. Colonial New Englanders who either lived in Indian communities or were formally married to Indian spouses were practically nonexistent, which meant that colonial governments had a relative lack of eyes and ears on the ground. Vast differences between English and Indian social structures and cultures obstructed colonists' views about how kinship, including the role of women, shaped Native politics. In fact, colonists showed hardly any interest at all in Ninigret's family life. We know that the Narragansetts in general associated the political and the sacred, but there are no accounts of how Ninigret's spiritual life affected his leadership. We do not even know when he was born. Clearly, then, the limits of the source materials do not permit a traditional biography in the sense of providing the story of a person's life, just as the Indian portrait does not permit an absolute identification of its subject.

However, the sources do afford enough evidence for a political biography—an account of the domestic and foreign policies, negotiations, and battles—of a major player in seventeenth-century New England. For instance, Ninigret appears frequently as a diplomatic actor in the records of the New England colonies, extending from his visits to colonial capitals, and from colonial ambassadors travelling to Ninigret's own seat. He also emerges in the correspondence of the Englishmen who conducted these proceedings and with whom he did business—men like John Winthrop Sr., the governor of Massachusetts; John Winthrop Jr., the founder of New London and governor of Connecticut; and Roger Williams, the founder of Rhode Island and an experienced Indian trader. Though discussions between Ninigret and English authorities almost always took place through interpreters—English and Indian—before being recorded by the English in a tangle of run-on sentences and phonetic spellings, these records sometimes manage to capture a semblance of Ninigret's voice. The English did not want to hear his critiques or threats, and yet those words made it onto the page. The sachem comes to us in metaphors that were characteristic of Indian speech and strange to Anglophone ears, and value judgments that could only have emerged from Indian perspectives. He also appears in the complaints of rival sachems who brought their grievances to the English. One must approach these records cautiously, for few colonists or Indians were interested in portraying Ninigret in a sympathetic light. Nevertheless, we proverbially throw out the baby with the bath water if we assume that every appearance by Ninigret in the English documentary record is fatally flawed. It is testimony to Ninigret's importance and resourcefulness that he managed to make his will known in colonial circles as much as he did.

Supplementing these documentary materials are Indian oral traditions and the archaeological record. Indian oral traditions recorded by colonists and later anthropologists often provide compelling details about Indian values, traditions, and worldviews, including the invisible world of spirits. The archaeological record, consisting of the remains of Indian habitations and cemeteries, adds critical details about Indian material culture, residential patterns, subsistence, trade networks, status systems, and rituals. It also provides an important indigenous counterpoint, difficult as it might be to interpret, to written records controlled by European colonists. No doubt, the historical and archaeological records are woefully incomplete, but they are rich with details that offer us glimpses of Ninigret's world, like clues to the identity of the subject of the portrait. The very process of trying to solve both puzzles, for all of its indeterminacy, reveals truths well worth telling.

•

The subject in the portrait is clearly an elite man and probably a sachem. Take, for instance, his ornamentation. His headband, earring, and necklace are decorated with white and purple wampum, beads that Indians manufactured from the whelk and quahog shells and then strung on lines of deer sinew or plant fiber for use as a status symbol. Roger Williams, who knew Ninigret well, observed that New England Indians "hang these strings . . . about their necks and wrists . . . about their middle and as a scarf about their shoulders and breasts. Yea the Princes [or sachems] make rich Caps and Aprons (or small breeches) of these beads thus curiously strung into many forms and figures: their black [purple] and white finely mixed together."[2] The subject of our portrait fits the description. Then there is the matter of this man being painted at all. As in most eras, average people rarely posed for portraits in the seventeenth century, a principle which applies severalfold to Indians given that portraiture was the colonists' tradition, not theirs. For an Indian to have his portrait painted would have required him to know a colonist of means who judged the Indian worthy of being commemorated.

Ninigret was an important man by practically any measure. Indeed, he was arguably the most influential Indian leader in southern New England during his era. His long life between roughly 1600 and 1676 saw him rise from sachem of the Niantics, a small Indian community in what is now southwestern Rhode Island, to become one of the major sachems of the much larger and more powerful Narragansetts, of whom the Niantics were a part. He also became a force regionally, through a combination of subjugating weaker Indian communities, alliance-building with other polities, and almost constant intrigue against neighboring sachems. Most of these initiatives took place against the backdrop of his rivalry with Uncas, sachem of the Mohegans, of what is now southeastern Connecticut. Their fight, which drew in confederates from a compass of sometimes two hundred miles, might be said to have been the dominant feature of Indian politics in southern New England during the mid seventeenth century.

Yet it would have been odd for the English to memorialize an enemy, and Ninigret definitely fell into that category. The United Colonies of New England, a military alliance of puritan Massachusetts, Plymouth, Connecticut, and New Haven, viewed the Narragansetts as the primary indigenous obstacle to colonial expansion and a buttress to the independence of heterodox Rhode Island. To hem in the Narragansetts, this confederation backed the very Indian sachems that Ninigret attempted to subdue, including Uncas, usually at the invitation of those leaders. Ninigret responded in kind. He offset the United Colonies' growing power by forging pacts with the formidable Mohawks (the easternmost nation of the Iroquois League, located on the Mohawk River just west of modern-day Albany), the Pocumtucks of the Connecticut River Valley, and the Dutch colony of New Netherland, leading the English to fear that Ninigret was plotting to wipe them out in 1653 and 1669. The United Colonies' repeated attempts to rein in Ninigret, and Ninigret's consistent refusal to heel, kept them on the edge of war throughout Ninigret's adult life. Ninigret also had a well-earned reputation for rebuffing Christian missionaries, who he wisely suspected of being a Trojan horse for English jurisdiction. English spokesmen denounced him as "insolent," "crafty," "proud and fierce," and one of the "professed enemies against praying to God."[3] Of all the region's Indian leaders, he was the one who gave them the most concern; he always seemed to be the most likely candidate to lead a general Indian uprising against the colonies.

Despite Ninigret's history of confrontation with the puritan colonies, legend holds that John Winthrop Jr., a major political figure in Connecticut, commissioned Ninigret's portrait. Supposedly Winthrop did this in appreciation for the sachem saving his life. This tradition does not say when, where, or from whom this rescue took place. Nor does the historical record make any note of this heroic act. Instead, the account was passed down through generations of the Winthrop family and only entered print in the nineteenth century, some 150 years after Ninigret's and Winthrop's deaths.[4] Given the lack of documentation relating to the painting and the clash between the Ninigret of this legend and the Ninigret of recorded history, and despite the seeming authority of the Winthrop account, the question cannot be escaped: just who is this in the portrait?

There is some circumstantial evidence to support the Winthrop tradition. Ninigret might have been at odds with United Colonies throughout his lifetime, but he did enjoy a close relationship with Winthrop characterized by visiting, intelligence sharing, gifting, mutual aid, and a shared disdain for Uncas. The story goes that Winthrop Jr. commissioned the portrait when Ninigret was visiting Boston in the summer of 1647, and in fact, Ninigret was in that place at that time to meet with the commissioners of the United Colonies. Winthrop was also there, having accompanied Ninigret to Boston at the sachem's request.[5] Moreover, Winthrop, a scientist with correspondents throughout the Atlantic interested in Indian life, might have wanted a portrait of Ninigret as part of his collection of American natural science specimens.[6] In these respects, legend and history seem to align.

There are also compelling visual clues that the man in this portrait dates from the 1640s or thereabout. In addition to the wampum jewelry so common to sachems of that era, the subject's dress is decidedly of coastal New England Indians in the mid seventeenth century. His breechcloth appears to have been made of wool, which was the most important object that Indians obtained from the English in terms of value and volume.[7] Massachusetts colonist William Wood explained that Indians with access to the trade would use this material "to cover that which modesty commands to be hid, which is but a piece of cloth a yard and a half long, put between their groinings, tied with a snake's skin about their middles, one end hanging down with a flap before, the other like a tail behind."[8] With the naked eye, it is harder to discern whether the mantle worn over the subject's shoulder is made of deerskin or wool. In what is believed to be the original painting, held by the Rhode Island School of Design, the mantle is colored brown, suggesting that it was made of deerskin, like the leggings and moccasins. Yet at some point that painting was restored and the color might have been altered. An oil copy of the portrait, painted by Charles Osgood in the 1830s and now hanging at the Massachusetts Historical Society, depicts a green mantle, possibly of wool.[9] Ironically, it might resemble the original's colors more closely than the restored (and thus altered) original. Williams and other colonial sources said that New England Indians "all generally prize a Mantle of English or Dutch cloth before their own wearing of skins and furs because they are warm enough and lighter"; Indians were especially fond of cloth mantles of a "sad [meaning deep] color without any whitish hairs."[10]

The objects of indigenous manufacture worn by the portrait's subject also point to a date from the early to mid seventeenth century. By that time, coastal Indians widely used metal tools obtained through colonial trade. For instance, they would have bored the holes of the subject's wampum beads with drills made of steel, which were a vast improvement over stone. They would have cut the leather for his moccasins and leggings using iron trade knives or scissors. The blade of the dagger in his right hand would have been of iron instead of flint. What this portrait shows, then, is an example of Indians in the process of adopting colonial textiles and tools to make their own material and artistic lives more vibrant. The Indian in this portrait is not colonized, subjugated, converted, or conquered. He draws on colonialism as it suits him. That description is quite fitting of Ninigret.

If this portrait dated from the late seventeenth or early eighteenth centuries, the subject probably would have appeared in a trade shirt with long sleeves and flaps hanging in front and behind down to his thighs, as was the fashion by that time. As a sachem, he also might very well have donned a wool mantle, a red or blue sleeved tailored coat, and an English hat, particularly in a diplomatic setting where European clothing symbolized alliance and status.[11] These temporal clues are only that—clues, not hard evidence. After all, there is always some variability within the fashion trends of a particular era and occasionally the subjects or painters of a portrait could very well have used staged dress and decoration to evoke an earlier time than the one in which they lived. Nevertheless, if realism was the goal of the painter and subject, there is a strong possibility that this subject posed in the mid seventeenth century and, if so, that this portrait is actually Ninigret.

Contrary cases can also be made. The subject is clearly a young man, yet by 1647 Ninigret was at least in his mid to late 40s. The ornate landscape of the background is more characteristic of English portraits from the late seventeenth and early eighteenth centuries than the early seventeenth century; this fact has led some art historians to date the portrait at circa 1681, five years after Ninigret's death. Dutch portraits from the mid seventeenth century sometimes contain this feature, and while it was certainly possible for a Dutch painter from New Netherland (of whom there were a couple) to have been in Boston in the 1640s, there is no documentation of such a visit. Based on these questions and skepticism that Ninigret is the subject, recent scholarship has posited that the subject is Ninigret's son, Ninigret II, who would been a young man in the 1680s, though he was a minor political figure. Other art historians have wondered whether the subject was instead the Pequot sachem Robin Cassacinamon or his son and namesake. Both of these men, though they each fell well short of Ninigret I's prominence, were especially close with the Winthrops during the mid to late seventeenth century. To add yet another obstacle to identifying the portrait, art historians are unsure whether the "original" in the Rhode Island School of Design Museum is actually an original or a nineteenth-century copy. If it is a copy, the question arises of what details, if any, were added.[12]

Scholars who rely on the Winthrop tradition to interpret the portrait must confront the confounding factor of the American romantic tradition in telling Indian history. The legend of Ninigret saving Winthrop's life became public only in the early to mid nineteenth century at the same time that white Americans began lionizing other Indians who seemed to consent to colonization. Indians celebrated by white Americans include Pocahontas, who supposedly saved John Smith from execution, married an Englishman, and then adopted Christianity and civility; Squanto, who brokered peace between the English of Plymouth and the surrounding Wampanoags, taught the English how to feed themselves by fertilizing their corn plants with alewives, and set the stage for the so-called "first Thanksgiving"; and Sacagawea who guided and interpreted for the Lewis and Clark expedition, the critical step in the expansion of the United States to the Pacific. The Ninigret who attacked English protectorates and lined up Indian allies to fend off the United Colonies does not fit this mold. This would seem to make him an unlikely subject of a unique nineteenth-century painting or a nineteenth-century copy of a seventeenth-century work. At the same time, a nineteenth-century painter who did his historical homework might also have discovered that Ninigret, though generally defiant of the English, sometimes knew when to accommodate.

Ninigret also bucks the romantic stereotype of the tragic Indian leader who goes down in defeat leading his people in a futile resistance against white expansion. The great irony of Ninigret's life is that he and his Niantics did not take up arms against the English in King Philip's War of 1675–76, the clash which finally determined the balance of power between Indians and colonists in southern New England, even though the rest of the Narragansetts fought on the opposite side.[13] Rather, Ninigret provided the English with grudging support during the war. His uneasy alliance with the English should rank as one of the conflict's key features. If Ninigret had joined other Indians against the English, he would have instantly become one of the Indians' war leaders by virtue of his lengthy record of opposition to English colonialism. Rhode Island would have suffered even greater bloodshed and property loss than it did at enemy hands, and eastern Connecticut, which went relatively unscathed, would have become a battle zone. In turn, the threat of the Niantics would have kept the Pequots and Mohegans, Connecticut's Indian allies, from performing their invaluable service during the war as warriors, guides, and trackers. The Niantics would have brought hundreds of warriors into the ranks of Indians fighting the English. Suffice it to say, it would have been a much different affair if Ninigret had decided to battle the English in what some English contemporaries called "the Narragansett War."

We might never know definitively whether this portrait is Ninigret, but, clearly, weighing the question in light of what we do know opens up windows into the life and times of a critically important man to the history of seventeenth-century New England. Moreover, the challenge of interpreting this portrait mirrors that of telling the story of Ninigret through the sometimes fraught documentary and archaeological records. Both stories are worth telling despite the obstacles, for to give up just because the evidence is incomplete, uncertain, or biased is to allow history to remain a story of the victors. Such resignation would be akin to painter Charles Osgood leaving our mysterious Indian subject out of the restored portrait even though he was originally there, filling most of the frame.

Ignoring Indians in our accounts of the colonial era or relegating them to mere bit players simply will not do. Only in the last few decades have scholars begun to grasp that Indians were *most of the people* in colonial America, that they experienced a *greater amount of change* than most colonists, and that they were among the *prime movers of change*. Numbers of people, degrees of change, and agents of change are among the basic measures of historical significance. As such, we need to move Indians from the periphery to the center of our histories of colonial America. We need to think of colonial America as consisting not just of colonists and colonies, but of Indians grappling with the forces of *colonialism*, sometimes in contexts in which colonists were scarce or even nonexistent. Those forces of colonialism included devastating epidemic diseases, new trade goods and technologies, unprecedented incentives for intertribal rivalry, colonial pressure on Indian land and jurisdiction, environmental change, Christian missionaries, and of course, war. At the same time, we need to consider how Indians harnessed colonists to *their* agendas and how Indian power affected colonial decisions. Stories like Ninigret's clarify how the abstract forces of colonialism shaped Indian lives, and of how Indians shaped colonialism. Indians are fundamental to any understanding of colonial North America.[14]

However, Ninigret has been widely overlooked in our histories of seventeenth-century New England, perhaps because he is such a difficult man to categorize. He remained, first and foremost, sachem of the small Niantic community. But during the prime of his career he was also one of the larger Narragansetts' principal leaders. Although the English considered Ninigret to be a dire threat throughout most of his political life, he was an ally (albeit a reluctant one) during their greatest crisis in King Philip's War. He was at the center of multiple war scares, yet none of those supposed plots ever materialized. At one time he could be found brandishing a gun in the face of Thomas Stanton, an English interpreter to the Indians, while only years later he would proclaim Stanton one of his most trusted friends. Ninigret, in short, was a flexible, resourceful leader whose strategies changed as he navigated his turbulent era. It might, in fact, have been easier to capture him in portraiture than to pin down his politics.

Fortunately, in our attempt to understand Ninigret we have the writings of Roger Williams. Though born in the crowded streets of Smithfield, England, Williams spent the majority of his adult life in Narragansett country in contact and conversation with the Narragansetts, including Ninigret.[15] A young Williams arrived in Massachusetts in 1631 seemingly destined to become one the colony's leading ministers, but by 1635 puritan officials banished him for his unorthodox views, including his conviction that Indian populations held legal title to their land. Rather than suffer deportation back to England, Williams fled to Narragansett Bay, where the sachems Miantonomi and Canonicus made him a gift of land contingent on his ongoing friendship. In turn, he spent much of the rest of his life in service to the Narragansetts as a trader, interpreter, scribe, and advisor.[16] Tellingly, Narragansett leaders often refused to meet with English officials unless Williams was there to assist them. Their own actions indicate that no Englishmen knew the Narragansetts better than Williams.

Certainly no Englishman wrote more about them. In addition to Williams's lengthy correspondence about the Narragansetts, in 1643 he published, as he titled it, A Key into the Language of America, which was at once a Narragansett-English dictionary, a Narragansett-English phrase book, and a series of cultural observations put to prose. With chapters dedicated to thirty-two aspects of Narragansett life, from childhood to burial, there is no greater source of information about the Narragansett language or Narragansett culture in the seventeenth century, though Williams's knowledge cannot be considered comprehensive or reflective of a Narragansett perspective.[17] Aware of these limits, we have quoted liberally from this source, including incorporating Narragansett phrases into many subtitles, to convey a sense of Ninigret's world.

Williams believed that providing his readers with some command of the Narragansett language, which was part of the broad Algonquian language family, would facilitate English relations with Indians across North America, particularly for missionary work. As he explained, "A little *Key* may open a Box, where lies a bunch of *Keys* . . . a man may, by this help, converse with thousands of Natives all over the Country: and by such converse it may please the Father of Mercies to spread civility (and in his own most holy season) Christianity; for one Candle will light ten thousand."[18] We draw extensively on Williams's writings as a historical source and inspiration for our interpretation of Ninigret's life. Just as Williams viewed the Narragansett language as the key into the language of America, we see Ninigret as a key into the balance of power in seventeenth-century New England.

If there was a unifying theme to Ninigret's career it was that he wanted to establish himself as a principal leader in intertribal affairs and that he wanted the English to stay out of this business. He might have been surrounded by colonial settlement, but his focus was indigenous politics, ranging from day-to-day Niantic governance to the cutthroat rivalries among sachems. To achieve his goals, he waged violent campaigns against neighboring Mohegans, Pequots, Montauketts, Nipmucks, and Wampanoags, and pursued alliances with distant indigenous powers. To the extent that Ninigret dealt with colonists, it was largely to trade for their goods or to negotiate an end to their interference in his diplomacy with other Indians.

•

Any discussion of Ninigret's politics is necessarily incomplete and speculative at critical points, indeed, at most points. Rather than avoid questions about Ninigret's uncertain motivations, our approach has been to propose his range of choices and suggest his thinking at moments of decision. Thus we have peppered our narrative with qualifiers: perhaps, might have been, probably, in all likelihood, and so on. We have done so in the interest of transparency. To have done otherwise would have required either making unsubstantiated statements or neglecting the story of Ninigret altogether. Ignoring Ninigret because his story is incomplete would be as misleading as asserting that we know all there is to know about him, for the history of colonial New England cannot be understood without him in it.[19]

To help readers trace how we have made our judgments, chapters 1 and 2 provide the cultural, social, and political background to the start of Ninigret's political career. Ninigret appears only intermittently in these chapters, reflective of his scant presence in the written record before the mid to late 1630s. Though Ninigret was not bound by the traditions of his society, understanding the context in which he lived makes his sometimes opaque decisions—and ours as authors—clearer.

This much is certain: Ninigret was central to the politics of seventeenth-century New England and considering his role brings that history into new focus. Ninigret's experience demonstrates the fragility of the forty-year peace between New England colonists and Indians from the Pequot War of 1636–37 to King Philip's War of 1675–76, a period marked by one war scare after another. It captures the multipolar character of the era's politics, involving not monolithic groups of Indians and colonists, or even of individual tribes and colonies, but shifting coalitions of tribes and colonies that often pit Indians against Indians and colonists against colonists, as one emergency bled into another. Ninigret's story also shows how deeply personal relationships and emotions—friendship, kinship, trust, and hate—shaped the politics of this time and place, as his bonds and enmities tended to revolve not around particular polities but individuals. Correspondingly, Ninigret's career illustrates the life cycle of a sachem, from a young man who needed to be at the center of crises to prove his mettle, to that of an old man interested in consolidating his gains and passing them on. Finally, treating Ninigret forces a reconsideration of King Philip's War. It highlights not only the Indians who took up arms against the English or even those who fought on their side, but those who maneuvered between these poles, preferring neutrality but settling for a strained alliance. Such Indians included Ninigret's Niantics, the Wampanoags of Cape Cod and Martha's Vineyard, and many of the Christian Indians of Massachusetts. If they had fought wholeheartedly against the English, Indian forces might have rolled back colonial settlement to the coasts of Massachusetts Bay, wiping out the English in Connecticut, Rhode Island, Cape Cod, Martha's Vineyard, Nantucket, and the Massachusetts interior. At the same time, if they had fought alongside the English without reserve, the English would have been able to claim victory far sooner. They and Ninigret had choices, however circumscribed, which raises another crucial point about the war: it was not inevitable, it did not have to happen. Forty years of history predicted that the great war would begin not with Philip, the sachem of the Pokanoket Wampanoags, but with Ninigret. The fact that it did not is a question worth exploring.

•

As a final remark, we would like to note that we have modernized the spelling and punctuation of quotations from seventeenth-century sources. Our purpose is to allow readers unfamiliar with the prose of that era to focus on other challenges, such as the meaning of the words and the rich variety of Indian names that constituted Ninigret's soundscape. For the same reason, we have standardized Indian proper names and place names, including Ninigret's own, which the English variously recorded as Ninigret, Ninicraft, and Niniglad, among several variations. We have included a glossary of the Indian (and several English) names that appear in this book to help readers stay on course. We encourage readers to make the effort to sound out such place names as Weekapaug, Misquamicut, Cocumscussoc, or Pettaquamscutt. What we too casually call New England was (and is) a region full of Indian place names. Respecting those names is a small step toward entering that region's history.

We use the term *Indian* rather than *Native American* or *Amerindian* because most (albeit not all) of the indigenous people we know prefer it. We use the terms *tribe* and *nation* interchangeably, aware that it is problematic to apply to such labels to what were often fluid bodies. We hope this history will illustrate what those groups meant in practice.

Our maps reflect the tension between trying to reflect Ninigret's geographical world without disorienting readers. Thus we have prominently featured indigenous community names and only the names of colonial places of importance to Ninigret. At the same time, we have included modern state lines for readers unfamiliar with the rivers and bays that constituted the major sociopolitical boundaries in seventeenth-century New England. Readers should not assume that these lines existed in the seventeenth century. Rather those lines were negotiated and contested between and among Englishmen and Indians, including Ninigret.

A Chronology of Key Events
in the Life of Ninigret

ca. 1600:	Ninigret born.
1602–19:	Increased pace of English, French, and Dutch exploration of the southern New England coast.
1608:	French found Québec.
1616–19:	An epidemic decimates the Wampanoag and Massachusett Indians east of Narragansett Bay.
1620:	English found Plymouth Colony.
1625:	Dutch found New Amsterdam.
1629:	English found Massachusetts Bay Colony.
1633:	Dutch establish House of Good Hope on the Connecticut River.
1634:	Murder of John Stone and his crew by Pequots and/or Western Niantics.
1634 35:	English begin settling the towns of Wethersfield, Hartford, and Windsor on the Connecticut River.
Winter 1635–36:	Narragansetts take in Roger Williams.
1636:	Manisees kill John Oldham and his crew.
1636–37:	Pequot War.

1638:	Treaty of Hartford. English found colony of New Haven and the town of Portsmouth, Rhode Island.
1639:	Skirmish at Pawcatuck pitting the Niantics, Pequots, and Narragansetts against the English and Mohegans. Founding of Newport, Rhode Island.
1640–42:	Rumor of the Narragansett sachem, Miantonomi, organizing a multitribal strike against the English and Dutch.
1643:	Founding of the United Colonies of New England, a military alliance of Massachusetts, Plymouth, Connecticut, and New Haven. Uncas executes Miantonomi.
1644:	Narragansetts subjugate themselves to the crown. John Winthrop Jr. receives grant from Massachusetts to Nameag in Pequot country.
ca. 1645:	Jannemo changes his name to Ninigret.
1645:	Narragansetts launch large-scale assault on Uncas. Pessacus commits the Narragansett to pay the United Colonies an indemnity in wampum.
1647:	Death of Canonicus. Ninigret in Boston to negotiate with commissioners of the United Colonies.
1648:	Aborted Narragansett-Pocumtuck-Mohawk strike against Uncas.
1649:	Beheading of Charles I.
1650:	United Colonies send expedition under Humphrey Atherton against the Narragansetts.
1653:	Rumors that Ninigret is organizing an alliance of Indian tribes and the Dutch against the United Colonies.
1653–54:	Ninigret launches raids against Long Island Indians.

1654:	United Colonies send expedition under Simon Willard against Ninigret. United Colonies authorize the Pequots to organize independently at Nameag and Noank under Robin Cassacinamon and at Pawcatuck and Weekapaug under Harmon Garrett.
1657–59:	Heightened Narragansett attacks on Mohegans.
1660:	Restoration of Charles II. Atherton mortgage.
1662:	Metacom (or Philip) becomes primary Wampanoag sachem. First rumors of Wampanoags plotting against the English. Connecticut obtains royal charter.
1664:	English conquer New Netherland and found the colony of New York. Mohawks shatter Pocumtucks.
1665:	Royal commissioners overturn Atherton mortgage.
1667:	Second rumor of Wampanoags under Philip plotting against the English.
1668:	Eight Nipmuck sachems submit to Massachusetts and welcome English missionaries.
1669:	Heightened intertribal diplomacy and English fear of a multitribal plot led by Ninigret.
1671:	Third rumor of Wampanoags under Philip plotting against the English.
1672:	Moweam murder case.
1675–76:	King Philip's War
June 1675:	Narragansetts promise not to aid Philip and to hand over Wampanoag refugees. Narragansett warriors make threatening march on Warwick.
September 1675:	Ninigret unveils peace plan to Thomas Stanton.

October 1675:	Narragansetts sign another peace treaty with the English.
December 1675:	English invade Narragansett country. Great Swamp Massacre.
February 1676:	Mohawks attack Philip's winter camp.
April 1676:	Execution of Canonchet.
August 1676:	Philip killed.
Fall 1676:	Ninigret dies. Succeeded by daughter Weunquesh.

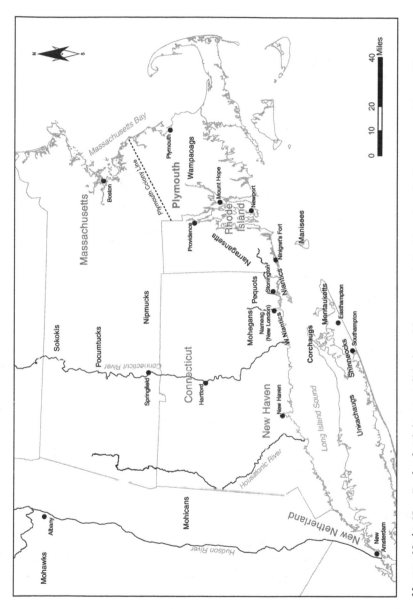

MAP 1 Native New England. Ninigret's political world was crowded with various Indian communities and European colonies over a range of some two hundred miles, from the coasts of Long Island Sound to the Mohawk River Valley of Iroquoia.

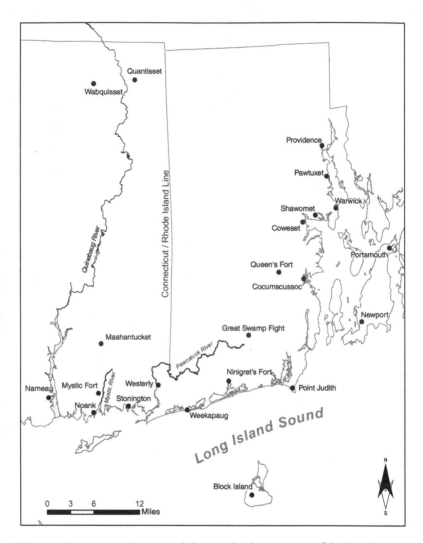

MAP 2   Narragansett Country. Ninigret's Niantics were part of the broader Narragansett community centered in present-day Rhode Island. Their landscape of beaches, bays, rivers, ponds, estuaries, islands, and woods gave them access to a rich variety of foods and connected them, via water, to friends and rivals throughout Long Island Sound and southern New England.

Ninigret, Sachem of the Niantics and Narragansetts

CHAPTER 1

Being and Becoming a Sachem

When Ninigret signed colonial documents, he left a war club as his mark, with the obvious intent of sending a message. At its most basic, this symbol warned colonists that Ninigret stood ever ready to defend his interests. More subtly, it also spoke to the central concern in his life: his responsibilities as sachem. Ninigret's qualifications for leadership must have included proving himself in battle, apparently while wielding a club. Thereafter, he fulfilled his role as sachem by leading his warriors against foreign enemies and using this weapon to "brain" the heads of egregious domestic criminals condemned to execution.[1] Ninigret's mark also might have referred to his people's commercial and diplomatic connections with the fearsome Five Nations Iroquois, particularly the Mohawks residing some two hundred miles to the northwest of Narragansett country. In exchange for wampum, the Mohawks traded the Narragansetts, weapons described as "hammers made of stone."[2] Ninigret appears to have modeled his signature on these clubs, perhaps because the weapons and the Narragansetts' alliance with the people who created them were sources of power for him. We cannot know for certain why Ninigret chose a war club as his autograph, but the possibilities speak to the dynamics of his political life.[3]

Just because Ninigret's world is not completely accessible to us is not to say that it has to remain completely closed. It is indeed possible to use historical and archaeological records, however incomplete or skewed, to trace the outlines of Ninigret's experiences with his family, local community, tribe, and region. If his personality is lost to us, we nevertheless can grasp his roles as a son, brother, husband, father, uncle, warrior, and most importantly, sachem. Living in an oral society, Ninigret did not leave behind a diary or correspondence, so we cannot get inside his head, yet we can situate him in the context of his people's values, beliefs,

FIG. 2   Ninigret's Mark. Westerly Town Records, September 23, 1663, Westerly, Rhode Island. Photo by Julie A. Fisher; photo editing by Dennis Fisher.

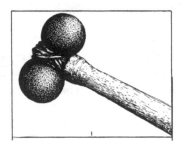

FIG. 3   Stone War Club. Ninigret and the Narragansetts obtained stone war clubs like this one from Mohawks and other nations of the Iroquois League. These clubs were potent as weapons and as symbols of the Narragansett-Iroquois alliance. Perhaps for these reasons, Ninigret used a stone war club as his signature. From *Bulletin of the Massachusetts Archaeological Society* 12 (1951): 34. Reproduced here with the permission of the Massachusetts Archaeological Society.

and practices. Exploring what we do know about the fundamentals of his life provides an essential backdrop to his political activities that did enter the historical record. Those activities are the foundation of this story.

Nickquénum. I am going home.
Family, Home Life, and Coming of Age

There was nothing as central to Ninigret's life as family, but we lack many basic details about which family members meant the most to him.

For instance, it is all but certain that Ninigret grew up under the supervision of his mother and aunts and in the company of siblings and cousins of several degrees. Yet we do not know whether his father lived with him and whether he lived among his mother's or father's extended kin or both, for anthropologists remain unsure whether the Narragansetts, in particular, and southern New England Indians, in general, were matrilocal or patrilocal. The office of sachem must have devolved on Ninigret by virtue of his father's and mother's elite status, yet no one recorded their names. Likewise, it is a mystery whether Ninigret belonged to a particular clan of the Niantics and, if so, whether he inherited that membership through his father or mother. For that matter, scholars question whether southern New England Indians even organized themselves into clans.[4]

If Ninigret spent his boyhood living with his sachem father, his house would have been a very busy place. A sachem's *wétu* (or wigwam) was his political headquarters, marked by a constant stream of well-wishers, ambassadors, couriers, petitioners, and complainants. Some of these visitors would have sat for a meal or spent the night, for it was the responsibility of a sachem and his wives to provide hospitality to political dignitaries. The wétu also would have hosted councils, some involving just a few men, others involving dozens. Williams observed that when there was an emergency, messengers would run from settlement to settlement, and then "coming within a mile or two of the court, or chief house, he hellos often, and they that hear answer him, until by mutual helloing and answering he is brought to the place of audience, where by this means is gathered a great confluence of people to entertain the news."[5] In all of these respects, and doubtless others, to live in a sachem's house was to know hustle and bustle.

In other regards, Ninigret's domestic life would have resembled that of Indian commoners. His home, like those of his neighbors, was either a round or oval wétu or, in the event that he lived with his sachem father, perhaps a spacious longhouse. The frame was constructed of poles, with one end secured in the ground and then bent over and tied at the top to poles anchored at the opposite end of the structure. Mats or strips of bark made up the outer walls depending on the season, while the interior walls were lined with mats woven and elaborately embroidered by the women, which, Williams judged, "make as faire a show as hangings with us."[6] A bench for sleeping and sitting ran along the inner perimeter of the dwelling. The residents stored their food and tools in reed or leather bags hung from the rafters or in reed or woodsplint baskets or clay pots kept underneath the benches. One or more fire circles for heat and cooking occupied the middle of the dwelling. Even in the absence of visitors, Ninigret's brothers, sisters, aunts, uncles, and cousins would have filled his home with activity.[7]

Despite his elite status, Ninigret would have spent his boyhood learning many of the same basic skills as other males. Indians expected practically all males to become hunters, fishermen, warriors, and craftsmen, and thus to develop a detailed knowledge of their people's territory: the best spots for trapping animals or harvesting fish, woodland signs that game was near, places to make defensive stands against an invading enemy, and more. The responsibilities of hunting and war were closely related insofar as they required young men to build the physical and psychological strength to travel tens and sometimes even hundreds of miles over rough, often dangerous, territory, then to track, ambush, and retreat quickly with their kill, enemy captives, or plunder in tow. Like his boyhood peers, Ninigret would have practiced fashioning the tools to conduct these activities: bows and arrows, war clubs, hatchets, knives, spears, fishing lines, hooks, seines, nets, and even dugout canoes. Possibly he also learned how to raise, and certainly to smoke, tobacco, which was the only plant cultivated by men, unlike the edible crops of corn, beans, and squash, which belonged to the care of women. Whenever the Narragansetts met in council, "every man has his pipe of their tobacco, and a deep silence they make, and attention give to him that speaks," the idea being that tobacco cleared the mind and carried prayers to the spirits.[8] Likewise, men customarily shared a pipe when they met each other on the trail. Ninigret certainly lived more comfortably than most people, but fundamentally his upbringing and day-to-day responsibilities were the same as those of any Indian male.[9]

Around the onset of their teenage years, Indian males went on a vision quest to obtain a guardian spirit. The Narragansetts and all of their indigenous neighbors believed that spirits called *manitous* animated the most prominent features of their world: the cardinal directions, animal species, metrological forces, bodies of water, and geological formations. As such, the manitous determined practically everything: whether the corn would grow, the rain would come, the warriors would be victorious, the hunters would find game, the sick would recover, or the new-born child would live. The key to individual and collective success was keeping the spirits appeased through ritual, but their demands and temperament could be fickle. Whenever something out of the ordinary happened—be it a comet, earthquake, meteor shower, unseasonal weather, or lightning strike—the people looked to their religious specialists for explanation. Yet dreams and visions available to common people were the typical channels of communication with the manitous. While a person slept, one of his or her two souls—the *Cowwéwonck* or dream soul—wandered out into the shadowy realm of manitous, while the other soul, *Míchachunck*, kept the body alive. A special dream involved a manitou offering the Cowwéwonck a favor, such as a successful hunt or discovery of a lost object, in return for a like kindness, though discerning this reciprocal obligation often required dream interpretation once the sleeper awoke. The vision quest was a comparable, if more intense, zone of contact between humans and the spirits. The quest began with a young man leaving home and going into the bush where he fasted and imbibed emetics or hallucinogens. His hope was that eventually a spirit would appear to him to offer its special protection, which the seeker could thereafter invoke in times of need by singing a special song or handling a particular fetish. Williams once encountered an ailing Indian man who "called much upon *Muckquachuckquànd* [the Children's God], who of other Natives I understood (as they believed) had appeared to the dying young man, many years before, and bid him whenever he was in distress [to] call upon him."[10] People also called on their spirits in wartime, sporting contests, and even gambling, for the support of manitous was what distinguished exceptional from ordinary men. "If they see one man excel others in wisdom, valor, strength, activity, etc.," Williams explained, "they cry out '*Manitou*, a god.'"[11] Ninigret might very well have possessed a guardian spirit, but unfortunately the historical record says nothing about it. However, given that he excelled in so many aspects of Indian life, it is reasonable to assume that he and the people around him attributed his success to his manitous.[12]

Ninigret probably adopted a new name after his vision quest, for Indians often changed their names at key transitions in life. Ninigret might have kept a private name, acquired at birth but known only to his family to keep it away from the conjurations of witches and other enemies. His public name, however, was most pertinent to his politics. When the English first encountered him, he was known as Jannemo, only later to adopt the name Ninigret. We do not know the meaning of the name Jannemo, though it was common enough to be shared by a leading Wampanoag on Nantucket in the early eighteenth century.[13] Whatever the precise import of the name Jannemo, Indians would have understood it to symbolize its holder's evolution as an individual and a public figure. It announced that he was learning to be a man and a leader.[14]

Ninigret's education also involved learning how to be a sachem. Throughout his young life, he would have observed councils of the Indian elite, consisting of sachems, specially trained warrior-counselors called *pniesok*, elders, and other family heads. For a rising leader like Ninigret, these sessions served as tutorials about how to conduct himself in public and what the most respected men in the community thought about the people's interests and values. Without a police force to impose his dictates, a sachem's influence depended on forging consensus among the communities' leading families. In turn, sachems had to listen as well as talk, to cull opinion as well as mold it, in short, to be "sober and grave."[15] After everyone was heard, the sachem issued his opinion and, according to Matthew Mayhew of Martha's Vineyard, "what was by him resolved, without the least hesitation was applauded."[16] Williams described this process as "gentle persuasion."[17] The sachem's persuasiveness rested in no small degree on his "courtly rhetoric" or "majestic deportment," a cultivated style of governance involving elaborate metaphors, theatrical gestures, and mnemonic devices.[18] The Narragansett sachem, Canonicus, dazzled Massachusetts governor John Winthrop with his performance in council, which involved a spectacle of "much state, great Command over his men: & marvelous wisdom in his answers."[19] The adults in Ninigret's boyhood would have encouraged him to study as high-ranking men modeled this sort of behavior.[20]

As Ninigret reached adulthood, his wives and their families would have joined his blood relations as the genealogical foundation for his status and leadership. We know little about how Indian commoners made their marriage choices, other than that family members participated. Arranged marriages might have been the norm. Among sachem elites, though, family considerations certainly were paramount. Close kin and in-laws, including several "petty" or "sub sachems," made up the inner circle of a sachem's constituency and the core of his council, with their followers or protectorates forming the next outer circle. Thus, for a sachem to consolidate and enlarge his or her sphere of influence meant marrying strategically, sometimes to unite elite lineages within the community, sometimes to broker alliances with foreign peoples. Either way, the goal was to link high-status families and their power bases. This priority is the moral of a Narragansett tradition that the people's first sachem, Tashtassuck, decided to join his son and daughter in marriage after he failed to locate other partners of suitable status for them. Most other eligible elites had greater luck on the marriage market. By the seventeenth century their unions had made the sachems of the Narragansetts, Pequots, Mohegans, Montuaketts, and probably other regional groups, an extended cousinage, sometimes kissing, sometimes clashing.[21]

Ninigret married well and often, wedding at least three women during his lifetime and producing at least six children, including five daughters and a son. His first wife was his niece by his brother Wepitamock. The only information about his second wife is that her father was a great sachem and her mother was of elite status. This bride might have been the sister of Miantonomi, one of the Narragansetts' two primary sachems. The background of Ninigret's third wife is a complete mystery. Reflective of the distance of these women from colonial authorities, we have no record of the wives' names. Suffice it to say, there is also no documentation about how they and Ninigret felt about each other, or what role they played in Ninigret's decision making. All we can say for certain is that their family connections were essential to Ninigret's claims to leadership.[22]

It is safe to assume that Ninigret's relationships with his blood kin, especially his children, and his wives, were the center of his emotional world. Though colonists generally paid scant attention to Indian family life, they found the Indians' "extreme affection" for children, including a refusal to mete out corporal punishment, to be utterly remarkable. They believed that the Indians' indulgence toward their children helped to explain why the Indians' young people were so "saucy, bold, and undutiful," at least by English standards.[23] The Indian counterargument was that, first, if adults expected their children to grow up to love them and take care of them in old age, it was best not to beat them. Second, they worried that children who suffered beatings would become timorous and depressed, even prone to suicide, lacking the bold initiative prized in Native society, at least among males. Put another way, fostering love and psychological health was among their goals in childrearing, quite unlike the English goal of breaking the child's will to discipline him and her to a society of strict laws and steep social hierarchy.[24] Ninigret's childhood and his own parenting would have reflected these principles.

Indian mourning rituals and calls to revenge crimes, particularly murder, also showcased the depth of their family relationships. Williams observed that after the Narragansetts buried a relative they would "all sit down and lament, that I have seen tears run down the cheeks of stoutest Captains, as well as little children in abundance."[25] The mourning state, which involved blackening one's face, wearing tattered clothes, and crying or wailing spontaneously, could last for months. Williams even saw "a father take so grievously the loss of his child, that he had cut and stabbed himself with grief and rage."[26] Whereas family members were powerless to bring the dead back to life, they could revenge crimes against their kin. The Narragansetts, like practically all Indians in the eastern woodlands, would not rest after one of their own was murdered until they had exacted a revenge killing against a member of the murderer's family, not necessarily against the perpetrator himself. As Williams put it, "They hold the band of brotherhood so dear, that when one had committed a murder and fled, they executed his brother; and 'tis common for a brother to pay the debt of a brother deceased."[27] Underlying this custom was the belief that the ghost of the dead would haunt the living until revenge was done.[28] Such anecdotes, combined with numerous colonial asides about "loving," affable Indian households and communities, leaves little doubt that close-knit, extended family networks were at the center of Ninigret's world.

Manìt-manittówock. God, Gods.
Ninigret's Spiritual Life

If family gave someone like Ninigret a sense of purpose, then the spirits supplied him with the courage to pursue his ambitions. Tattoos of "bears, deers, mooses, wolves . . . eagles [or] hawks," similar motifs painted on clothing, and sometimes the new names that Indians adopted at key transitions in life, symbolized an individual's spirit protectors.[29] The subject of the portrait traditionally identified as Ninigret has a tattoo on his thigh which appears to be of a Thunderbird, the great spirit of the Narragansett upperworld and the protagonist for humankind against the dark enemies of the underworld.[30] Ninigret would have petitioned these spirits for strength and guidance at decisive moments. Additionally, Ninigret probably carried a medicine bag containing spiritually potent objects. New England Indians believed that spirit power, or *manit*, could be located in any one of a number of forms, including rocks, minerals, and human artifice. For instance, Indians thought quartz was the crystallized form of lightning bolts shot from the eyes of the Thunderbird streaking across the sky. It followed that crystal and other light-colored, transparent articles, like white wampum, connoted the social: life, knowledge, harmony, the sun, and the benevolent spirit named

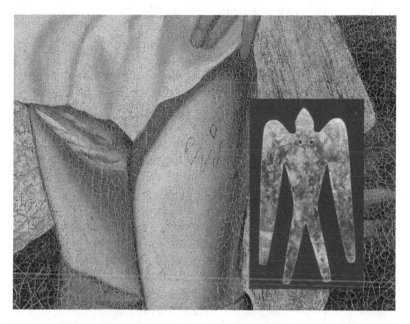

FIG. 4   Tattoo. A faint image of a tattoo is visible on the portrait subject's upper thigh (shown in close up here). The tattoo may be the incomplete outline of a Thunderbird, the great spirit of the Narragansett upper world and the protagonist for humankind against the dark enemies of the underworld. The tattoo appears in American, Native American Sachem, ca. 1700 (see figure 1). Oil on canvas, 84.1×76.5 cm. (33 ⅛×30 ⅛ in.). Gift of Mr. Robert Winthrop 48.246. Photography by Erik Gould, courtesy of the Museum of Art, Rhode Island School of Design, Providence. The Thunderbird image is courtesy of the Peabody Museum of Archaeology and Ethnology, Harvard University, Peabody ID No. 33-54-10/1536. Design by Dennis Fisher.

Cautantowwit. By comparison, Indians associated dark objects, such as purple wampum, with the asocial, and, by extension, with the Thunderbird's underwater analog and antagonist, Hobbomock, the horned serpent and god of the dead. The moon, the color black, and jealousy also fell within purple wampum's and Hobbomock's symbolic spectrum. Red materials, such as copper and ochre, symbolized the antisocial, or violence, with some Algonquian-speaking peoples imagining that copper originated as flakes shed from the tail of the mythical underwater horned serpent. Any variety of items in these colors and forms might have appeared in Ninigret's medicine bag alongside works of human artifice, like statuettes capturing the form of certain manitous. These were the private sources of the public man's confidence.[31]

A sachem's charisma also rested on the display of rare, powerful objects. Indians associated exotic items with spiritual and political power, for such things were imbued with manit and often obtained through foreign alliances or tribute networks. The sachem in the portrait, for instance, wears an earring, a headband, and a gorget interlaid with wampum, which originated in Hobbomock's underworld and then passed to the sachem through the collection of tribute. Written descriptions of sachems also emphasize their distinctive dress and ornamentation. There are accounts of one sachem adorned with "a humbird [hummingbird] in his ear for a pendant," and of others outfitted with black hawk headdresses "accounted of worth sufficient to ransom a Sagamour [sachem]."[32] These birds symbolized flight and, by extension, the soul wandering prized by Indians as a source of knowledge and power.[33] Elites even took prestige goods to the grave so they could continue to enjoy them in the afterlife or, alternately, the relatives of elites buried their kin with finery to exhibit their own generosity and spiritual potency.[34] Plymouth's Edward Winslow wrote of the Wampanoags, "When they bury the dead, they sew up the corpse in a mat, and so put it in the earth. If the part be a sachem, they cover him with many curious mats, and bury all his riches with them, and enclose the grave with a pale [or fence]."[35] Likewise, when Roger Williams attended the burial of the sachem Canonicus's son, he witnessed the lad interred with goods "to a great value."[36] Archaeological excavations of Narragansett and Wampanoag cemeteries from Ninigret's era have confirmed these accounts. Skeletons showing evidence of superior nutrition tended to be buried with most numerous and valuable grave goods, such as Native wampum and stone effigy pipes and colonial fire-arms, glass beads, brass kettles, and spoons.[37]

Just as personal ties to the spirits grounded Ninigret's identity, so too did the Narragansetts think of themselves as bound to each other and their land through collective spiritual relationships. They told Roger Williams that the great anthropomorphic spirit, Cautantowwit (or Kiehtan), had created the territory on which they lived and then pro-vided the ancestors with gifts of corn, beans, and squash, the staffs of their existence.[38] He rewarded Narragansetts in the here and now with sunshine so they could cultivate these crops. He welcomed the spirits of their dead into his house far off to the southwest, where they reunited with their ancestors in an afterlife blessed by peace and abundance. For these reasons and more, Edward Winslow observed, whenever the Nar-ragansetts would "obtain any great matter . . . and so likewise for plenty victory etc.," they would gather to "sing, dance, feast, give thanks, and hang up garlands and other things," in praise of Cautantowwit.[39] By contrast, when a drought or disease ended, the people thanked Hobbo-mock (also Abbomocho or Cheepi) for sparing them further suffering. As eighteenth-century Narragansetts explained, "The Evil Power hurts us, does all the Mischief, and who should we seek to prevent or remove Mischief but to him that does it."[40]

The Narragansetts considered the landscape and the animals that inhabited it to be imbued with spiritual power. To them, swamps, the ocean, and caves were thresholds between the terrestrial habitation of people and the underworld of Hobbomock. Likewise, trees and moun-tains were avenues to the upper realm of the Thunderbird. They held that some prominent features of the landscape had been formed in an-cient times by great giants, especially, "one Wétucks, a man that wrought great Miracles amongst them."[41] In all likelihood, they also believed that Little People, akin to the elves and dwarves of European folklore, could sometimes be seen in wooded hollows and other remote places.[42] Each species of animal was governed by a lookalike boss spirit, which some-times appeared in humans' dreams and visions to offer its fleshy self in return for certain rituals or prayers. Some animals seemed to embody the very power of these *manitous*. "The Indians say," wrote Williams, "they have black Foxes, which they have often seen, but never could take any of them: they say they are Manittóoes, that is, Gods, Spirits, or Divine powers, as they say of everything which they cannot comprehend."[43] In the Narragansetts' world, there was no firm line between the natural and the spiritual. Moreover, part of what gave the Narragansetts proprietorship in their land was their close relations with the spirits of the place, or to put it more pointedly, with their spirits of their place.

Shamans, or spiritual intermediaries, who the Indians called *powwows*, were the key to channeling *manit* toward productive ends, including political ones. A man became a powwow when Hobbomock appeared to him or her (there is one known example of a female powwow) in a vision in the form of a snake and offered the power, variously held, to cure, poison, divine the future, discover lost objects, and conjure the weather. Individuals often turned to the powwows to assist them with their afflictions. So did sachems, as when they wanted to predict the outcome of a battle, or poison their enemies, or organize a ritual. Although only a few sachems in the historical record were also powwows, and none of them were Narragansett, it is clear that Indians in southern New England associated great sachems with shamanistic power. Ninigret would have consulted Narragansett powwows whenever he contemplated a major political move.[44]

Natuphéttitch yo fandukamick. Let them feed on this ground.
Narragansett Economic Life

The authority of sachems in and around Narragansett country rested on large human populations fed by rich estuarine and woodland resources. Before the arrival of Europeans, coastal southern New England was among the most densely populated places in Native North America, largely because it contained a rich variety of wild foods with a soil fertile enough and an environment temperate enough to sustain the raising of corns, beans, and squash.[45] The key to this abundance was water. The Narragansett country, colonists marveled, was "wondrous full of brooks and rivers, so doth it also abound with fresh ponds, some of many miles compass."[46] And not just fresh ponds, but brackish ones too, strung out for dozens of miles, separated from the ocean by just a thin strip of barrier beach. The result was an estuarine zone teeming with life. In the nearby ocean and coastal ponds, Narragansetts could harvest fish such as cod, striped bass, bluefish, scup, sturgeon, pike, perch, and bream.

Shark, flounder, eel, and skate were available almost year round, as were turtles, seals, and shellfish such as oysters, crabs, snails, lobsters, and clams, "which all Indians, generally all over the Country . . . delight in."[47] Seasonal runs of alewives could feed the people for weeks. Fowl such as ducks, geese, swans, and cormorants were abundant and easily taken. Moving inland from the coast, the sandy beach and grassy marsh-land gave way to rocky hills with a forest cover of maple, oak, ash, birch, and pine. The people relied on these hardwoods for their dugout canoes, house poles, bows, axes, harpoons, spears, knives, pestles, clubs, handles, and of course, firewood. The woods also housed the Narragansetts' game animals such as turkey, bear, rabbit, and especially deer. The large deer population was not happenstance, but a deliberate result of the Narragansetts' controlled burns of the forest, which cleared out under-brush and encouraged the growth of tender greenery that deer craved. Game animals provided the Narragansetts with meat to consume, skins, furs, and feathers to wear, bones for tools, and sinews for bowstrings and thread. Native plant resources were equally rich and versatile. The Narragansetts enjoyed wild foods such as beach plums, strawberries, blueberries, raspberries, blackberries, cherries, wild onions, Jerusalem artichokes, hickory nuts, hazelnut, chestnuts, and acorns. Women turned sea grasses and hemp into mats, baskets, clothing, and line. With such wild plenty, there were multiple safety nets if one or another resource failed.

Yet the people left little to chance, choosing to supplement what they could hunt and gather with what they raised themselves. Though some archaeologists still question whether coastal Indians were committed farmers before the arrival of Europeans, the general consensus is that they had made this transition at least a couple of hundred years earlier. During the warm months, the Indians' fields of corn, beans, and squash stretched out for miles along the coast. Women (and, for the most part, only women) spent most of their spring and summer planting and weeding these crops. Then, as the weather turned cooler, women har-vested the corn and ground it into meal with mortar and pestle for stor-age in handcrafted clay pots and woven grass bags. Ideally, there would be enough corn meal to last the people until the next planting season, for the standard Indian dish was a corn mush stew containing some combination of meat, fish, vegetable, and fruit. Agricultural production was not the singular focus of economic life among coastal New England

Indians, but it was an essential component of it. Moreover, farming cultivated the people's sense of proprietorship in the land. "They say themselves," wrote Williams, "that they have sprung and grown up in that very place, like the very trees of the wilderness," or, put another way, like the vegetables they raised.[48]

In peaceful times, the people's economic cycle determined where and with whom they lived. In the winter, the Narragansetts lived inland amid the shelter of hills and woods, close to the game animals. Then, in the spring, they relocated to the coast where they could be near their cornfields, fishing stations, and shellfish gathering spots.[49] Williams described Narragansett country as comprised of "many towns, some bigger, some lesser, it may be a dozen in 20 miles travel."[50] Yet he appears to have been describing kin-based hamlets spread out in pockets along the coastal estuary rather than large, centralized settlements of hundreds or thousands of people, judging from the lack of village sites in the archaeological record.[51] As far as scholars can tell, the only time the Narragansetts lived in concentrated groups was when they clustered near the protection of palisaded forts during war. Ninigret's Niantics, for instance, sometimes moved their houses close to a walled fortress enclosing an area 152 feet long by 137 feet wide at the head of modern-day Fort Neck Cove on Ninigret Pond in Charlestown, Rhode Island.[52] Otherwise, they fanned out as they moved from place to place during their people's seasonal round. It was a pattern that gave them a deep stake in defending the full range of their territory, they being "very exact and punctually in the bounds of their Lands, belonging to this or that Prince or People."[53]

Sâchim-maûog. Sachimaûonck. King, Kings. A Kingdome or Monarchie.
Ninigret's Role as Sachem

The vast majority of records about Ninigret relate to his foreign affairs, for he tended to attract English attention when he was making trouble for them or their Indian protectorates. Yet Ninigret would have spent much of his life as sachem focused on the local concerns of his people. Although we have no firsthand accounts of him acting in this capacity, the information that exists about neighboring sachems gives us a good sense of his public responsibilities.

In the half century or so preceding European colonization, the dense Indian population afforded by the coastal economy gave rise to sachems like Ninigret, whose domestic duties included managing their follower's resources, arbitrating disputes, and meting out justice for the most serious crimes. Though it appears that most Indian families held their planting lands in perpetuity, they still went to their sachem periodically to have the grant renewed. At such times, the people expressed their love to the sachem and paid him or her a tribute of produce, furs, or labor, whereupon the sachem responded with a reciprocal "gift" of the land. Likewise, if a new family moved into the community, the sachem would assign that family planting ground. In these respects, the people's territory symbolically belonged to the sachem who, in turn, shared it with his or her followers. That said, there was no risk of the sachem permanently alienating the people's land from them through sale because there was no market for land before the arrival of Europeans.[54]

The sachem also ritually gifted hunting grounds to the people in exchange for tribute from the hunt. Occasionally, a sachem would hold a "great hunt" in which he and a group of select followers—"twenty, forty, fifty, yea, two or three hundred in a company"—would drive deer from the woods into a pen or other trap to be slaughtered en masse.[55] Usually, Indian hunters operated on their own or in small groups, but even then they had to keep the sachem in mind. Edward Winslow's understanding was that the Wampanoags gave their sachem the "fore parts" of any deer they killed within his territory.[56] The sachem also received the skins from any deer that his people killed in the water, possibly because water represented the threshold to the underworld and rituals conducted by the sachem and his powwows maintained the balance between the terrestrial earth and that dark zone. For similar reasons, perhaps, sachems oversaw distribution of the remains of beached whales, which appear to have washed ashore in Ninigret's era with much more frequency than nowadays. It took someone trained to manage the dangers of the world to handle such a potent gift from the underworld.[57]

As the human embodiment of the people, the sachems oversaw public matters like poor relief and justice. Feasts sponsored by the sachems were one of the reasons that "there are no beggars amongst them, nor fatherless children unprovided for."[58] In all likelihood, another duty of the sachem was resolving disputes between families so revenge killings would not spiral out of control. For certain, sachems took charge of punishing great public crimes such as murder, witch-craft, and treason. "The most usual custom amongst them in execut-ing punishments," wrote Williams, "is for the sachem either to beat, or whip, or put to death with his own hand . . . though sometimes the sa-chem sends a secret executioner . . . to fetch off a head, by some sudden unexpected blow of a hatchet, when they have feared mutiny by public execution."[59] A sachem who governed more than one community would take periodic tours of his dominions to collect tribute and pun-ish criminals, always accompanied by an entourage of guards and war-riors. There was no greater embodiment of the sachem's authority than when he was on the march, "his queen and children in company, with a guard of near two hundred . . . and sentinels by course, as exact as in Europe."[60]

Ninigret wielded great powers at home in part because he was re-spected abroad, and vice versa. He was a leader who could protect the people from their enemies, project their strength against neighboring peoples, and form the kinds of military and trading alliances that brought them peace and wealth. In turn, the people granted Ninigret the resources and deference he needed to pursue their interests in foreign affairs. Ninigret's prominence in intertribal and Indian-colonial politics indicates that he had a strong base of support at home.

The sachem was the people's representative to the outside world in matters of trade and politics. When the people received visitors from abroad, the sachem fed and lodged them in his own home. In dealings with neighboring communities, he issued messages of peace and threats of violence, usually backed up by young warriors recruited from the families that followed him. Sometimes these warriors accompanied him on diplomatic missions to lend strength to his words. At other times they conducted raids on communities targeted by the sachem. The reasons for these attacks varied widely, but some of the common causes included revenging a grave insult (such as mentioning the name of a sachem's dead relative), reducing another community to the status of tribute payers, or punishing a rival sachem who grew too zealous in the competition for followers. The form of these strikes varied from ambushes by small bands of warriors to invasions by hundreds of men, characterized by the plundering and burning of enemy property and the killing and capture of enemy populations. As long as victories kept com-ing, a sachem's boldness was a virtue, contributing both to his prestige and that of his people. If he met repeated losses or even too costly victories, however, he jeopardized his following.[61]

All of these activities—providing for the poor, sponsoring warriors and guards, hosting embassies, and more—were costly to the sachem. Indeed, sachems might be said to have spent their tribute almost as quickly as they collected it. This pattern has led some scholars to assume mistakenly that sachems collected tribute primarily to redistribute wealth. While there is no question that sachems assumed some responsibility to provide for the needy, the main purpose of tribute was to fund the sachem's political activities. At the same time, the sachem and his family benefited mightily from their control over this wealth. Eyewitness observations and the archaeological record agree that Indians of sachem status enjoyed better nutrition, less physical stress, and greater material comfort than their people. These status distinctions among the Narragansetts were less stark than those between elites and commoners in Europe, but they were of a kind.[62]

Sachems risked losing their followers to other sachems if they fell short in their public responsibilities or in their character. Sometimes rivals came from within the group, as when a member of the sachem's lineage claimed a superior right to rule by genealogy or accomplishment. In such cases, the danger was less that the rival sachem would displace the sachem in power than that he would set up a new community and attempt to draw off the sachem's people. Neighboring sachems posed a similar threat. Just as most sachems in southern New England were related to each other to some degree, so too did people of lesser status have kin ties that cut across community boundaries. If the people grew dissatisfied with the sachem of one place, they might move to live with their relatives under the sachem of another, who him- or herself might be related to the disowned sachem. A sachem did not make a single decision without considering this possibility. Thus, even though the people generally deferred to a sachem's will, it was also true, as Williams explained, that sachems avoided rulings "to which the people are averse, and by gentle persuasion cannot be brought."[63] The only constant feature of a sachem's power was that it was a work in progress, ever in need of maintenance and cultivation. Ninigret spent his entire career with this principle in mind.[64]

The relationship of Ninigret's Niantics to the Narragansetts might be characterized as a sachemship within a tribe. Indians along the southern New England coast lived in sachemships, which is to say, in territories and among people under the authority of a particular sachem. In this sense, the Niantics were a sachemship. Individual sachemships sometimes grouped together in larger units that we might call tribes, whether voluntarily, based on defensive or other political consider-ations, or out of forceful subjugation. In the case of the Niantics, they belonged to a regional network of sachemships known as the Narragan-sett tribe. The Narragansett tribe got its name and leadership from a cluster of sachemships located on the southwest side of Narragansett Bay under the direction of the sachems Canonicus, Miantonomi, and their close relatives. These sachems not only governed their local com-munities, but collected tribute from and exercised authority over the war, trade, and foreign diplomacy of a number of other sachemships in the neighborhood, including the Manisees of Block Island, and the Cowesets, Shawomets, and Pawtuxets on the northwest side of the bay. By contrast, the Niantics under Ninigret do not appear to have been tributaries to Miantonomi and Canonicus but instead coequal confeder-ates, despite their relative weakness. According to Indian sources, the Narragansett tribe could field up to five thousand warriors in the early seventeenth century, putting their overall population around twenty-five thousand people.[65] The Niantics would have contributed a mere frac-tion, perhaps a fifth, to these totals. The obvious question, then, is why the Narragansetts treated the Niantics with such respect. One possible scenario is that the Narragansetts offered Niantics an alliance of equals in exchange for military assistance against the Pequots, with whom the Narragansetts appear to have had a long-running rivalry by the time the English arrived in New England in the 1620s.[66] Miantonomi's expla-nation was the Niantics "were, he said, as his own flesh, being allied by continual intermarriages."[67] Whatever the impetus, the Niantics were one of the few, if only, groups outside of the Narragansett core who boasted such independence within the greater Narragansett tribe.

A few facts are known about how Ninigret came to be sachem of the Niantics. Ninigret was born into the Indian elite by virtue of both his father's and mother's sachem status, which means that they hailed from families with claims to political leadership. They also had close ties with leading Narragansetts. Ninigret's mother, whose name is unknown to us, was the sister of Canonicus, the great sachem of the Narragansetts during the early to mid seventeenth century. She was also the aunt (and

Ninigret the cousin) of Miantonomi, who jointly headed the Narragansetts with his uncle Canonicus during the 1630s. Further tightening this
familial knot was Ninigret's sister, Quaiapen (also known as Matantuck
and Magnus), who married Canonicus's son, Mixano, sometime in the
1630s. As for Ninigret, he appears to have married one of Miantonomi's
sisters (another of Ninigret's cousins) at some point in his life. In short,
Ninigret was closely related to the most powerful sachems of the Narragansetts through his mother and eventually through marriage. His
father's identity is more elusive. It is likely, though uncertain, that Ninigret's father was a Niantic, since Ninigret's brother, Wepitamock, became
sachem of the Niantics at some point before 1635 and the most common pattern of sachem succession was for a son to follow his father.
Ninigret strengthened his right to a share of power over the Niantics by
marrying one of Wepitamock's daughters and producing at least two
girls with her. He also married two other women of whom we know
nothing except that they were of high status. Such marriages strengthened
Ninigret's prestige among his own people and among the neighboring
communities from which these women hailed.[68]

The question is what role, if any, the Narragansetts played in putting
Wepitamock and Ninigret in these positions. In other times and places
in North America, including New England, the leaders of powerful
tribes appointed relatives to rule over weaker partners.[69] The Narragansetts took such a measure among the Pawcatuck Indians who lived on
the western edge of Niantic country along the frontier with the Pequots
(the modern day border of Rhode Island and Connecticut). The context
was this: some time before the 1630s, the Narragansetts broke the hold
of their Pequot rivals over the Pawcatuck Indians and then placed a war
leader named Sosoa (or Sassawwaw) as sachem over the Indians there.[70]
It is uncertain whether the Pawcatuck Indians greeted this change with
enthusiasm or grudging acceptance, as the historical record is vague as
to whether they self-identified as Pequot, Narragansett, or neither. All
that we know is that Sosoa was born a Pequot but later in life defected to
the Narragansetts, which he announced by turning on his supposed Pequot allies in battle and beheading one of their war leaders. The point is
that the Narragansetts might very well have directed Niantic politics in
the same way, hand-choosing Wepitamock and Ninigret as elite men of
dual Niantic and Narragansett descent to exercise authority over a Niantic community of strategic value in the rivalry against the Pequots. In

1706, a Rhode Island colonist named Nathaniel Waterman contended that Ninigret's father "was never a sachem nor of the blood of said sachem" and that therefore Ninigret was not the natural-born leader of the Niantics. Rather, Waterman continued, Ninigret was "a man of courage as the Indians said," who the Narragansetts placed over the Niantics after he performed a special mission for them against the Pequots.[71] In the 1760s, Yale College president Ezra Stiles repeated Waterman's testimony, writing that "Ninigret for service done was made Captain & afterwards had land given him in the Niantic country & so called Sachem."[72] Stiles's account probably drew on Waterman's, and Waterman's telling likely either confused Sosoa and Ninigret or purposefully diminished Ninigret's standing. Waterman's testimony was designed to strengthen Rhode Island's claim to land, disputed by Connecticut, that it had purchased from most of the Narragansett sachems, but not Ninigret; if Rhode Island could debunk Ninigret's sachem status, it would free itself of the historic responsibility of gaining his consent to the cession. Given the level of respect shown by the Narragansetts toward Ninigret and, later, his sister, the most likely back story is that the Niantics chose Wepitamock and Ninigret as leaders out of their own accord, valuing their descent and marriages as bases for alliance and affiliation with the neighborhood's dominant power, the Narragansetts. The full truth must remain a mystery. What is known, and what is most important for an understanding of Ninigret's politics, is that he and his brother counted themselves as sachems of the Niantics and as part of the community of Narragansett sachems.

The brothers might very well have divided their responsibilities as sachems along the lines of peace chief and war chief, just as the Narragansetts did. Among the Narragansetts, the elder sachem Canonicus functioned as a peace chief, meaning that he usually oversaw domestic affairs, whereas the younger sachem, Miantonomi, tended to relations with outsiders, including leading the people in war.[73] This distinction reflected a number of dualities—peace and war, settlements and the woods, old and young, life and death—that Indians held to be at once opposite and complementary if kept in balance through ritual. Wepitamock might very well have been the Niantics' peace chief and Ninigret their war chief, judging from Ninigret's emergence as the Niantics' bold public face in the mid 1630s. However, after the death of Wepitamock probably in the early to mid 1650s, Ninigret appears to have performed both duties.[74]

As a young man, Ninigret's responsibility as a Niantic sachem was more important than his role within the Narragansetts; first he had to prove himself locally before he could command respect regionally. He also had to age and mature. As Ninigret reached these milestones, and as other Narragansett sachems proved to be less competent than he was, he advanced to become one of the Narragansetts' main leaders, though never neglecting his leadership of the Niantics. All of this is to say that Ninigret's political life had mutually reinforcing local and regional components. The English sometimes referred to him as a Niantic and at other times as a Narragansett but he would have considered himself to be both.[75]

Náwwatuck nôteshem. I came from farre.
Nippenowàntawem. I am of another language.
Narragansett Foreign Affairs

The Narragansetts were an expanding power when the English first arrived in New England. An epidemic between 1616 and 1619 had decimated the Narragansetts' rivals to the east while leaving the Narragansetts relatively unscathed. The Narragansetts took advantage of this disaster by trying to absorb the survivors or subjugate their communities to the status of tributaries. This campaign was still ongoing in the 1620s and 1630s against the Wampanoags on the east side of Narragansett Bay and the Massachusett Indians to the northeast.[76]

The Pequots of the Mystic River and Thames River valleys in what is now Connecticut were the Narragansetts' great nemesis to the west. They too had built a network of allies and tributaries that included the Mohegans further up the Thames, the Western Niantics of what is now Lyme, Connecticut, the Podunks and Wangunks of the Connecticut River Valley, and the Montuaketts and perhaps the Shinnecocks, Corchaugs, Setaukets, and Unkechaugs of Long Island. The Pawcatuck River, which today marks the boundary between Rhode Island and Connecticut, was then the contested frontier between these expanding powers.[77]

Tiny shell beads known as wampum or peague were among the great stakes in this rivalry. Coastal Indians made purple wampum from the outer edge of the quahog shell and white wampum from the inner column of the whelk, periwinkle, and conch, all of which were found on the shores of Long Island Sound. Indians then strung these beads on deer gut or plant fiber to make belts, headbands, and necklaces. The English generally calculated wampum in bushels or six-foot strings which they called fathoms. In whatever form, Indians throughout the Northeast coveted wampum as a status symbol, a spiritually charged item associated with the watery underworld of Hobbomock, and a primary medium in the gift exchanges that characterized Indian diplomacy. The latter feature is particularly important for understanding Ninigret's activities. When a coastal sachem adorned himself in wampum or gifted it to a foreign power, it symbolized his authority at home and abroad. It showed that his followers—women as well as men—put enough trust in his leadership to donate their time and effort toward producing wampum and wampum belts for his activities. By the same token, a sachem's supply of wampum reflected his network of tribute payers and, by extension, the military power he wielded to keep them in subjugation. Wampum also had practical use as a gift in diplomacy with foreign powers, particularly the formidable Mohawks. Wampum was essential to Iroquois ceremony, and thus the Mohawks were eager to exchange their political support and specialized goods, like stone pipes and stone war hammers, in exchange for the beads. By the time the English arrived in New England, the Narragansetts boasted a thriving trade with the Mohawks and, it followed, an alliance, a relationship which only grew stronger as the Narragansetts increased their production of wampum following their acquisition of metal drills. Whereas Iroquois archaeological sites from the late sixteenth and early seventeenth centuries contain at most only a few hundred wampum beads, mid seventeenth century sites can yield as many as 250,000.[78] The support of foreign powers like the Mohawks, brokered through the exchange of wampum, could make the difference for a sachem like Ninigret when it came to defeating an enemy or at least keeping him at bay. At the same time, a sachem who could boast an alliance with the Mohawks and display Mohawk goods enjoyed increased status at home.[79] In short, by Ninigret's lifetime coastal sachems were deeply concerned with acquiring, exhibit-

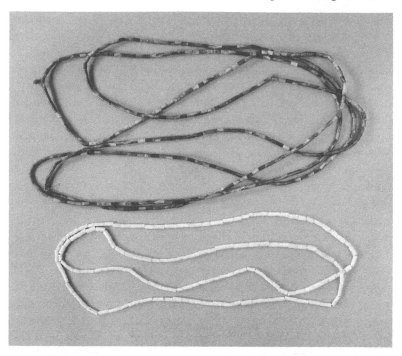

FIG. 5 Wampum strings. The Indians of Long Island Sound, including the Niantics and Narragansetts, made purple wampum from the outer edge of the quahog shell and white wampum from the inner column of the whelk, periwinkle, and conch. They then strung these beads on deer gut or plant fiber to make belts, headbands, necklaces, and strings measured in fathoms. Indians throughout the Northeast coveted wampum as a status symbol, a spiritually charged item, tribute, and a primary medium in the gift exchange that characterized Indian diplomacy. Courtesy of the Peabody Museum of Archaeology and Ethnology, Harvard University, Peabody ID No. 99-12-10/53011 and 99-12-10/53014.

ing, and circulating wampum. Control of the flow of these beads could determine political fortunes.

The competition between sachems for wampum and, in turn, tribute payers, picked up considerably after 1600 as a direct result of European technology and markets. Before the advent of trade with Europeans, Indians relied on their own stone drills to manufacture wampum, which was time consuming and cumbersome. European metal drills considerably sped up the process. Moreover, Europeans themselves represented a nearly bottomless market for wampum, at least for a few decades, less because Europeans intended to wear the beads than because they could trade them to inland Indians for fur which could then be sold for profit back in Europe. The English and Dutch turned wampum into a commodity, assigning it abstract value, accepting it as currency, and standardizing the units in which it was traded.[80] In turn, coastal sachems with wampum to trade increasingly had access to coveted European goods: brightly colored cloth, metal knives and axes, copper pots, beads, glass bottles, fishhooks, and more. These goods made Indians' lives easier to a significant degree. Metal edge tools cut better and were more durable than stone ones. Copper cooking pots could go directly over the fire, unlike the Indians' clay and wood ones in which one cooked by dropping in heated stones. Indians also prized these goods for aesthetic reasons. In many cases, Indians traded for European goods similar to items that they already possessed, as in the case of beads and even cloth. Yet the fact that these goods were foreign, made of exotic materials and colors, gave them added prestige. So too did the fact that they came from a distant source that the Indians associated with a strange spiritual power. The point is that sachems could consolidate their following at home and abroad by acquiring these goods for display and distribution as gifts. Though Ninigret is invisible in the historical record throughout this process, there is no doubt that he witnessed its unfolding and listened intently as the old men discussed what it meant for the people.[81]

Mishâupan, A great wind; *Mishitashin,* A storme.
The Beginning of Colonialism in Narragansett Country

The opportunity for southern New England Indians to acquire European items grew with practically every passing year after 1600 in lockstep with the increased pace of contact. The first recorded meeting between Europeans and the Narragansetts took place in 1524, when the French-employed, Italian explorer Giovanni da Verrazzano stopped for a two-week visit in Narragansett Bay. During this time his crew traded with the local inhabitants under the supervision of two Indian "kings," estimated to be forty and twenty-four years old. The account of the voyage described

the older man as having "on his naked body a stag [or deer] skin, skill-
fully worked like damask with various embroideries; the head was bare,
the hair tied back with various bands, and around the neck hung a wide
chain decorated with many different-colored stones," which probably
refers to wampum.[82] In other words, this man looked a great deal like
the figure in the portrait identified as Ninigret; it might very well have
been one of his close ancestors. There are no subsequent contact epi-
sodes on record for the region until the early seventeenth century, and to
the extent that they took place at all, they must have been rare. The archaeological record indicates that during this interim period the con-
nection of southern New England Indians to the European trade was
mostly through Indian middlemen from Nova Scotia and Maine, who
were already in regular contact with English, French, and Basque fisher-
man. We know this because there are almost no intact European goods
in southern New England archaeological sites from this period. The region's Indians did, however, obtain bits of copper and other metals
from objects like trade kettles that Indians further up the coast had
dismantled before trading the raw materials far afield. Indians then
fashioned this metal into beads and amulets, just as they did with indigenous surface copper mined by Indians in places like the Great Lakes
and traded through networks that stretched across the continent.

After 1602, however, southern New England Indians obtained steadier
access to the European trade. The establishment of French bases at Aca-
dia (Nova Scotia) in 1604 and Québec in 1608 increased the number of
goods accessible through long-distance exchange. More important, English, Dutch, and French ships began to visit the southern New England
coast annually, during which they traded and often fought with local
people. Already by 1614 the Dutch had established trading relationships
with several groups along Long Island Sound, including the Pequots,
Mohegans, Montauketts, Narragansetts, and Wampanoags. For the most
part, these trading sessions involved the Dutch dropping anchor, trading, and then sailing off when the business was done. Yet the impact of
such fleeting exchanges was dramatic. First off, they began a consumer
revolution in coastal Indian life in which the Indians began to procure
increasing amounts of European manufactured goods, particularly tools,
weapons, cloth, and clothing. Indians sought to open up new trade lines
to Europeans, acquire the furs and especially the wampum that Europeans wanted in trade, and protect their access to the European market

from indigenous competitors. As such, Indians had greater incentive than ever before to subjugate their neighbors for wampum tribute, thus setting the stage for decades of violence between area peoples, especially the Narragansetts, Pequots, and later, Mohegans.[83]

Increased contact with Europeans came with yet another cost: epidemic disease. Indeed, the devastation of American Indians by epidemic diseases might be the most significant disaster of modern world history. Before colonization, the Indians' geographic isolation from the rest of the world meant that they been spared ancient European scourges such as smallpox, measles, scarlet fever, chickenpox, bubonic plague, the flu, mumps, and whooping cough and African diseases such as yellow fever and malaria. Many of these diseases developed because peoples on other continents, unlike Indians, crowded together in filthy cities and lived in close contact with domestic animals. Indians had only to cope with their own comparatively mild diseases of venereal syphilis, hepatitis, and polio. The downside was that when Indians finally came into contact with Europeans, Africans, and their diseases, the results were horrific. Between the late fifteenth century and the late nineteenth century, diseases from Europe and, to a lesser extent, Africa, were the major factor in reducing the Indian population of the Western Hemisphere from as many as 70 million people on the eve of 1492, or about one-seventh of the entire globe's estimated 500 million people, to just 2 or 3 million people in 1900, with a mere 250,000 within the boundaries of the modern United States.[84]

The Indians of southern New England suffered more than their fair share of this disaster. Between 1616 and 1619, a case of what was probably either the plague or smallpox, introduced by a European vessel skirting the coast, tore through Indian communities between Maine's Saco River on the north and the east side of Narragansett Bay on the south, sweeping away as much as 90 percent of the population of the infected communities and obliterating some communities altogether. Wampanoags inhabiting the area between Massachusetts Bay and Narragansett Bay were especially hard hit. According to Plymouth colonist Thomas Morton, the surrounding country was littered with the bones and skulls of the unburied dead, which "made such a spectacle . . . it seemed to me a new found Golgotha," in reference to the biblical hill where Jesus was crucified and which was covered with the rotting remains of the Romans' other execution victims.[85] Yet this was just the beginning of the Indians' ordeal. In 1622, what contemporaries described as a "great sicknesse . . . not unlike the plague" erupted in coastal Massachusetts, mercilessly killing up to 50 percent of infected communities just beginning to come to terms with their losses from the previous epidemic. Strikingly, the Narragansetts were spared both times, which probably reflects that they were on hostile terms with their Wampanoag neighbors to the east and thus not swapping germs with them. In 1633, however, smallpox tore down the Connecticut River Valley and into Narragansett country. Seven hundred Narragansetts died in this disaster, suffering, in the words of Plymouth's William Bradford, "like rotten sheep." It was a trauma probably unlike any other in their people's history.[86]

Each epidemic produced a power vacuum that the survivors struggled to fill. When disease swept off a community's sachem, the people had either to appoint a new one or put themselves under the protection of a neighboring leader. In turn, established sachems and upstarts competed with each other for followers. Though we do not have eyewitness accounts of these contests, it is safe to assume that they sometimes grew violent. That is certainly true of the rivalry between the Narragansetts and the Wampanoags around Narragansett Bay. According to Indian testimony, after the epidemic of 1616–19 the Narragansetts began intimidating the weakened Wampanoags in an attempt to reduce them to the status of tribute payers.[87] Sachems who wanted to avoid this fate needed outside help and fast.

At the same time, Indians faced the challenge of explaining what this disaster meant. Some Indians near Massachusetts Bay associated the plague with a curse put on them by some French sailors who they had captured and enslaved, while others linked it to a comet.[88] At least until 1633, the most common explanation appears to have been that Cautantowwit was angry. The reason was that the Narragansetts had escaped the plague, and they alone among the Indians of the coast had been preforming a ritual in which they destroyed "almost all the riches they had . . . as kettles, skins, hatchets, beads, knives," and dedicated the sacrifice to Cautantowwit. Given the survivors' need for spiritual succor and political protection, a number of them chose to abandon their decimated communities and join the Narragansetts.[89]

It was at this critical moment, as sachems were looking to reconsolidate or expand their followings, that English colonists began arriving on the coast, opening up new possibilities for trade and alliance. The first of these colonies was Plymouth, which the English established in 1620 on the site of Patuxet, a Wampanoag town the plague had eviscerated and the few survivors had abandoned. Wampanoags had every reason to be apprehensive about the newcomers, as they had clashed with English explorers several times between 1602 and 1619, including an incident in 1614 in which English captain Thomas Hunt abducted twenty-seven of their people off Cape Cod and transported them to Spain as slaves. Nevertheless, the sachem Massasoit of the Wampanoag community of Pokanoket overcame his trepidation out of need for assistance against the Narragansetts. They had already pushed his people from the head of Narragansett Bay eastward to the Taunton River and appeared determined to keep up the pressure. Thus, after keeping the English under watch for a year, Massasoit finally offered his friendship to them, using as his go-between a Wampanoag named Squanto, a former captive of Hunt who had managed to return home in 1619 after a long sojourn in Europe. Given that Plymouth numbered less than two hundred people, many of them women and children, and most of them diseased and malnourished, the colony did not appear threatening. Plymouth did, however, possess exotic goods and armed soldiers that Massasoit could use to strengthen his authority among the Wampanoags and fend off the Narragansetts.

Massasoit reaped the benefits of this alliance as early as September 1621, when Plymouth raised an armed force to intimidate two Wampanoag sachems, Corbitant and Nepeof, who threatened to defect to the Narragansetts in protest of Massasoit's rapprochement with the English. The Narragansetts responded by sending the English a bundle of arrows wrapped in snakeskin, the arrows symbolizing war and the snakeskin the shamanistic power to implant these dangerous objects. On Squanto's advice, Plymouth's governor William Bradford responded by returning the snakeskin filled with gunpowder and shot. The message should have been clear. Lest anyone mistake its meaning, the following year Massasoit convinced the English to attack and kill the sachem of Wessagusset on the south shore of Massachusetts Bay, who he charged with organizing a conspiracy of Wampanoag sachems to wipe out the young colony. With this, Massasoit enhanced his authority by illustrating his power to direct the English. Henceforth, Wampanoags sachems followed Massasoit's judgment in colonial affairs, sending him tribute from as far away as Nantucket. For their part, the English now considered Massasoit a fast friend and pledged to defend him against Narragansett attacks. They also relied on him to broker their trade and diplomacy with other Wampanoags. Massasoit had turned English colonization into a source of personal strength and sachems across the region, including Ninigret, took notice.[90]

Controlling the small English colony of Plymouth was one thing, but the populous Massachusetts Bay Colony was quite another. Between 1629 and 1640 more than thirteen thousand English, most of them in family groups, crossed the Atlantic to form a puritan bastion along Massachusetts Bay, centered on the peninsular town of Boston. The local Massachuset Indians, weakened from repeated bouts of epidemic disease, tried to form an alliance with these newcomers to fend off their own enemies, the Micmacs of Nova Scotia, but soon the colonists overwhelmed them. The problem was not just the sheer number of English migrants, but their animals too—cows, horses, pigs, and sheep. These animals grazed in the woods unfenced and competed for food with the Indians' wild game. They often wandered far beyond the bounds of English settlement to feast on Indian crops. Not the least of all, they became a source for trouble whenever Indians killed or injured them and colonists demanded compensation. Englishmen and their animals seemed to sprout from the graves of Indians who had died during the previous years' epidemics. The Massachusetts Bay Colony had become as powerful a force as any of the region's major tribes.[91]

Coastal Indians, including the Narragansetts and Niantics, found the Dutch colony of New Netherland more to their liking. The Dutch extended their commerce to the Indians of New England after founding Fort Nassau (later Fort Orange) on the upper Hudson River in 1614 near the site of modern Albany, followed by New Amsterdam (or Manhattan) on the lower Hudson in 1625. With Indian permission, the Dutch also set up a handful of small and, for the most part, short-lived, trading posts on Block Island, Narragansett Bay, Buzzard's Bay, and the Connecticut River, but otherwise they dealt with Indians throughout Long Island Sound from shipboard. Sometimes this trade involved the coastal Indians trading the Dutch their wampum, which the Dutch then exchanged with interior Indians for furs. At other times, coastal Indians traded the Dutch furs which they themselves had acquired from the interior tribes in exchange for wampum or European goods marked up at a premium.[92] Competition between the Pequots, Mohegans, Montauketts, Narragansetts, and Wampanoags for control of this trade—indigenous and European—was becoming a new source of rivalry that would reconfigure the politics of the region.[93]

Even distant New France and its indigenous trading partners influenced these coastal developments. After decades of exploring the southern New England coast and trading and fishing along the bays and inlets of Maine, Nova Scotia, and Labrador, in 1608 the French established a permanent colony on the St. Lawrence River at Québec, followed by new settlements upriver at Trois-Rivières and Montreal. Though New France was small in terms of population, with only twenty-five hundred colonists in 1663, the French evangelized and traded with a variety of Indians stretching westward into the Great Lakes region and eastward into the Canadian Maritimes.[94] French commerce also reached the Sokokis and other Abenaki bands of the upper Connecticut River and, through them, the Pocumtucks downriver, who, in turn, traded with the Narragansetts. Thus, Narragansett wampum ended up traveling all the way into the St. Lawrence River Valley while French goods, such as Jesuit rings, sometimes made it to Long Island Sound.[95] Equally important in the world of indigenous politics, the Narragansetts' distant Indian allies, the Mohawks and the upper Connecticut River tribes, were directly affected by the French, with the Mohawks and the rest of the Iroquois at war with New France and its indigenous trading partners, including the Sokokis, throughout much of the seventeenth century. Ninigret's efforts to enlist these northern powers in his causes often pivoted on their own northerly concerns.[96]

This was the world in which Ninigret came of age, a world shaped by intense competition between sachems for tribute-paying followers and between entire communities for control of trade. These contests hinged on marriage alliances, warfare, long-distance trade, religious authority, loyalty oaths and betrayals. That was certainly the case before the era of colonization and would remain throughout Ninigret's lifetime. Yet as the Pequot War of 1636–37 would illustrate, the colonists' involvement dramatically raised the stakes in this game. It is at this moment that Ninigret comes into view.

CHAPTER 2

"To obtaine it by force"

Ninigret emerged as a major sachem during the 1630s, as surrounding European colonies, particularly English ones, began to expand in size and influence. Throughout the decade, English puritans arrived by the thousands in the new colony of Massachusetts and then began spreading into the Connecticut River Valley, Narragansett Bay, and eastern Long Island, thereby encircling Narragansett country. Meanwhile, the Dutch of New Netherland extended their Indian trade eastward through Long Island Sound and up the Connecticut River. These developments were followed quickly by the Pequot War of 1636–37, the first large-scale clash between Indians and colonists in the region. Given this context, one might reasonably assume that colonists became the focus of Ninigret's political life. To be sure, they claimed a great deal of his attention, mostly because the English kept trying to direct the Narragansetts' affairs with other Indians after the Pequot War, and because sachems competed for English and Dutch trade, political influence, and military might. Yet throughout his career Ninigret's main priorities had to do with other Indians, specifically increasing his influence among the Niantics and Narragansetts and expanding his circle of tributaries. Ninigret's colonial diplomacy focused on defending his autonomy against English interference in these matters, all the while using the newcomers to his best advantage in relations with other Indians.

Europeans did not alter the organizing principles of Ninigret's politics, just the means of achieving them. Ninigret's main purposes were to advance the interests of his people—the Niantics, specifically, and the Narragansetts, generally—and to strengthen his own influence. He constantly weighed these priorities in the competition between sachems for followers, tribute payers, and prestige. Colonization changed this dynamic only insofar as it introduced new players into the contest. Once the English and Dutch began partnering with sachems along the coast, many of whom were Ninigret's foes, sachems began vying for colonial goods, protection, and the power to direct colonists against their enemies. Cutthroat and savvy as any of his rivals, Ninigret was just the man to play this sort of game.

Tawhìtch chachepiséttit nishquéhettit? Why are you angry? Ninigret and the Beginning of the Pequot War

The Pequot War, in all its phases, was an outgrowth of indigenous politics.[1] Among the conflict's defining features was the decision of the Narragansetts and Mohegans to side with Connecticut and Massachusetts against the Pequots, but an indigenous perspective could argue that it was the colonies who joined the Narragansetts and the Mohegans in their ongoing struggles with the Pequots. After all, the Narragansetts and Pequots appear to have been at odds at least throughout the 1620s and 1630s over control of the flow of wampum, access to colonial trade, tributaries, and dominion over the area stretching east from the Pawcatuck River to Weekapaug, on the edge of Ninigret's territory. According to William Wood, the Pequots derided the Narragansetts as loathe to fight, insulting them as "women-like men," but anecdotal evidence suggests that the Narragansetts were worthy opponents. Recall that the Narragansetts welcomed the Pawcatuck Indian war leader, Sosoa, over to their side after he turned on his supposed Pequot allies and decapitated one of their captains. Also remember Nathaniel Waterman's testimony that Ninigret was known among the Narragansetts as a "man of courage" for his deeds against the Pequots. The point is that the Narragansetts doubtlessly welcomed English hostility against the Pequots but did not need it to hold their own in the indigenous contest for Long Island Sound.

The same cannot be said of Uncas, sachem of the Mohegans, who the Pequots had humbled repeatedly. The Mohegans, a community of between four hundred and six hundred people residing twenty miles north of the mouth of the Pequot (or Thames) River, were one-time allies of the Pequots, but in Uncas's lifetime they had fallen to the status of tributaries. Uncas had no intention of staying that way. Indeed, he seems to have aspired to become the Pequots' leading sachem, for his ancestors included at least two Pequot sachems and one of his wives was the daughter of the great Pequot sachem, Tatobem. According to Indian testimony, Uncas rose up against Tatobem's son and successor, Sassacus, five times preceding the Pequot War, only to have the Pequots force him on each occasion to retreat into Narragansett country and beg for pardon before allowing him to return home. Uncas would stoke Pequot-English tensions during the 1630s and then use the ensuing war as the sixth and final chance for him to escape his subordination and rise to the head of the Pequot tributary network. His ascendency would also introduce him to a new rival in the form of Ninigret.

Power struggles between the Pequots and their western tributaries, the Podunks and Wagunks, or so-called "River Indians" of the middle Connecticut River Valley around modern Hartford, also factored into the start of the Pequot War. The Connecticut River Valley was the geographical center for the war's opening events as a contested site between various Indian communities, between the English and Dutch, and between the English colonies of Plymouth, Massachusetts, and Connecticut. Setting this process in motion were the efforts of River Indians to free themselves from subjection to the Pequots. As early as 1631, the Podunk sachem, Wagincut, had tried and failed to entice the English of Massachusetts and Plymouth to build a trading post near modern Windsor, Connecticut; earlier, the Pequots had driven him from the area, and apparently he hoped English protection would enable him to return. One scholar surmises that he had Narragansett backing in this initiative, which would be consistent with Narragansett entreaties to disaffected Pequot tributaries in the disputed Pawcatuck region.[2] Thereafter, the Pequots took the lead in directing European activity in the Connecticut River Valley. In 1633, the Pequot sachems authorized the Dutch to build a trading house, named Good Hope, among their tributaries on the site of modern Hartford, though Pequot territory was some sixty miles to the southeast. The Pequots also permitted a rebellious Connecticut River sachem, Sequin, who they had forced from the area, to return and live at the House of Good Hope, apparently in the expectation that he would serve as their eyes and ears. By giving their tributaries conditional access to the Dutch trade, and the Dutch conditional access to Pequot tributaries, the Pequots probably hoped to strengthen their control over the region and, by extension, weaken the possibility of their subordinates reaching out to the English or the Narragansetts. In other words, the

Pequots' management of the Dutch and the River Indians was supposed to be mutually reinforcing. Yet their plans went awry.

Things began to go wrong after some Pequots attacked a party either of Narragansetts or their protectorates near the Dutch House of Good Hope. Earlier, the Pequots and Dutch had agreed (at least as the Dutch understood it) to permit free access to this site. The Pequots, however, were not about to watch their rivals stock up on Dutch goods and open up another avenue of influence into the Connecticut River Valley. Rejecting the Pequots' right to dictate their trade, the Dutch took the Pequot sachem, Tatobem, hostage, and demanded a ransom of wampum. The Pequots paid up and received Tatobem's head in return.

Unwilling to let the matter rest there, the Pequots took revenge on the next Dutchmen who dared to sail up the river. There was only one problem: the men the Pequots killed were English, not Dutch. The Pequots apologized to Massachusetts authorities that this was a case of mistaken identity, that "we know no difference between the Dutch and the English, they are both strangers to us, we took them all to be one."[3] They also appealed that the victims of this attack, Captain John Stone and his crew of seven, had brought it upon themselves. Apparently Stone's men had seized some Western Niantics to force them to serve as guides on the Connecticut River. This community, which was distinct from Ninigret's Eastern Niantics, was a Pequot protectorate. Yet Massachusetts did not care why the Pequots had killed Stone and his sailors, only that they had done so. The colony wanted to send Indians a message that it would not tolerate "savages" taking English lives. Thus, Boston demanded the Pequots to turn over the killers to colonial justice.

No sachem could relinquish his people to a foreign power without risking his following or even his own neck. Instead, the Pequots tried to appease the English through Indian protocols. In the fall of 1634 they compensated for the murders in accordance with Indian custom by presenting Boston with a valuable gift, including furs and an invitation to settle on the Connecticut River. Put another way, the Pequots were trying to resolve this crisis by recruiting the English as a military and trade partner to answer the Dutch. Massachusetts was generally receptive, especially to the Pequots' gift of land. The Pequot offer helped clear the way for the founding of the towns of Windsor, Hartford, and Wethersfield, which formed the core of the new colony of Connecticut. Yet Massachusetts authorities refused to drop their demand for Stone's killers.

For two more years they pressured the Pequots to extradite the suspects until, finally, another case of Indians murdering Englishmen convinced them to resolve the issue violently.[4]

Ninigret might very well have been involved in this second murder, but the extent of his participation is shrouded in mystery.[5] Here are the known facts: in July 1636, John Gallop, captaining a trading barque in Long Island Sound, spied John Oldham's pinnace in the distance sailing erratically. As Gallop approached Oldham's ship he noticed that the deck was full of Indians, while another body of Indians paddled a canoe full of goods away from the vessel. Fearing the worst, Gallop and his men opened fire on the pinnace and took possession of it, killing about a dozen of the Indians and capturing two more in the process. As for John Oldham, Gallop discovered his body tangled in the ship's netting, his limbs mangled, and "his head cleft to the brains."[6] A couple of other Indians remained barricaded in the ship's hold, ready to fight, until Gallop decided that he had tested his luck far enough. After securing Oldham's remaining goods, Gallop set the bloody vessel adrift with the last two Indian defenders still below deck. Then he began interrogating his lone Indian captive, having sent the other one to a watery grave.

The prisoner's testimony was potentially explosive as it implicated some of the highest-ranking Narragansetts in Oldham's murder.[7] He confessed that the attackers were Manisees from Block Island, a small spit of land located thirteen miles off the coast of Narragansett country. Yet the Manisees had only executed the killing, they had not orchestrated it. Gallop's prisoner charged that "all the Sachems of the Narragansetts except Canonicus and Miantonomi," including Ninigret, had masterminded a plot to kill Oldham after he began trading with the Pequots the previous year.[8] As proof, the prisoner pointed out that two Narragansetts had been aboard Oldham's ship as hired hands at the time of the assault. Conspicuously, the Manisees had spared them along with two young English crewmembers, who they had spirited away in canoes before Gallop fell upon the pinnace. This was no mere coincidence, the Indian told, for the Narragansett crew members had volunteered to sail under Oldham as part of the plot, which was becoming wider and more insidious with every mounting detail.

Some of this testimony rings true. It makes sense that the Narragansetts would attempt to cut off Oldham for extending his trade to their primary rival, the Pequots. The Narragansetts had been doing business with

Oldham for at least a few years before his killing. Canonicus and Miantonomi had gone so far in 1634 as to grant him use of an island in Narragansett Bay, doubtlessly with the hope of setting up an exclusive commercial relationship with him.[9] Yet Oldham insisted on remaining a free agent to the point of supplying the Narragansetts' enemies. At least some Narragansetts must have believed, therefore, that he deserved to die. To be sure, attacking an Englishman carried some political risk for the Narragansetts, but for years the Pequots had managed to avoid any serious repercussions for the murder of Stone and his crew, and there was no reason to think that an attack on Oldham would prove any different.

In weighing this decision, the Narragansetts had not yet come to respect the English as a major military power. Though the population of the Massachusetts Bay colony was expanding at a rapid pace because of the regular arrival of new migrants, in 1636 its population still stood at only five or six thousand people, less than the Narragansetts.[10] The English populations of Plymouth (probably between five hundred and six hundred people by the mid 1630s) and Connecticut (approaching eight hundred by the middle of 1636) were smaller still, and there was no guarantee that they would support Massachusetts in the event of hostilities.[11] The Narragansetts might have surmised that killing Oldham would adversely affect their trade with the English, but the Dutch were available as substitutes. In short, it would have been understandable for the Narragansett sachems to conclude that dispatching Oldham was worth the risk, particularly if they could pawn it off on their Manisee tributaries.

There is no way to know whether there was a full-fledged conspiracy and whether Canonicus and Miantonomi were innocent of it, but it is clear that these sachems did everything they could to distance themselves from the charge. No sooner had Boston authorities received word from Gallop about Oldham's murder than an urgent message arrived from Canonicus and Miantonomi, written by Roger Williams who had recently settled at the head of Narragansett Bay. Remarkably, the carriers of this message were the same two Narragansetts who had survived from Oldham's crew. It was as if the sachems wanted to prove either that they had nothing to hide or, at the very least, that the English did not intimate them. The sachems expressed "how grievously they were offended" at the Manisees, so much so that Miantonomi had sent two hundred men in seventeen canoes to punish the Block Islanders.[12] Yet the English remained unsatisfied. Winthrop had Williams warn Canonicus and Miantonomi that Oldham's murder might be cause for war, "for Blocke I[s]land was under them" and therefore the English held the Narragansett sachems responsible.[13] Might was the operative word here, for Winthrop still considered the innocence of Canonicus and Miantonomi to be open to question. However, he had already judged that other high-ranking Narragansetts, Ninigret among them, had something to do with Oldham's murder.

Ninigret certainly was involved at some level. Shortly, another message arrived from Canonicus and Miantonomi that they had ordered "the Sachem of Niantic," probably Ninigret, to fetch from Block Island the two English boys who survived from Oldham's crew.[14] Apparently the Narragansett sachems wanted Ninigret to put out a fire he had started. Connecticut's John Mason learned that Ninigret had some of the plunder from Oldham's boat, which clearly implicated him in the murder. Later, Canonicus and Miantonomi sent additional intelligence that the Narragansett crewmen who had sailed with Oldham had been hired "by the sachem of Niantic" and some other, lesser sachems killed during Gallop's attack on Oldham's pinnace. Unfortunately for the English, Canonicus and Miantonomi refused to turn over these crewmen for questioning. Collectively, this testimony convinced the English that they knew the contours of the plot. Winthrop told Canonicus and Miantonomi that the English held them to be innocent in light of their cooperation. As for the "6 other under Sachems" of the Narragansetts, particularly Ninigret, they "were guilty."[15]

Perhaps Canonicus and Miantonomi were making Ninigret their fall guy, but it is equally possible that Ninigret had designed Oldham's murder to enhance his own and the Niantics' profile among the Narragansetts. Young sachems like Ninigret rose to power by leading their people against outsiders despite calls for restraint by more mature sachems, like Canonicus. Ninigret might have seen killing Oldham as a way to damage the Pequots' trade, burnish his credentials for leadership, raise the Niantics' voice in Narragansett affairs, and challenge Canonicus's and Miantonomi's policy of rapprochement with the English.[16] Given these possibilities, we need to consider that Canonicus's and Miantonomi's eagerness to punish the Block Islanders and direct English aggression against Ninigret might had more to do with putting down a domestic challenge than cowering before the English.

Ninigret avoided a more serious confrontation, both with the Narragansett sachems and the English, but just barely. As it turned out, he not only had possession of Oldham's goods, but at least some of Oldham's killers. One of them was Adussah, the Manisee sachem, who had taken refuge with Ninigret's nephew, a minor Niantic sachem named Wequash-cook.[17] Miantonomi ended the impasse by paying some unidentified person six fathoms of wampum "for the slaying of Adussah."[18] The recipient might very well have been Ninigret, for it is unlikely that anyone would have dared to execute Adussah in Niantic territory without Ninigret's consent. All of which is to say, Ninigret might very well have been involved in the plot to kill Oldham *and* the killing of Oldham's killer. It made sense for Ninigret to betray Adussah because he was in no position to challenge Canonicus, Miantonomi, and Boston simultaneously. In any case, by murdering Oldham and keeping his goods from the Pequots, Ninigret had already proven his ability to lead.

Whether or not Adussah's death would have satisfied Massachusetts became a moot issue when a punitive English expedition against the Manisees and Pequots for the murders of Oldham and Stone expanded into an English-Pequot war. Oldham's murder convinced colonial authorities that they had let the Stone affair drag on for too long. They judged that their peaceful diplomacy with the Pequots had only emboldened Indians throughout the region to slay Englishmen whenever they pleased. Failing to act in the Oldham case, they concluded, would only invite more killing. Thus Massachusetts raised a force to thrash the Manisees and then proceed to Pequot country to demand Stone's killers at gunpoint. The mission did not include pursuing Ninigret, probably out of respect to Miantonomi and Canonicus. Though the English would have liked to make an example of Ninigret, they could not afford to antagonize the Narragansetts while their hands were full with the Pequots. In other words, Ninigret had successfully challenged the English, drawn their parry, and escaped injury. He must have risen in the eyes of his countrymen as a result.

Nickqueintouôog, I will make Warre upon them.
The Bloody Pequot War and Political Realignment

The colonists' first strikes against the Manisees and Pequots were minor in scale, probably in line with what Indians expected, given that their own conflicts rarely took large numbers of lives. In late August 1636, Massachusetts sent an expedition of one hundred troopers under John Endecott against the Manisees with orders to kill the men and enslave the women and children. Yet the Manisees slipped their grasp, even within the narrow confines of Block Island (which is less than ten square miles in area). After launching arrows at the English from a safe distance, the Manisees disappeared into their island's scrub forest. Frustrated, the English killed the Manisees' dogs, looted and torched their homes, and then sailed away to confront the Pequots. There too the English came up empty-handed. Landing near the mouth of the Pequot River, the English ordered the Pequots to turn over Stone's murderers and pay an indemnity in wampum. Instead, the Pequot sachems stalled while their people retreated into the woods. Without anyone to attack, the English again resorted to plundering and burning, which did nothing to bend the Pequots' will. The Pequots revenged this attack by besieging the colonists' Fort Saybrook at the mouth of the Connecticut River and then, in April 1637, raiding the Connecticut town of Wethersfield, to the loss of several English lives and head of livestock. These were the opening blows in the first major war between Indians and colonists in the history of New England.[19]

After expressing a preference for neutrality, the Narragansetts lined up with the English in this campaign despite entreaties from the Pequots. Though the Narragansetts' relations with the English were strained over the Oldham affair, the Pequots were their primary rival in the contest for wampum-paying tribute payers and the Dutch trade. This war seemed like a prime opportunity to deal them a heavy blow, particularly after the English rejected an offer from Miantonomi to leave the fighting to his warriors and limit themselves to providing sea transport.[20] The English would come to battle with a formidable array of sophisticated metal weapons, including firearms, swords, pikes, and armor. The Pequots were isolated, having no foreign allies willing to come to their defense, which meant that the Narragansetts could war against them without having to guard another front. Seeing the gravity of their situation, the Pequots reached out to the Narragansetts, pleading, according to English accounts, that the colonists "were strangers and began to overspread the country," and that if the Narragansetts joined those strangers in this war, "they [the Narragansetts] did but make the way for their own overthrow," for soon the English would turn on them too.[21] The Narragansetts, however, could not see that far into the future, and in any case they had more pressing concerns. They viewed this crisis as a rare chance to dispatch their enemy and establish their preeminence in the region.

Ninigret appears to have opposed this policy of Canonicus and Mian-tonomi. After all, if the Pequots were right that the English would eventually turn on the Narragansetts, Ninigret was likely to be their first target given his purported role in the Oldham killing. Additionally, Nini-gret probably saw the danger of permitting the English to invade what amounted to his backyard. As if to accentuate the point, in May 1637, a force of more than a hundred Englishmen from the Connecticut towns and Fort Saybrook sailed into Narragansett Bay and then began march-ing westward toward Pequot country. They hoped to recruit Narragan-sett warriors along the way. Miantonomi contributed two hundred men to this campaign, but when the expedition stopped overnight at a fort in Niantic country, Ninigret and his brother were less supportive.[22] Ac-cording to Captain John Mason, the sachem of this stronghold, either Ninigret or Wepitamock, "carried very proudly towards us; not permit-ting any of us to come into their fort." The English carried it proudly as well, stationing guards all around the palisade and threatening to kill anyone who tried to send warning to the Pequots.[23] They knew that a number of sachems in this Niantic-Pequot border region, such as Sosoa, had only recently aligned with the Narragansetts and still had relatives among the Pequots.[24] Despite these issues, an unspecified number of Niantic warriors joined the expedition when the march resumed, but prob-ably more out of deference to Miantonomi than to the English. Even then, most of them returned home before any fighting occurred. What-ever their hostility toward the Pequots, they had no interest in lending support to the English.[25]

The English were the victors in the subsequent war, but the results were decidedly mixed. In May 1637, English forces from Connecticut and Massachusetts marched into Pequot territory and massacred hun-dreds of Pequot innocents at Mystic, leaving Mohegan and Narragansett warriors to capture the survivors. In the months that followed, the En-glish and Mohegans hunted down the remaining Pequots they could find, killing scores of them, including the leading sachems and war-riors, and enslaving hundreds of others. Though some Pequots man-aged to find refuge among sympathetic Indian neighbors, the Pequots were finished as a regional power. Startled at the carnage, lesser sa-chems throughout the region sent presents and declarations of friend-ship to colonial authorities to ensure that they were not next. In this sense, the English accomplished their primary aims in the Pequot War, which, at minimum, had been to force Indians to hand over community members accused of murdering colonists, and more symbolically, to show Indians the bloody costs of defying colonial authority.

Yet Ninigret, Miantonomi, and Canonicus were not so easily browbeaten. The English acted as if their victory over the Pequots gave them automatic rights to all the spoils. For instance, they banned the Narragansetts from hunting in Pequot country, ordered them to turn over all Pequots they had taken in, and tried to prevent them from subordinating former Pequot protectorates such as the wampum-rich Montauketts and Shinnecocks on Long Island. The Narragansetts had no intention of conceding to these demands. Their purpose in cooperating with the English had been to remove the Pequots and then fill the power vacuum.[26] In short, the English defeat of the Pequots had set the stage for the Narragansetts to take their place as the colonists' primary indigenous rival.

Compounding these tensions, the Narragansetts also denied the English a say in how they responded to a new and unexpected contender to replace the Pequots—the Mohegans. English hostility toward the Pequots had revived Uncas's bid to throw off his tributary status and become the Pequots' ranking sachem. To these ends, he incited the English throughout the Stone murder crisis, such as warning that the Pequots were plotting a strike against the new colonial settlements on the Connecticut River. Then, at Mystic, Uncas raised scores of warriors for the invading force and kept them in the fight even as Narragansetts fled in disgust at the indiscriminate killing. Uncas's strategy was to establish himself as the colonists' indispensable ally and then use their backing to absorb as many Pequot survivors as possible and become a tribute-collecting sachem himself. By definition, that aspiration made him a rival of Ninigret and the Narragansetts. Stepping forward to meet Uncas's challenge would become one of the keys to Ninigret's transformation from a local leader of the Niantics to a tribal leader of the Narragansetts.[27]

Mat méshnawmônash, I did not see those things.
The Emergent Narragansett Rivalry with the Mohegans and English

The end of the Pequot War was the beginning of a struggle over the peace, centered on who would collect tribute from which Indian communities and who would control former Pequot lands. In this, Sassacus's warning that the English were playing the Narragansetts in a game of divide and conquer began to materialize. In a 1638 agreement known to posterity as the Treaty of Hartford, Canonicus, Miantonomi, and Uncas pledged to submit their intertribal disagreements to the colonies and pay an annual wampum tribute for any Pequots they harbored. Yet the Indian signatories, particularly the Narragansetts, appear to have interpreted the treaty less as a binding agreement than as a symbol of peace, as a means, in the words of the document, for "all former injuries and wrongs offered each to other [to be] remitted and buried and never to be renewed any more from henceforth."[28] Indian diplomacy often pivoted less on specific policy issues than on creating a ritualized environment of fellowship in which foreign people could forgive each other's injuries.[29] For them, the main accomplishment of the meeting at Hartford was opening communication between the parties and representing their intentions to work together in the future. The Narragansetts also signaled their friendly intentions to the English shortly after signing the treaty by deeding Prudence and Aquidneck Islands in Narragansett Bay to Roger Williams and Massachusetts governor John Winthrop.[30] Though the Narragansetts were unwilling to march to English orders, they expected the English to overlook their affronts in light of such gestures. In this expectation, they were gravely mistaken.

The Narragansetts had a number of factors working against their plan to reap the spoils of the Pequot War. Weak Indian communities had no desire to pay the Narragansetts tribute that had once gone to the Pequots or to affiliate with the Narragansetts at a time when a Narragansett-English war seemed to be brewing. Throwing their loyalty to the English seemed the best way to reduce the burden of tribute and distance themselves from colonial enemies while gaining protection against Narragansett retaliation. Wyandanch of the Montauketts is a prime example of a sachem who adopted this strategy. Like Uncas, he saw the war as an opportunity to break free of tributary status of the Pequots. During the conflict he ingratiated himself with the English by befriending Lion Gardiner, the commander of Fort Saybrook, and pledging to keep Pequots from fleeing to Montaukett territory. After the fighting ended, the emergent threat of Narragansett attack led Wyandanch to sell the English land that became the towns of Southold, Southampton, and East Hampton, and to submit to English authority. Ultimately, this alliance would cost the Montauketts and other Long Island Indians dearly in land and sovereignty, to the point that many of them became debt peons to the English by the late seventeenth and early eighteenth centuries. In the meantime, however, Wyandanch viewed the Narragansetts as his biggest threat and the English as a resource to exploit.[31]

The problem for the Narragansetts was that other minor sachems followed Wyandanch's lead. Over the course of the 1640s, Narragansett tribute payers such as the Pawtuxets under the sachem Socononoco and the Shawomets under the sachem Pomham, also submitted themselves to Massachusetts to free themselves from Narragansett dominance. Like the Montauketts, they could not anticipate that the English would eventually become a greater threat to their interests than the Narragansetts ever had been. Their immediate priority was to escape their subordinate status to the Narragansetts, and the English seemed the best means to that end, given the colonies' growing strength and the fact that they made few demands, as yet, of their Indian protectorates. Little did these subsachems realize that the English, in the long-term, were less interested in offering weak Indians protection than in weakening the Narragansetts and Indians overall.[32]

Another factor working against the Narragansetts was that the English colonies, spearheaded by Massachusetts, were eager to take up the role as the tributary-Indians' defender—at least when it came to intimidation from the Narragansetts. The English knew that their influence in Indian country—and, with it, access to Indian land—depended on chipping away at the tribute relationships that structured Indian politics. With the Pequots defeated and Uncas wise to his dependence on the English, the Narragansetts were now the colonists' main target.

Uncas posed the final challenge to the Narragansetts, for he, no less than them, wanted to lord over Pequot survivors and land. Uncas was by far the weaker party in this rivalry, but his alliance with the English offset Narragansett strength. Yet Uncas first had to convince the English that the Narragansetts represented a threat to them too, not just him. Asking for English protection was one way for Uncas to accomplish this end because any Narragansett move against him became a challenge to English honor and authority. Uncas also fed the English an endless stream of information and misinformation that the Narragansetts plotted against colonial interests. Uncas was not the first or last sachem to adopt this sort of strategy, but his shrewdness, ruthlessness, and deviousness set the standards for his day. The Narragansetts and English would teeter on the brink of war almost constantly for forty years in part because of Uncas's truth and lies.

Ntacquêtunk ewò, He is my subject;
Kuttáckquêtous, I will subject to you.
The Postwar Contest for Tributaries

Ninigret threw himself right into the fray to realign the political hierarchy following the Pequot War, organizing an amphibious assault of eighty men, twenty of whom were Pequot, against the Montauketts in the late spring of 1638.[33] After paddling their dugout canoes across the sound's nearly twenty miles of ocean and then landing on eastern Long Island's outer forks, Ninigret's warriors marched to the home of a Montaukett sachem (probably either Wyandanch or Youghco) and announced that they would seize the sachem's wampum and take prisoners. The sachem managed to flee into the woods, but his people "for fear of their lives" turned over sixty fathoms of wampum. Afterward Ninigret's men "went up and down the island, robbing and pillaging, and got more, about some 30 fathom of wampum." In the process, Ninigret humiliated an unnamed Long Island sachem (possibly Wyandanch) by stripping him naked, "which is accounted among them the greatest disgrace." The point of this raid was not to kill or even necessarily to profit but to assert dominance. The message was that the Montauketts would henceforth pay tribute and deference to the Niantics and Narragansetts, no longer to the Pequots and certainly not to the English.

Ninigret was sending a message to the English too. Doubtless he knew that the Montauketts had put themselves under English protection. Indian sources said that during the raid Ninigret had dismissed Montaukett warnings that Connecticut and Massachusetts would make him pay. Reportedly, he derided Connecticut Colony as of "no matter" and predicted that its government would "but do little." As for Massachusetts, he boasted that he could satisfy its "great man" governor with a simple present of wampum. He chastised the Montauketts that it was foolish for them to depend on the colonists' protection. "English men are liars," he declared, for they promised friendship only "to get your wampum."[34] One of the points of his assault was to test this theory.

The English took Ninigret's dare, but only partially. After receiving a plea from Wyandanch for help, Connecticut sent John Mason and seven men into Niantic country to demand satisfaction. At the same time, Massachusetts governor John Winthrop used the threat of war to convince Miantonomi to bring Ninigret to heel.[35] Under this pressure, Ninigret, after consulting with Roger Williams, visited Connecticut "in person" to return the wampum he had plundered from the Montauketts.[36] However, the Montauketts did not think that this was the end of their troubles with the Niantic sachem. In December 1640, they granted another tract of land to the new English town of Southampton for payment in trade goods and "in consideration that the above named English shall defend us the said Indians from the unjust violence of whatever Indians shall illegally assail us."[37] Certainly the Montauketts had Ninigret in mind. The Montaukett perspective was that Ninigret had come out of this affair just as strong if not stronger than he had entered it. After all, the English had not attacked Ninigret's community, but had only threatened to do so, which suggested that they were reluctant to clash with him. Yes, Ninigret had returned his plunder under English pressure, but he did not concede the larger point about his right to raid the Montauketts at will. Even in the wake of the massacre at Mystic Fort, Ninigret did not view the English as his master.

Narragansett muscle flexing, as in Ninigret's assaults on Long Island, convinced the English that the Narragansetts had joined them in the Pequot War less out of friendship than as a stalking horse "to augment their own Kingdom."[38] The Narragansetts aspired to become "the only lords of the Indians," in the judgment of colonist Daniel Patrick, and "affect not others' greatness," as Israel Stoughton put it.[39] The English believed, with good reason, that the Narragansetts were their most formidable Indian rival now that the Pequots were vanquished. The Narragansetts, for their part, concluded that the English were itching for a fight with them, for why else would they devote such energy to hemming in Narragansett influence so soon after the Narragansetts had assisted them in the Pequot War and granted land to their high-ranking men?

The threat of a new war continued to mount as the English insisted on refereeing the competition between sachems for Pequot survivors and Pequot lands. According to the Treaty of Hartford, each of the various allies was to receive a share of Pequot prisoners, with eighty allotted each to Miantonomi and Uncas, twenty to Ninigret, and the rest to the

45

English. The sachems were also supposed to pay an annual tribute to the English in exchange for these captives. The problem, as the English saw it, was that the sachems seemed determined to adopt as many Pequots as possible all the while laying the charge on their rivals. Nearly everyone was in on the game. By 1640, Uncas was said to have married six or seven high-ranking Pequot women to widen his appeal to Pequot survivors.[40] Likewise, Ninigret reportedly harbored "divers[e] of the Pequots."[41] Yet perhaps the most active sachem in recruiting Pequots was Wequashcook, Ninigret's nephew. Like Uncas, Wequashcook boasted Pequot ancestry and territory on the border of Pequot country, a small area between Weekapaug Brook and Pawcatuck River, slightly west of Ninigret's fort. He also resembled Uncas in viewing the Pequots as a means to elevate himself into a major sachem. The goal of established leaders like Canonicus, Miantonomi, and Ninigret was that such upstarts did not succeed.

More than any other sachem, Ninigret clashed with the English over the fate of the Pequots. He not only refused to turn over Pequots who had killed Englishmen in the war or who were in excess of the allotments specified in the Treaty of Hartford but attempted to set them up near the Pawcatuck River as a new tributary community under his control. This provocation was more than the English were willing to brook, particularly in light of their previous troubles with Ninigret. Furthermore, Uncas urged them to confront the Niantic sachem over this issue, for he saw Ninigret and Wequashcook as his primary rivals for domination of the Pequots.

In what could have easily become the next chapter of the Pequot War, in late August 1639 forty Connecticut soldiers under John Mason and one hundred Mohegans under Uncas landed at the mouth of the Pawcatuck to disperse the nascent settlement. The Pequots wisely fled in advance of the attack, whereupon the invaders began plundering their wétus and cornfields, assuming the day was won. It was not. Midway through the looting, a party of sixty armed Narragansetts, Niantics, and Pequots appeared on a nearby hill and began racing toward the ransacked village, probably hollering at the top of their lungs. The Mohegans watched, waited until the runners were within thirty or forty paces, and then surged forward to meet this force head-on. Yet the fight disappointed Mason, who had a taste for blood sport. He judged the Indians' combat to be "feeble" insofar as it only involved them "striking and cutting with Bows, Hatchets, Knives, etc.," as opposed to the carnage of

Mystic. Nevertheless, the Mohegans emerged from the fray with seven captives, "who were Ninigret's Men." Bold like their leader, the prisoners began to grow "very outrageous," which probably is to say that they taunted and boasted at their captors. An antagonized Mason was ready to behead them when suddenly the Narragansett sachem Yotash, brother of Miantonomi, arrived to negotiate for their lives. Yotash protested that the captives were "his Brother's Men, and that he [Miantonomi] was a Friend to the English." In other words, putting the captives to the sword risked drawing the wrath of the most powerful sachem in the region. Thinking the better of it, Uncas and Mason agreed to spare the men's lives and keep them as hostages until the Niantics turned over any Pequots implicated in the murder of Englishmen.

This compact prevented a general blood-letting, but just barely. For the next twenty-four hours, the Mohegans and English continued to ravage the Pequot settlement, all the while flanked by some three hundred enemy warriors daring them to fight. Then, as the invaders withdrew to their boats, the two sides began shouting at each other. The English declared that they were merely enforcing the terms of the Treaty of Hartford. The Narragansetts responded that "the Pequots were good Men, their Friends, and they would Fight for them, and protect them." The Narragansetts also added a critical detail which the English heard but refused to heed. "They would not fight with English Men," the Narragansetts announced, "for they were spirits, but would fight with Uncas." From their perspective, this was an Indian matter involving Indian contestants and the fate of Indian people and Indian territory. It was not an English concern. The English response said it all. As his vessel began drifting away from the shore, the interpreter Thomas Stanton shot at two Indians "jeering and reviling at us" from a distant hill, hitting one of them in his thigh. It was as if to punctuate that there was no longer any such thing as Indian affairs that did not involve the English.[42]

"So must we be one as they are, otherwise we shall be all gone shortly"
Miantonomi's Failed Anticolonial Campaign

The clash on the Pawcatuck River crystallized the problems facing Canonicus and Miantonomi after the Pequot War. Outside of the Narragansett community, Uncas was doing everything in his power to manufacture a Narragansett-English crisis, the better for him to acquire more followers and tribute payers.[43] The English were willing partners of Uncas because they seemed to believe that their rise depended on the Narragansetts' fall. From inside the Narragansett community, Ninigret and Wequashcook were building their own bases of strength through attacks on neighboring communities and the absorption of Pequots. These activities not only represented power struggles within the Narragansetts but aggravated Narragansett-English relations, for English authorities expected Canonicus and Miantonomi to control Narragansett sachems of lesser status. Given the English refusal to consent to a Narragansett war against Uncas and a substantial Narragansett share of the spoils of the Pequot War, the only alternative for the Narragansetts seemed to be war with the colonists.

In the 1640s, rumors began swirling that Miantonomi was in negotiations with the Mohawks to enlist them in a multitribal strike against the English. The rumor was at least partially true, but the Narragansetts' main concern was Uncas, not the English. In all likelihood, Miantonomi hoped that the threat of the Mohawks would convince the English to abandon the Mohegans to the Narragansetts. As for the Mohawks, though they do not seem to have had any quarrel with Uncas, they did have an abiding interest in maintaining the flow of wampum from the Narragansetts. Consequently, while it is impossible to know whether the rumors of a Narragansett-Mohawk alliance were true, they certainly made sense and definitely got the colonists' attention. The English knew of the Mohawks' fearsome reputation, referring to them as "a cruel bloody people," "Men-eaters," and "the terror of the neighbor Natives."[44] An anticolonial alliance between the most powerful tribe in southeastern New England and the best-armed tribe in the entire Northeast was nothing short of the colonists' greatest nightmare.[45]

Miantonomi professed his friendship to the English when they confronted him with the charge in July 1640, pledging "not to use any hostility towards the English, except [if] they began [it]." Yet two years later, fresh rumors appeared that he had been traveling as far west as the Hudson River to rally Indians for a united strike against colonial settlements.[46] The English first heard of this plot from an Indian who had nearly died after an ox-drawn cart ran over him. This injured man said that "the Englishman's god was angry with him, and had sent Englishman's cow to kill him because he had concealed such conspiracy against the English."[47] Shortly, news of Miantonomi's intrigues began pouring in from all directions. In the spring of 1642 Dutch authorities in New Amsterdam learned that Miantonomi was in the neighborhood with an entourage of one hundred men, "passing through all the Indian Villages, soliciting them to a general war against both the English and the Dutch."[48] Hudson Valley Algonquians and the Dutch were already in the early stages of a devastating conflict now known as Kieft's War, which had also started, in part, over the question of Indians turning over accused murderers to colonial justice.[49] Miantonomi's argument appears to have been that the Pequot War and Kieft's War revealed a systematic colonial threat to all Indians. Lion Gardiner, from Long Island, reported Miantonomi paying two visits to Wyandanch. In the first meeting, Miantonomi merely pressured the Montauketts to halt their wampum tribute payments to the English, "for they are no Sachems." On the second visit, Miantonomi raised the stakes. He offered the Montauketts gifts but would not receive reciprocal presents, which indicated that he had something important to say; if the Montuaketts kept the gifts after the sachem's talk, they symbolized their agreement with him. Miantonomi then shared his vision for a regional military alliance of Indians based on their mutual suffering since the onset of the colonial era. The account of his speech, as related by Wyandanch to Gardiner, is worth quoting at length, for no Indian statement from this time and place provides a more comprehensive view of colonialism's threats to indigenous people:

> He gave them gifts, calling them brethren and friends; for so are we all Indians as the English are, and say brother to one another; so must we be one as they are, otherwise we shall be all gone shortly, for you know our fathers had plenty of deer and skins, our plains were full of deer, as also our woods, and of turkeys, and our coves full of fish and fowl. But these English having gotten our land, they with scythes cut down the grass, and with axes felled the trees; their cows and horses eat the grass, and their hogs spoil our clam banks, and we shall all be starved; therefore it is best for you to do as we, for we are all the sachems from east to west, both Mouquakues and Mohawks joining with us, and we are all resolved to fall upon them all, at one appointed day . . . when you see the three fires that will be made forty days hence in a clear

night; then do as we and the next day fall on and kill men women and children, but no cows, for they will serve to eat till our deer be increased again.[50]

It was a moving plea that must have resonated with many of his listeners. The problem, however, was what the speech failed to say. The Montauke-tts were no fools. They knew that Miantonomi's greatest frustration with the English was not with wandering cattle or declining game populations. Rather, it focused on English interference with the Narragansetts' subjugation of the very people he was now trying to recruit. Calling on Indian communities to rally together as "brethren and friends" against a common English threat was one thing, but what then? Indians across Long Island Sound wanted to hear that a future free of colonists would also mean freedom from Narragansett dominance. That is not what Miantonomi had come to offer and, thus, he was asking too much.

In the near term, the English responded to this rumor with uncommon, if calculated, restraint. Though they seized arms and took hostages from Indians near Boston, they used a much lighter hand when dealing with Miantonomi. The reason was that they attributed the rumor to Uncas and they knew that Miantonomi and Uncas "continually sought to discredit each other with the English."[51] Hoping to uncover the truth, they called Miantonomi to Boston, where, predictably, he charged Uncas with dissembling. Yet that was not enough to satisfy the English magistrates. They wanted a major concession from Miantonomi that proved his commitment to peace: a pledge to stand aside if and when they sent an armed force against Ninigret and the Niantics. Here was English Machiavellianism at its finest. The English wanted to weaken the Narragansetts without having to confront their collective might. Reducing the Niantics while the rest of the Narragansetts looked on would accomplish just that, for in the long term the humiliation suffered by Miantonomi and Canonicus would be sure to undermine their following. Miantonomi was no more eager for war than the English, at least not until he had allies lined up, but this was asking too much. The Niantics "were, he said, as his own flesh, being allied by continual intermarriages." All he would grant was that he would leave the Niantics to the English if, and only if, they wronged the English and Miantonomi himself could not bring them to terms.[52] Despite the qualifications, it was enough of a concession to defuse the emergency, at least for the meantime.

Regardless of whether the war scare was less about the Narragansetts and the colonies than sachem politics, the rivalry between Miantonomi and Uncas soon eclipsed the crisis. Shortly after Miantonomi returned home, Uncas complained that the Narragansett sachem had hired a Pequot to kill him. Once again, Miantonomi countered that Uncas was lying, but his beheading of the suspect assassin shortly after the English brought him in for questioning seemed to confirm the accusation. Then, in July 1643, Uncas responded to an ambush by a Narragansett protectorate, the sachem Sequassen on the Connecticut River, by assaulting Sequassen's Wagunk village, killing seven or eight men, wounding several others, and putting wétus to the torch.[53] Uncas certainly meant this action to double as an insult to Miantonomi, which is precisely how the sachem took it. Miantonomi had watched Uncas rise from an insignificant village leader to a regional power in the space of a few short years, largely by employing the English against other Indians. Furthermore, most of Uncas's gains came at the Narragansetts' expense. He absorbed Pequot survivors that the Narragansetts wanted for their own; he claimed Pequot land that the Narragansetts considered theirs; he gave the English intelligence and false intelligence about Miantonomi's diplomacy; and now he was attacking Narragansett tributaries. To allow this pattern to continue was intolerable. Nevertheless, Miantonomi proceeded cautiously, first asking Massachusetts "if we would not be offended, if he made war upon Uncas." John Winthrop answered, "If Uncas had done him and his friends wrong and would not give satisfaction, we should leave him to take his own course."[54]

Miantonomi's course ultimately led to his own death and opened a new stage in Ninigret's life. In August 1643 Miantonomi gathered an army of a reported one thousand men and invaded Mohegan country, only to be defeated by a much smaller Mohegan force. Worse yet, Miantonomi found himself a captive of Uncas. Shrewd to the new colonial politics, Uncas carried his prize to Hartford to consult with English authorities about what to do. Uncas knew where his strength lay.

Uncas arrived at an auspicious time, for Hartford was hosting the first ever full meeting of the commissioners of United Colonies of New England. This organization, made up of two commissioners from each colony, was dedicated to the shared diplomatic and military concerns of the puritan colonies of Massachusetts, Plymouth, Connecticut, and New Haven. It excluded Roger Williams's tiny colony of Rhode Island as punishment for its religious dissent. Ninigret's attacks against Long Island and Miantonomi's supposed conspiracy were among the reasons that the colonies created this league. Now, in what must have seemed like an act of providence, the commissioners had one of their prime Indian antagonists in their hands. They asked Uncas to march Miantonomi back to Mohegan country and kill him there, seeing an opportunity to eliminate their greatest Indian rival while deflecting Narragansett wrath for the deed. He readily complied.[55]

Kuttannótous: I will revenge you.
Ninigret's Purpose

Even before the killing, the Narragansetts had every reason to want Uncas dead. Now he had killed their hero, leaving them outraged and bent on revenge. Moreover, they charged that Uncas had received a large ransom in wampum for Miantonomi's life, only to renege on his part of the bargain. They no longer wanted the wampum back. They wanted Uncas's head.

Yet the United Colonies warned Canonicus not to seek revenge on Uncas unless he wanted a battle with them as well. Fighting Uncas was one thing. Waging a multifront war against the Mohegans and perhaps four colonies was quite another. There was no way for the Narragansetts to do that without the full backing of the region's other Indians, and securing that kind of support would take time and resources. Then there was the matter of leadership. Canonicus was near eighty years old and would be dead by 1647. He was too old to lead his people into this critical phase of their history. Somebody else had to step forward.

Ninigret saw himself as that man and, to symbolize this new stage in life, he adopted a new name. Up until Miantonomi's death, he had gone by the name of Jannemo. Yet by 1645 the English had begun to refer to him as Ninigret. Name changes of this sort were common among Indians across North America. They took place at rites of passage or after an individual had experienced a profound vision. Political leaders also chose new names when they embarked on challenging new agendas. For instance, when Massasoit died in 1660, his sons, Wamsutta and Metacom, visited Plymouth authorities and asked them to recommend new names. Henceforth these sachems were known as Alexander and

Philip. Conspicuously, they also became immediately associated with trying to organize a multitribal strike against colonial encroachment. Jannemo appears to have had similar reasons for choosing the name Ninigret. The name seems to refer to the direction, southwest, which the Narragansetts associated with the spirit Cautantowwit and the land of the dead. West-southwest was also the route to the Mohegans and Montauketts from Narragansett country. In these respects, Ninigret's new name invoked spiritual strength and its targets.[56] So did the symbol that Ninigret chose as his mark: a war club, which Indians used to smash in enemy skulls. The skulls Ninigret intended to smash belonged to Uncas, any of the Long Island sachems who resisted him, and perhaps, the English who protected them. Ninigret's name change announced that he would lead the Narragansetts in their quest for revenge. He was also warning the English not to stand in his way.

"I doe but Right my owne quarrell"

Ninigret said nothing on record about his ambitions following the death of Miantonomi in 1643. Nevertheless, his actions suggest that he was driven by the goal of extending his network of tribute payers and broadening his influence domestically to include the Narragansetts as well as the Niantics. He behaved like a young sachem on the make, seeking to accumulate and wield power, rather than as an older leader focused on consolidating previous gains. To a certain degree, the path for Ninigret's ascent was clear of major obstacles because of the defeat of the Pequots, the loss of Miantonomi, and the shortcomings of Miantonomi's would-be successors, Pessacus and Mixano. Yet in the multipolar politics of colonial New England there were always several contenders to fill a power vacuum. Ninigret's primary enemies, Uncas of the Mohegans and Wyandanch of the Montauketts, recruited the English to their side, which, in turn, became one of Ninigret's most vexing problems. Ninigret's attempts to neutralize the English in intertribal politics involved him allying with the Pocumtucks of the upper Connecticut River Valley and especially the Mohawks of the Iroquois League. The English, he reasoned, might think twice about confronting the Narragansetts if that meant drawing the wrath of these other indigenous nations. Ninigret also tried to outmaneuver the United Colonies of New England by reaching out to their English and Dutch rivals such as Rhode Island, New Netherland, and even King Charles I. This was the very sort of divide-and-conquer strategy that the United Colonies employed against the Narragansetts. Ninigret's effective use of all these tactics made him the puritan colonies' chief nemesis and the most powerful Indian leader in southern New England during the 1640s and 1650s.

The challenge for Ninigret and his contemporaries—and for their historians—was that Indians conducted politics through a dizzying combination of rumor, bluster, innuendo, and intrigue that seamlessly blended fact and fiction. The inability to separate information from misinformation often prevented sachems and colonial magistrates from acting with any certainty even as they feared that indecision courted disaster. The result was one war scare after another in which the English imagined alliances of several tribes and even the Dutch striking out against Uncas and his colonial protectors. Some of these conspiracies might have been real to greater or lesser degree and some of them might have been phantasmal. Given deep contradictions in the evidence, we are unlikely ever to know for certain any more than English sources did. We do know, however, that these crises frequently brought the region to the very brink of war. Though Uncas is often cast as the consummate player in this scheming—and for good reason—Ninigret could give as well as he got. He too cast aspersions on his rivals, intimidated his indigenous neighbors, and matched the English threat for threat. Ninigret's skillful navigation of this hazardous political terrain largely explains why he and his people escaped the dismal fate of the Pequots and Miantonomi even though so many surrounding Indians and Englishmen wanted them dead. Without Ninigret, the Narragansetts likely would have been subjugated by the English-Mohegan alliance, thereby handing the English control of southern New England long before the colonies' victory in King Philip's War.

"The Young Sachems, being but boys, will need warre"
Narragansett-English Diplomacy over the Narragansett
Conflict with Uncas

English authorities warned the Narragansetts not to take revenge on Uncas for the killing of Miantonomi, but Indian values and politics all but required it. For one, Indians widely held that the spirit (or "blood" in their parlance) of someone killed by the enemy haunted its living relatives until the family settled the score by killing or capturing one of the enemies' people. The deed simply had to be done. It was bad enough if common people ignored this obligation, but a sachem's disregard for the murder of one of his sachem kin—and Miantonomi was Ninigret's cousin and possibly also his brother-in-law—was probably a disqualification for office. There was also the matter of filling the leadership void left by Miantonomi's death. An elder sachem like Canonicus had such a long track record of bold action that he could counsel peace even as his people clamored for war. Younger sachems like Ninigret, Pessacus, and Mixano had no such security. If they wanted to take Miantonomi's place, they had to earn it by leading the people's warriors against Uncas. As Canonicus himself explained to John Winthrop, "The Young Sachems, being but boys, will need war, and so sett all the Country in Combustion."[1]

The Narragansetts did everything short of granting Uncas a reprieve to avoid clashing with the United Colonies over this issue, even going so far as to seek out other English colonists as allies. Fortunately for them, they had options in the growing number of religiously disaffected colonists leaving Massachusetts for life in other parts of southern New England, including Narragansett country. Some of the migrants were moderate puritans, such as those who founded the colony of Connecticut with the Reverend Thomas Hooker in the 1630s. They disagreed with Bay Colony congregations restricting church membership to those who had given public testimony on their state of grace, and with the state restricting male suffrage to church members. By contrast, the puritans who formed the town and colony of New Haven judged that Massachusetts had not gone far enough in enforcing biblical law. Under the leadership of the Reverend John Davenport and Theophilus Eaton, in 1638 they left the Bay Colony for the mouth of the Quinnipiac River on the north shore of Long Island Sound and created the sternest puritan society of their era out of the towns of New Haven, Southold, Stamford, Milford, and Guilford. For the Narragansetts, the most important participants in this "hiving out" from Massachusetts were the hundreds of colonists who left for Rhode Island after pushing puritan ideas to their (some would say, logical) extremes. Back in England, such radicals had been considered puritans for their opposition to the Anglican Church's Catholic holdovers; yet in America, fissures emerged within the puritan ranks over what they were *for*, that is, over what a puritan colony should be. Roger Williams, for instance, challenged the right of the state to enforce religious laws. Others, like the so-called Antinomians of Boston led by Anne Hutchinson in the mid 1630s, claimed to receive direct revelation from God and questioned whether established puritan ministers placed too much emphasis (like Catholics) on works righteousness instead of on faith. Unwilling to brook open dissent among the ranks, Boston forced Williams, Hutchinson, and their sympathizers to follow their consciences and move to Narragansett Bay. Then there was Samuel Gorton, whose radical ideas and raucous wit made Williams seem conservative by comparison. Gorton's principles included universal access to grace in opposition to the puritans' belief in limited salvation, rejection of infant baptism as a Catholic relic without scriptural warrant, and denunciation of university-educated, salaried ministers as a manifestation of the Antichrist. These leveling ideas and more have led some scholars to characterize Gorton as occupying the "lunatic fringe" of reformed Protestantism. Puritan leaders certainly would have agreed with that description and, for that matter, so would magistrates in Rhode Island, who, despite their own heterodox reputations, found Gorton so insufferable that they forced him out of the communities of Aquidneck and then Providence after he had already worn out his welcome in Massachusetts and Plymouth. In this, Gorton's plight represented the fracture of the puritan movement from its base in Massachusetts into a constellation of new communities and colonies emphasizing different aspects of puritan belief and practice. New England puritans were not a monolith, religiously or politically, and their rifts were just as vulnerable to exploitation by Indians as the Indians' factions were to their divide-and-conquer tactics.[2]

The Narragansetts' problems merged with Gorton's beginning in January 1643, when Miantonomi forced Pomham, the tribute-paying sachem of Shawomet, to sell a portion of his land to Gorton, which became the foundation for the town of Warwick, Rhode Island. Massachusetts was outraged at the Narragansetts' support of a potentially cancerous dissident community right on the Bay Colony's southern flank, and discovered a solution a few months later when Pomham and Socononoco, the sachem of nearby Pawtuxet, subjected themselves to Boston in exchange for help in driving away Gorton and his followers. The colony was happy to oblige given its dual interest in diminishing the Narragansetts' influence and ridding itself permanently of a dangerous schismatic. Therefore, in October 1643, shortly after Uncas killed Miantonomi, Massachusetts authorities arrested and tried Gorton and ten of his followers on charges of blasphemy and sentenced them to hard labor. However, by the spring of 1644 the Bay Colony had released the prisoners back to Rhode Island, partially out of concern that they were going to appeal their conviction to London. When Canonicus and Pessacus asked Gorton how he had managed to outwit such powerful foes,

Gorton responded that he was under the protection of the king of England, whereupon the Narragansetts expressed interest in becoming royal subjects too, having concluded that Gorton "belonged to a better Master than the Massachusetts did."

Gorton took it from there. In April 1644, just a month after Williams successfully lobbied Parliament for a patent incorporating the Narragansett Bay towns as "Providence Plantations," Gorton delivered the crown a letter (probably self-authored) in which the sachems offered their subjection in exchange for protection against "any of the natives in these Parts" and "some of His Majesty's pretended subjects," which clearly meant Massachusetts. Gorton's thinking was that the king's defense of the Narragansetts would help to keep Massachusetts out of his and Rhode Island's affairs. As for the Narragansetts, they were looking for any allies to maintain their network of tribute payers and, equally important, dissuade Massachusetts from trying to referee their quarrel with Uncas.[3]

The Narragansetts did not need the status of royal subjects to claim political equality with Massachusetts, but it did give them added confidence that puritan authorities would extend them diplomatic respect, however grudgingly. That point became abundantly clear in June 1644 when Massachusetts ordered the Narragansett sachems to Boston to answer for their attacks on Uncas, only to have them refuse on the basis that they were "subjects now, that with joint and voluntary consent, unto the same king, and state as yourselves are."[4] In other words, they rejected the puritan colonies' authority to interfere in their intertribal affairs, for only the king, an ocean away, held such a right, if he chose to exercise it—and they had no reason to believe that he ever would.

Massachusetts disregarded the Narragansetts' claims as coequal subjects of the king, correctly assuming that Charles I would never come to the aid of a distant Indian tribe while he was busy struggling with Parliament for control of his kingdom—a conflict that in 1649 would see him lose his crown and the head underneath it. Instead, Boston sent envoys to the Narragansetts to demand an explanation for their dealings with Gorton. Yet the sachems refused to answer any Englishman lacking the title of king. Rather, they used this encounter to pay back Massachusetts for a diplomatic insult it had committed against Miantonomi more than three years earlier, in November 1640. On that occasion, Massachusetts had insisted on using a Pequot woman interpreter who Miantonomi distrusted and then refused to seat the sachem at the governor's dining table until he acquiesced to the choice. Now, with Bay Colony men at the mercy of their hospitality, the Narragansetts responded in kind. According to John Winthrop, writing in the spring of 1644, "When our messengers came to them, Canonicus would not admit them into his wigwam for two hours, but suffered them to stay in the rain. When he did admit them, he lay along upon his couch, and would not speak to them more than a few forward speeches, but referred them to Pessacus, who, coming after some four hours, carried them into an ordinary wigwam," as opposed to a formal council house. The Narragansetts were reminding their guests that they had honor too.[5]

The Narragansetts merely wanted English authorities to recognize them as coequal at the table, not to provoke hostilities. To that end, in 1643 and again in 1644 Pessacus and Ninigret presented the United Colonies with gifts of otter pelts and wampum as part of a request to leave Uncas to defend himself. They also charged that Uncas had accepted a ransom in wampum for the life of Miantonomi before treacherously killing him. The commissioners, however, remained unmoved. They had concluded that their dominance of the region depended on restricting both the Narragansetts' independence and London's oversight of colonial-Indian affairs. The practical and symbolic core of this policy was defending Uncas from the Narragansetts on the hollow excuse that the colonies were peace loving.[6]

The Narragansetts were determined to attack Uncas, with or without the United Colonies' permission. Thus, in May 1645, a Narragansett force wielding thirty guns made a surprise assault on the Mohegans, killing four high-ranking men and two commoners and injuring numerous others, "most of which were wounded with bullets."[7] For the English—and doubtlessly the Mohegans—this was a startling development, not the least of all because the Narragansetts had managed to acquire guns, powder, and shot despite colonial restrictions on the sale of those items to Indians. English authorities were unsure whether the Narragansetts had built their armament through the Dutch, the French, black market English trade, Indian middlemen, or (most likely) a combination thereof. Regardless, the point was that the Narragansetts' strike against the Mohegans had displayed their power to resist the United Colonies.

Roger Williams, who knew the Narragansetts as well as anyone, could not have been any plainer in explaining their actions to Massachusetts. "There is a spirit of desperation fallen upon them," he wrote. "[They] are resolved to revenge the death of their prince and recover their ransom for his life etc. or to perish with him."[8] Rather than take Williams's word for it, Massachusetts appointed a team of ambassadors to meet with the Narragansett sachems only to discover firsthand just how desperate they had become. Pessacus opened negotiations in a spirit of "moderation," but the tone shifted dramatically as soon as Ninigret arrived. From that point on, "there was nothing but proud and insolent passages . . . frowns and threatening speeches."[9] Suddenly the Narragansetts were the ones demanding that the English withdraw their soldiers from Mohegan country. If they refused, Ninigret warned, his people "would take it as a breach of former Covenants, and would procure as many Mohawks as they English should affront them [the Narragansetts] with, that they would lay the English cattle on heaps as high as their houses, that no English man should stir out of his house to piss, but he should be killed."[10] Then, as if to add insult to injury, Pessacus sent the English home with an old Pequot woman as a guide, a clear allusion to the unacceptable interpreter that Boston had once pressed on Miantonomi.[11] Williams was so convinced of the imminence of war that he struck a deal with the Narragansett sachems to spare Rhode Island in exchange for its neutrality.[12] As for the rest of the New England colonies, he left it to them to test Ninigret's resolve.

The United Colonies feared that abandoning Uncas would produce a domino effect of defections among their Indian protectorates in favor of the Narragansetts, thus turning a defensive wall of allies into the advance guard of an anti-English Indian coalition. After all, the main reason the English counted so many Indian friends was that the colonies offered protection against the Narragansetts. That reasoning applied not only to Uncas, but Massasoit and the Wampanoags, Wyandanch and the Montauketts, Pomham and the Shawomets, and Socononoco and the Pawtuxets. Miantonomi had already tried to recruit these Indians and others into a league to resist colonial expansion. There could be no depending on their loyalty a second time if the commissioners left Uncas to face the Narragansetts alone. The commissioners' explained their reasoning this way:

> The eyes of other Indians . . . are . . . fastened upon the English with strict observation, in what manner and measure they provide for Uncas's safety: If he perish, they [the Indians] will charge it upon them

who might have preserved him, and no Indians will trust the English if they now broke engagements, either in the present or succeeding generations. If Uncas be ruined in such a cause, they [the Indians] foresee their heads upon the next pretense shall be delivered to the will of the Narragansetts, with whom they shall be forced to comply, as they may for their future safety, and the English may not trust an Indian in the whole country.

Given such logic, the United Colonies saw themselves as having no more choice in this matter than the Narragansetts did. Ironically, they judged their own security to rest in confronting the most powerful tribe in the region.[13]

There was still time for one more round of diplomacy before resorting to war. In the late summer of 1645, Boston hosted a conference attended by a Narragansett delegation led by Pessacus and Mixano, plus one of Ninigret's deputies and "a large train of men." The Narragansetts arrived believing that the United Colonies were finally ready to treat them as equals, but they were operating under false assumptions. Their interpreter and go-between, Roger Williams, had decided independently not to tell them that the commissioners expected to dictate, not negotiate, the terms of peace. He knew that the sachems would never have agreed to come if they thought otherwise. They soon had a rude awakening. The commissioners gave the Narragansetts the choice between war or complying with a list of six humiliating conditions: first, payment of a fine of two thousand fathoms of wampum (representing between fifteen thousand and twenty thousand days of labor) to reimburse the United Colonies for protecting Uncas and sending punitive expeditions into Narragansett country; second, regular tribute payments for any Pequots in the Narragansett ranks; third, the return of all Mohegan captives and plundered property; fourth, an end to raids on any and all Indians under English protection; fifth, acceptance of the United Colonies' arbitration of the Narragansetts' disputes with Uncas; and, sixth, the surrender of hostages to ensure compliance, including Pessacus's son and nephew.[14] Years later, Pessacus insisted that "when he made his covenant he did it in fear of the Army," or, put another way, that he consented to these degrading provisions only because he was surrounded by Englishmen bearing weapons.[15] Reading down the list, it is difficult to imagine otherwise.

Ninigret skipped this conference on the excuse that he was ill, but perhaps he had foreseen what Pessacus had not and thus come down with a diplomatic sickness.[16] Whatever the case, after this meeting, he became the Narragansett standard bearer for revenging Miantonomi's death and, by extension, resisting the English. The same could not be said of Pessacus, who seems to have lost face, as evidenced by his increasing deference to Ninigret in English and intertribal affairs. It is telling of the two men's shift in fortunes that whereas the Mohegans began to "speak well of the Narragansett Sachem [Pessacus]," they remained "jealous of the Niantic Sachem [Ninigret]."[17] For Narragansett sachems dependent on popular support, the Mohegans were bad friends but good enemies to have.

"A great business"
Ninigret's Alliance Building

Uncas's distrust of Ninigret was well founded, for while Boston was dressing down Pessacus, Ninigret was cobbling together alliances to counter the English-Mohegan axis. Strikingly, he reached out to none other than John Winthrop Jr., scion and namesake of the very Massachusetts governor and United Colonies commissioner who had so often bedeviled the Narragansetts. Winthrop Jr. would have been familiar to Ninigret by virtue of his parentage, but he became an important figure in Indian affairs only in the 1640s when he broke ground on a new English settlement at Nameag, in the heart of Pequot country.[18] This territory, contested as it was between the Mohegans, Narragansetts, and United Colonies, as well as between Massachusetts and Connecticut, meant that Winthrop Jr. had entered a political maelstrom.

Tribes, colonies, and competing alliances of Indians and Englishmen had struggled bitterly for control of the Pequot country ever since the Pequot War. The Mohegans and Narragansetts battled for Pequot survivors, former Pequot tributaries, and Pequot hunting grounds, with Uncas marrying as many high-ranking Pequot women as he could in order to absorb their followings, a strategy that increased the Mohegan population from an estimated four hundred to six hundred people in 1637 to more than twenty-five hundred in 1643.[19] Ninigret answered by setting up his nephew Wequashcook as a sachem over a community of Pequots between Weekapaug and the Pawcatuck River, subject to Ninigret's over-sight. Connecticut and Massachusetts also wrangled for jurisdiction over the Pequot country. Massachusetts's campaign included securing a Narragansett grant to former Pequot lands in 1638 and granting Winthrop Jr. the right to build a settlement on the Pequot (or Thames) River. Connecticut asserted its claims by granting John Mason, a veteran captain of the Pequot War, five hundred acres of Pequot land in 1642 and then using him as their point man in relations with Uncas. Uncas, in turn, deeded Connecticut title to all of his people's lands in 1640 with the exception of territory on which his people lived or planted, claims that by then extended into Pequot territory on the basis of Uncas's Pequot marriages. In return, Uncas expected Hartford to continue its support of him. These efforts paid off for Connecticut in 1646, when the commissioners of the United Colonies awarded it jurisdiction over the Pequot country. However, with Massachusetts still angling to revive its claims, and Connecticut lacking a royal charter until 1662 that would confirm its boundaries, Hartford's authority over the area remained tenuous. Suffice it to say, Winthrop Jr. had to choose his friends and enemies carefully if he intended to remain long in Pequot country.[20]

Winthrop Jr.'s title from Massachusetts automatically put him at odds with Connecticut and, by extension, Uncas, while his plan to turn his settlement into a Christian alchemist headquarters also strained his relations with Massachusetts and the United Colonies. Winthrop Jr. was at once a churchman and an alchemist, devoted to purifying minerals and metals and studying medical and natural science. Having discovered a source of lead (and, he hoped, of silver) at the head of the Pequot River, Winthrop Jr. envisioned that his "New London" at the river's mouth would become an export center of this precious material and a place for alchemists to collaborate. The problem, however, was that puritan authorities feared his relative tolerance for religious dissenters would turn New London into another Rhode Island. Winthrop Jr. would eventually make peace with Hartford once it was clear that New London fell within Connecticut's jurisdiction, not the Bay Colony's; in fact he would go on to be elected governor of Connecticut in 1657 and then every year from 1659 until 1676. Along the way, he also served a number of terms as Connecticut's commissioner to the United Colonies. Yet for the meantime, the puritan colonies kept a close eye on Winthrop Jr.'s enterprise, uncertain of its direction.

With few trustworthy friends from which to choose, Winthrop Jr. turned to an unlikely ally, the very Pequots whom Massachusetts had conquered under his father's governance a decade earlier. Winthrop Jr. picked Nameag as a site for his alchemical headquarters, in part, because there was a welcoming community of some five hundred Pequots already living there. These Pequots had managed to survive the Pequot War and then to escape captivity among the Mohegans, Narragansetts, and English, to establish themselves by the mid 1640s as a distinct community under Uncas's rule.[21] Their leader, Robin Cassacinamon, had spent the postwar years as a servant, messenger, and interpreter in the Winthrop household in Boston, quite possibly as a spy for Uncas, during which time he formed a close working relationship with John Winthrop Jr. Now, in the late 1640s, the two men united to create a new English community and quicken an old Pequot one. Cassacinamon wanted to free the Pequots from Uncas and establish himself as a bona fide sachem. Given the United Colonies' hostility toward the Pequots and support of Uncas, this could only be done with the aid of some powerful Englishman. Winthrop Jr., for his part, needed Indian friends to help him establish a settlement in what remained Indian country despite the colonies' overlapping jurisdictional claims. As he explained to his friend, the Reverend Thomas Peters, the security of his plantation required having "a party of the Indians there" with "their chief dependence upon the English" because "they will easily discover any Indian plots." Winthrop Jr. also hoped local Indian allies would strengthen his problematic title to the land and help him to find valuable natural resources. Yet Winthrop Jr. could not depend on the nearby Mohegans under Uncas to fulfill these roles. He knew that Connecticut's claims to the Nameag site depended on Uncas, and that Uncas's power rested partially on support from Connecticut. Thus neither Connecticut nor Uncas were likely to favor Winthrop Jr.'s settlement. The alternative was Robin Cassacinamon and his Pequots, who were as desperate as Winthrop for a counterweight to the Connecticut-Mohegan axis. Winthrop Jr.'s plan to bring the Pequots out of the Mohegan fold and under his protection guaranteed him a future of trouble with Uncas.

Ninigret's interest in these matters was to see Uncas lose his Pequot followers (if only into Cassacinamon's camp) and to pit an influential Englishman against him. Ninigret seems to have thought that in Winthrop Jr. he had an independent colonial authority to rival that of the United Colonies, which would have been a reasonable assumption. After all, Winthrop Jr. descended from the great leader of the rising Massachusetts Bay Colony, and in Indian country the mantle of sachem tended to pass from father to son. Indians also associated power with eclectic spiritual and medical knowledge and far-flung connections, which Winthrop Jr. possessed in abundance. Indians who entered Winthrop's house—and he had many Indian visitors—discovered a working laboratory with cabinets, bottles, and bundles of herbs containing substances for alchemical experiments, and burning chemical fires emitting smoke and strange odors. Winthrop's role as a healer enhanced his reputation in indigenous circles. Over the course of his life, he doctored numerous Pequots, Mohegans, and probably Narragansetts, as well perhaps half of the colonists of Connecticut and many others in Massachusetts. Indian letter carriers ferried letters to and from Winthrop Jr. throughout New England and even New Netherland, illustrating the breadth of his influence and knowledge. In these respects and more, writes Winthrop Jr.'s historian, he appeared to Indians "not just as an English sachem but also as a magico-religious specialist, similar to an Indian shaman, or powaw."[22]

Perhaps the greatest demonstration of Winthrop Jr.'s power was flouting the will of the United Colonies, including his father, to become the advocate of the Nameag Pequots. John Winthrop Sr.'s last request to his son, made from his very deathbed, "was that you would strive no more about the Pequot Indians but leave them to the Commissioners' order."[23] His wish died with him. To Ninigret, John Winthrop Jr. seemed like a young sachem accumulating honor and power by bucking his elders and seeking confrontation. Ninigret likely envisioned Winthrop Jr. becoming someone akin to Roger Williams, who could represent Indians before the United Colonies and even help them outmaneuver that body. Probably Ninigret also assumed that the Nameag Pequots and perhaps even Winthrop Jr. would eventually join his campaign against Uncas. But in order to accomplish these ends, Ninigret first had to cultivate a relationship with Winthrop Jr. Thus the sachem took every opportunity to pay this newcomer compliments, including delivering a present of corn from "all the women of [Ninigret's] town as a token of his fidelity to Mrs. Winthrop."[24] In Indian country, fur and wampum were diplomatic gifts, whereas corn was for friends and family. Given Winthrop Jr.'s close study of Indian ways, he probably understood the message.[25]

Uncas could see the threat posed to him by this new alignment and took forceful measures to neutralize it. In the late spring or summer of 1646, Uncas and some three hundred Mohegans chased a band of Pequots under Wequashcook out of former Pequot hunting territory all the way back into Nameag, where they hoped to receive protection from Winthrop Jr.'s small New London settlement. Yet the surrounding colonists gave Uncas no pause. According to eyewitness accounts, the Mohegans brutalized the Pequots by "cutting and slashing and beating in a sore manner . . . taking their skins, their baskets, taking their britches [and] their hose from their legs, their shoes from their feet, forcing them in the water and there shooting at them, also forcing into English men's houses frightening the women." Additionally, the Mohegans looted "a great deal of Mr. Winthrop's wampumpeag."[26] Uncas intended this raid to humiliate the Pequots and their newfound protectors. It was also a warning about the dire consequences for Pequots trying to buck his authority.

Ninigret exploited this raid to test English support for Uncas. Claiming that "he was sorry to hear of this business, that Uncas did, that it was a great business," Ninigret asked Winthrop Jr. for permission for the Niantics to hunt in Pequot territory claimed by Uncas. Apparently, Ninigret wanted to dare Uncas to treat his men with as much disrespect as the Pequots.[27] Ninigret knew that the United Colonies would say no if he posed the question to them. Winthrop Jr., however, responded favorably, though he hedged that Ninigret should first clear the matter with the commissioners. Ninigret did no such thing and instead went right along with his plans to the outrage of John Mason, Uncas's main advocate in Hartford. Mason and the commissioners sputtered that "the treacherous, and mischievous counsels and plots of the Narragansett sachems, in general, and Ninigret in particular, against Uncas," not only disgraced the Mohegan sachem but the New England Confederation backing him, which for Ninigret and, to a lesser extent, Winthrop Jr., was precisely the point.[28] Ninigret hoped to raise his stature at home by outwitting the United Colonies and demeaning Uncas.

Divisions between Winthrop Jr. and the United Colonies over the fate of the Pequots gave Ninigret a wedge to seek Winthrop's support against

Uncas. Not only did the commissioners fail to sanction Uncas for his 1646 attack on Nameag, but in September 1648 they effectively authorized him to repeat this affront in order to bring the Pequots back under his subjection, provided he took care not to harm any of the English in New London.[29] In October, Mason accompanied Uncas to Nameag so the sachem could round up any Pequots living there without his permission, an action which Winthrop's constable apparently resisted. Then, a few months later, Uncas launched another brutal raid against Nameag to complete the dragnet.[30] Even though Uncas had tacit approval from the United Colonies, some English authorities, including John Winthrop Sr., saw his behavior toward the English of New London as an "outrage."[31] For Ninigret and the Narragansetts, though, this was a chance to solicit Winthrop Jr. as an ally in his own campaign of retribution against Uncas. As Roger Williams wrote to Winthrop Jr. in January of 1649, "All our neighbors the Barbarians," which certainly included Ninigret, were "ready to fall upon the Mohegans at your word."[32] Put another way, the Narragansetts wanted some assurance that Winthrop Jr. would stand with them against the United Colonies.

Ninigret was operating on the understandable, though mistaken, assumption that Winthrop Jr. and New London were as free of the United Colonies as Roger Williams's Rhode Island. After all, Winthrop Jr., like Williams, seemed to follow an independent course when it came to Indian affairs and religious dissidents. Just as Rhode Island's security rested on the Narragansetts, so too did the future of New London hinge on the fate of the Pequots. As such, the leaders of both places were hostile to Uncas. Ninigret could have imagined a scenario in which he warred against Uncas with the support of New London and Rhode Island over the opposition of the United Colonies. It was a reasonable interpretation of divisions within the English ranks informed by the norms of Indian politics.

Jûhettîtea: Let us Fight.
Ninigret Takes the Lead against Uncas

Ninigret had the foresight to recruit other allies against Uncas, using wampum that the United Colonies believed was first due to them under the agreement reached with Pessacus. By June 1646 the Narragansetts had paid the United Colonies only one hundred fathoms of wampum of the thirteen hundred they owed, which Pessacus blamed on "the Niantics & others failing to contribute their parts."[33] When the commissioners pressed Ninigret for an explanation, he cried poverty, pleaded sickness, or in one instance, said he was delayed because his mother-in-law had died.[34] Yet as these excuses piled up month after month, the English began to suspect that something sinister was afoot. Their intelligence, probably obtained from Uncas, said that the Narragansetts, led by Ninigret, were funneling their wampum to the Mohawks in the hopes of drawing them into war against the Mohegans. If Uncas was right, Ninigret's strategy was double-edged. Certainly the Narragansetts would have been grateful for Mohawk assistance against Uncas. Ultimately, though, the Narragansetts could handle that job themselves. Their main goal was to have the Mohawks scare off the English from coming to the Mohegans' defense.

Ninigret's meeting with the commissioners in August 1647 to discuss the overdue wampum and rumors of his dealings with the Mohawks showcased his growing leadership within the Narragansetts. Canonicus had died sometime that summer, leaving Pessacus, Mixano, and many other leading Narragansetts in deep mourning. They were in no state to conduct diplomacy. Additionally, Pessacus had already proved incapable of facing down the commissioners, and doubtless he had fielded criticism from Ninigret on this front. Given all of this, and Ninigret's already long history of fending off the English, the sachems chose him as their proxy. One after another, they informed colonial authorities that "what Ninigret shall doe" they would "stand to it."[35] It was a wise decision.

Ninigret's arrival in Boston to meet with the United Colonies was his unofficial debut as the Narragansetts' primary leader. It was also the beginning of a pattern in which he would promise to abide by English demands only to continue down his own path. He entered the bustling seaport town, which he would have known by its Algonquian name of Shawmut, with a delegation of Niantics, two of Pessacus's men, and, tellingly, John Winthrop Jr., who was there at his request.[36] His confrontational side was nowhere on display. Rather, he "professed his desire to be reconciled to the English."[37] He also had an answer for every English charge. His explanation for his earlier rough treatment of English messengers was that they had "provoked him." As to why the Narragansetts had failed to pay the fines and tribute they owed to the United Colonies,

Ninigret "pretended ignorance as if he had not known what covenants had been made." Yet he was ready to argue that the Narragansetts should owe less than the commissioners' said by quibbling over whether former presents should count as payments. By leading the commissioners into this thicket of particulars, Ninigret managed to avoid the larger question of the Narragansetts' determination to remove Uncas at any cost, including war with the English.

On the second day of negotiations, Ninigret staked his own reputation to score a diplomatic victory over the commissioners. He claimed that he, not Pessacus, would have the Narragansetts pay what they owed to the English within three to ten days. If anyone doubted his sincerity, he volunteered to serve as a living bond. This dramatic gesture had the desired effect. Declaring themselves "well satisfied for the present," the commissioners excused Ninigret to return home with the children of Narragansett sachems who had lived for over a year as hostages among the English.[38]

Ninigret returned to Narragansett country having won the release of the people's high-ranking hostages and without any more demands from the English. Yet once their children were safe and secure, Ninigret and the Narragansetts suddenly became less compliant than he had led the English to believe. Already, by August 20, Ninigret was having Roger Williams ask John Winthrop Jr. to request the commissioners to extend the due date for the wampum payment from ten days to a month.[39] Token payments trickled in, but nowhere near the amount promised. Almost a year later, a seething John Winthrop Sr. was writing to his namesake to "speak with Ninigret and tell him how ill we take it at his hands, that he has dealt so unfaithfully and ungratefully with us."[40]

The English took it even worse when they discovered that the Narragansetts continued to send wampum to the Mohawks and now also to the Pocumtucks of the upper Connecticut River Valley. It appeared that Ninigret had designed his promises to the commissioners to buy time for the coordination of a multitribal strike against Uncas. The Narragansetts, of course, had been plying the Mohawks with wampum for years to draw them into such a campaign. Recruiting the Pocumtucks had required a stroke of luck. The context was this: in 1646, the United Colonies had sent Uncas to the Pocumtucks to demand the surrender of Sequassen, sachem of the Wagunks near Hartford. Sequassen had fled to the Pocumtucks after Connecticut charged him with a plot to kill its commissioners to the United Colonies and then frame Uncas for it. Rather than negotiate with the Pocumtucks for Sequassen's extradition, Uncas seized him in a nighttime raid. Ultimately, Connecticut acquitted Sequassen for lack of evidence, but in attacking the Pocumtucks Uncas had made himself another enemy.[41]

With but a slight twist of fate, the Narragansett-Mohawk-Pocumtuck alliance might have dispatched Uncas and realigned the regional balance of power in the Narragansetts' favor. Eight hundred warriors from the three tribes planned to rendezvous at Pocumtuck in late August or early September 1648, after the harvest, whereupon they would descend the Connecticut River and invade Uncas's territory. One source claimed that they had "four hundred guns & for each gun three pounds of powder, and answerable shot."[42] In the expectation of a Mohegan or English counterstrike, the Narragansetts began stashing their corn and removing their women, children, and elderly to the safety of swamps. They also warned the English to think twice before they acted, as when Ninigret met with John Winthrop Jr. and "inquired whether the English would defend Uncas, expressing himself that if they did, they," the allied Indians "could soon burn the houses at Connecticut, &c."[43] Clearly the Narragansetts were prepared for a reckoning more than a decade in the making. Yet their plan came to naught. As the Mohawks made their way to Pocumtuck, they came under attack by unnamed Indians allied with the French (probably the Sokokis) and lost two of their sachems in the fight. Their delay and demoralization, combined with news that the English would not sit out this affair, led the Pocumtucks to call off the attack. The Narragansetts were left alone to deal with the United Colonies' response.[44]

Ninigret must have known that the English would try to call him to account, but in the meantime he focused on his main concerns: ridding himself of Uncas and extending his influence over the Pequots. Having failed to mass an army against Uncas, Ninigret apparently hired an assassin to finish him. In April 1649 a Narragansett named Cuttaquin, working as a deckhand on an English trading vessel, reportedly waited for Uncas to come aboard and then stabbed him. Uncas, despite groaning "that the Narragansett had killed him," somehow escaped with a minor wound to his breast and nothing more. While Uncas's men cut off his fingers, Cuttaquin confessed that Ninigret and the other Narragansett sachems had hired him for a price of a thousand fathoms of wampum. Needless to say, the commissioners were particularly angry to learn how much the Narragansetts had paid given that the tribe was in arrears to the United Colonies. Yet Ninigret and the Narragansett sachems called the entire affair a ruse, alleging that Uncas had injured himself with "a small stab on his breast in a safe place" and framed Cuttaquin to "render the Narragansetts still odious to the English." Roger Williams believed the charge, but the commissioners did not.[45] The United Colonies were developing a healthy skepticism for whatever Ninigret had to say.

The commissioners grew all the more frustrated with Ninigret as they learned about his ongoing efforts to absorb Pequots. First and foremost, he was planning a marriage between one of his daughters and Tausaquaonawhut, the son of the deceased Pequot sachem Sassacus. Meanwhile, he began intimidating Wequashcook and his Pequot band to choose between taking up arms against Uncas or leaving Niantic territory. The timing coincided with Ninigret's invitation to the Nameag Pequots to move to the Niantic side of the Pawcatuck River, perhaps to occupy land from which he would remove Wequashcook. The threat seemed real enough that the commissioners finally approved a request of the Nameag Pequots to settle at a new location at Noank, a peninsula just west of Mystic in the heart of their ancestral territory. Ironically, to the commissioners, it was becoming less of a risk to grant the Pequots more independence, contrary to the declaration in 1638's Treaty of Hartford that they "shall no more be called Pequots," than to have them fall under Ninigret's sway.[46]

"Doe they thinke wee are madd to sell our lives?" The Narragansetts and English Face Off

With Ninigret and the Narragansetts challenging the United Colonies on so many different fronts, the commissioners authorized an armed expedition into Narragansett country in 1650, ordering twenty men under Humphrey Atherton to demand immediate payment of the Narragansetts' overdue wampum fines and the cost of seeking their compliance. If the Narragansetts refused, Atherton was to seize the amount and even take sachems as hostages. Atherton's instructions also included demanding Ninigret to end his overtures to the Pequots. The commissioners wanted to send a clear message that they were willing to risk war over these issues.[47]

They very nearly got one. It was bad enough for the United Colonies to send a military force into Narragansett country, but the timing coincided with an elite funeral for one of Wepitamock's sons (Ninigret's nephew), a sacred event at which emotions ran high. Atherton camped his men at Roger Williams's trading house at Cocumscussoc (modern day Wickford) and then had Williams go to the funeral three or four miles to the west to broker a meeting. The conference took place the next day in a wétu near the funeral site, with Atherton, Williams, and one or two other colonists sitting across from Pessacus, Ninigret, and the other Narragansett sachems. Numerous warriors stood "ready with guns and bows" yet, unbeknownst to them and even Williams, Atherton had instructed his troopers to encircle the wétu once talks were underway. When they arrived, Atherton ordered a stunned Williams "to tell the Sachems [that] he would take by force Ninigret and Pessacus." It is doubtful that Williams relayed the message in full, for he had no interest in committing suicide and throwing Rhode Island into a war of the United Colonies' making. Contrary to a legend first propagated by the minister Increase Mather in 1677 and repeated by historians ever since, there are no firsthand accounts that Atherton seized the hair of one of the sachems and pointed a pistol at his breast.[48] Nevertheless, the standoff was tense enough for Williams to characterize it as resting "upon the tickling point of a great slaughter."[49]

Fortunately for everyone, clear heads prevailed and the parties reached a compromise. Atherton agreed to withdraw to Williams's trading house for four days, during which time the Narragansetts would gather the wampum they owed. What the Narragansetts performed, however, was something less than full compliance. They did manage to deliver 380 fathoms of wampum, representing between 2,850 and 3,800 days of labor, which they had been resisting for years. Yet this amount was considerably less than the 508 fathoms that Atherton demanded and, furthermore, Williams and Atherton convinced the commissioners to forgive the rest of the debt rather than force the issue.[50] In this sense, both sides won. Narragansett sources told Thomas Stanton that though the Narragansett sachems were willing to give up their wampum, if the English dared "go about to seize upon the person of Ninigret, or any of the other Sachems, he thought they would be mad, and rather hazard all their wives and children, and lives and all they had."[51] Williams believed that such a conflict would ultimately draw in the Mohawks and "if not dispossess many a planter and displant plantations: yet hazard much blood and slaughter and ruin to both English and Indian."[52] Little did he know how right he was.

Whauwudutowawánouat. There is an alarm.
Askwhítiteass. Keep watch.
Ninigret's Dutch and Indian Diplomacy and the Panic of 1653

No sooner had this crisis passed than another emerged in 1653 with Ninigret at its center. It represented the most serious alarm that the region had faced since Miantonomi's plot ten years earlier. The charge was that Ninigret had been coordinating a Dutch-Indian strike against the United Colonies to take place as soon as a fleet carrying men and weapons from the Netherlands arrived in the Hudson. Several sources agreed on the following points: that Ninigret had spent the winter of 1652–53 in and around Manhattan, the Dutch colonial capital; that he had met with Peter Stuyvesant, governor of New Netherland, and given him "a great present of wampum" to seal an alliance; that Ninigret returned home in a Dutch sloop with his own present from the governor, being "twenty guns with powder and shot answerable"; that he had visited Indians throughout Long Island Sound distributing wampum and making "exclamation against the English and Uncas desiring their aid and assistance against them"; and that he promised his Indian audiences Dutch trade and military support for this campaign, adding "they are furnished with [gun]powder as plentifully as if it were sand."[53] There were very good reasons to pay credence to this rumor. For one, the Dutch and English were fighting the first of their three naval wars during the seventeenth century, stemming largely from English attempts to close their colonial markets to Dutch merchants. This conflict had yet to reach American shores, but it made sense that the Dutch would strike against English interests wherever they were. Furthermore, there were acute tensions between New Netherland and the New England colonies over such issues as Dutch rights to the Connecticut River Valley, English claims to the Delaware River Valley and Long Island, and especially the sale of firearms to Indians.[54] Not the least of all, Ninigret had a long history of attempting to line up allies against the English and fresh motivation for such a campaign following the Atherton expedition of 1650.[55]

Ninigret claimed that this entire affair was a misunderstanding. He admitted to visiting the Hudson Valley Indians and Dutch Manhattan during the winter, but explained that his main errand was to see a French doctor on the recommendation of John Winthrop Jr.[56] This excuse was plausible given Winthrop's international network of alchemists. As to supposedly conspiring with Stuyvesant, Ninigret claimed to have called on the governor's headquarters out of courtesy, only to be left knocking at a door that never opened. Yes, Ninigret acknowledged, Indians were talking excitedly about the prospects of a Dutch-English war, but none of them were interested in getting involved. They said only that "the English and the Dutch were fighting together in their own country and that there were several other ships coming with ammunition to fight against the English here and that there would be a great blow given to the English when they came." Ninigret protested that he would never wrong the English for they were his "friends" and, in a fit of bad history, "he doth not know any wrong the English hath done him." He made a more convincing argument that he knew "the English are not a sleepy people" and that they would respond aggressively to any perceived threat. Ninigret challenged the commissioners, "Do they think we are mad to sell our lives and the lives of our wives and children and all our kindred and to have our country destroyed for a few guns, powder, shot, and swords? What will they do us good when we are dead?"[57]

The English might have asked Ninigret the same thing given how much evidence was lined up against him. Predictably, the main source of the charge was Uncas. He claimed to have discovered the conspiracy when his men waylaid a Narragansett canoe carrying another assassin hired by Ninigret, only to find that the boat also contained a large supply of wampum bound for Manhattan. Nor was Uncas the lone accuser. When the Mohegans brought their prisoners to Hartford for questioning, two of them "confessed the whole plot." Additional details poured in from all across the region. An unnamed sachem on Long Island "who professes respect to the English, told his friend that the Dutch counseled the Indians to fire some of the English houses in all parts and when the English come forth to quench them, to shoot them."[58] An unidentified Pequot woman "found trusty to the English" warned a colonist in Wethersfield "that the Dutch and Indians generally were confederated against the English," and that they intended to launch their attack when the colonies held their Election Day, "because then it is apprehended the plantations will be left naked and unable to defend themselves."[59] Some nine Indian sachems living near Manhattan told New Haven authorities "that the Dutch had solicited them by promising them guns, powder, swords, weapons, waistcoats, and coats, to cut off the English." A number of Long Island Indians laid the charge on the Dutch fiscal officer, and others on Governor Stuyvesant himself.[60] One of the sachems, named Ronnessoke, testified that the previous winter Ninigret had come to visit him at Canarsee (modern day Brooklyn) on the pretense of trading for corn, but then took him aside to draw him into the plot, telling him that "he had brought a bag of wampum to hire as many Indians as he could upon Long Island." Ronnessoke added that Ninigret instructed him to go to the Dutch to "fetch ammunition, lead and guns as many as they would."[61] Additional reports had Stuyvesant sending war belts of wampum and guns, powder, and shot up the Hudson River to the Mohawks and Mohicans, and eastward as far as the Pocumtucks, to draw them into the alliance. Still others told of him encouraging nearby Indians to "let Uncas be killed."[62] As for the rumored meeting between Ninigret and Stuyvesant, an Indian named Adam, "who speaks English very well," said that, contrary to Ninigret's testimony, the two leaders had in fact met together for two straight days," with much wampum passing back and forth between them.[63]

Even Ninigret's own messengers to the United Colonies incriminated him. Awashaw let it slip that while Ninigret was at Manhattan he had given fifteen fathoms of wampum to the Dutch governor and in exchange received a "sleeved coat."[64] Another ambassador from Ninigret, who the English called Newcomb (his Indian name was Mattakist), a "cunning and bold" fellow, threatened an Englishman in the Dutch language that a Dutch plot against the English was in the works and that the Dutch would gladly pay him an annual salary of a hundred pounds to join their campaign.[65] Newcomb had been living at Flushing in New Netherland for at least a couple of years, apparently as Ninigret's agent, or, as he put it, as "Ninigret's Man."[66] His boast only strengthened the case against his patron.

The obvious question is whether there was really a plot. The United Colonies commissioners from Connecticut, New Haven, and Plymouth thought so and therefore favored a war against New Netherland and Ninigret. The commissioners from the Bay Colony were more skeptical. They did not trust Ninigret, but neither did they place any confidence in the Indians who levied the charges against him. Boston judged that un-substantiated rumors were insufficient grounds for an offensive campaign, particularly against a small Dutch colony that posed little threat to Massachusetts.[67] The case cannot be closed today any more than it could then. Nevertheless, it seems likely that Ninigret and Stuyvesant had been reaching out to each other as *defensive* allies rather than as part of a joint offensive to sack New England.

As in Ninigret's diplomacy with the Mohawks and Pocumtucks, his main concern with the Dutch would have been to offset the threat of the English so he could attack Uncas. He had grown tired of the series of back and forth raids, robberies, murders, and attempted assassinations between him and the Mohegan sachem.[68] It was time to bring this pattern, and Uncas's life, to an end. Note the Dutch governor's supposed charge to other Indians to "*let* Uncas be killed." If anyone was going to do the killing, it was Ninigret and his men. All they wanted was for the English and their Indian allies to get out of the way. The Dutch had no quarrel with Uncas, but it was politic for them to support Ninigret's campaign as a means of enlisting the Narragansetts and their Indian allies in the cause of New Netherland. This does not mean that the Dutch planned to invade New England. New Netherland contained less than five thousand people, a mere fraction of New England's colonial population, which was about four times that number.[69] Fragile Indian alliances were no answer to this problem over the course of a long war. Thus, while it is possible that the Dutch were hoping to launch a surprise strike, it is equally likely that they were lining up Indian allies for the defense of New Netherland in the event of an English attack.

Among the most compelling evidence of growing diplomatic ties between Ninigret and the Dutch is the sudden strength of Ninigret's armament. Ninigret claimed that the only guns he brought back from his trip to the Hudson were two muskets given to him by other Indians. Yet eyewitness accounts from the fall of 1653 saw evidence of the Niantics stockpiling arms. That September, the United Colonies sent Sergeant Richard Wait, Sergeant John Barrell, and interpreters Thomas Stanton and Valentine Whitman to question Ninigret about his attacks on Long Island and his role in the Dutch plot. "About forty or fifty Indian all in arms" met them at the edge of Ninigret's territory, the leader "having a gun in his hand on the cock . . . as if he would have cocked it." After refusing to stand aside, these gunners escorted the English to Ninigret's headquarters while "shouting and hallowing and using scornful words." The sachem greeted the ambassadors not with gifts and warm speeches, but a company of "many armed men . . . and himself a pistol in his hand." When the English sat down to council, "the Indians did then surround them and some of them charged their guns with powder and bullets and some primed their guns" in a manner "so tumultuous" it was impossible to conduct business. Making matters worse, Ninigret's men identified one of the most agitated warriors as a Mohawk, which, as designed, left the English "much disturbed." Ninigret's right-hand man, Awashaw, added that this Mohawk was there to ascertain if "the English were coming to war against the Narragansett Indians, which if true the Mohawks take what is done among the Narragansetts as done against themselves." The colonial ambassadors felt lucky to escape this encounter with their lives. Ninigret's point, however, was for them to report his readiness for war if the English insisted on it.

Tellingly, Ninigret bought a mastiff, a dog of war, at the very same time that he was accumulating arms. In and of itself, the mastiff made a statement. Weighing as much as 250 pounds, standing some 30 inches high at the shoulder, and with a formidable jowled head and jaws to match, mastiffs had been brought to the Americas by Europeans who bred them to intimidate.[70] Whereas in England one of the most common uses of this dog was in the blood sport of bull, bear, or lion baiting, in America the English employed mastiffs to terrify Indians. For instance, when English captain Martin Pring was exploring Cape Cod in 1603, he would release two mastiffs to chase away the local Wampanoags whenever he wanted them gone.[71] Likewise, during the Pequot War, Lion Gardiner took mastiffs on expeditions to flush out Pequots who were lying in ambush in the reeds and woods surrounding Fort Saybrook.[72] In these and probably innumerable other cases, Indians had come to associate mastiffs with military prowess and, perhaps, the spiritual power of manit.[73] It was with this symbolism in mind that Ninigret bought one of these dogs for forty shillings from an Englishman named Robert Cole, though it soon ran away.[74] Clearly, Ninigret was readying for battle.

The question is battle with whom. The most likely target was the Mohegans and anyone they enlisted in their cause, including the United Colonies. At the same time, Ninigret was in the early stages of a war with the Indians of Long Island, who also claimed the protection of the United Colonies. New Haven's understanding was that "Ninigret has hired some other Indians, as Mohawks or Wampeages [Hudson Valley Indians], to assist him in cutting of[f] the Long Island Indians, or at least those that we count our best fr[i]ends, and that having done that, they intend, as it is thought, to cut of[f] Uncas."[75] It seems farfetched that Ninigret planned to initiate war with the English, except insofar as they interpreted an attack on Uncas or the Long Island Indians to be an attack on them. His buildup of arms and allies was thus probably aimed at the Mohegans and only secondarily at the English. The threat of uniting the Indians and Dutch of Long Island Sound in a grand campaign against the English was supposed to avoid a war with the United Colonies, not spur one.

Ninigret remained preoccupied with other Indians rather than with the English. As bad as his relations were with the commissioners, and as close as his territory was to several colonies, his people still suffered few of the most common problems that afflicted Indians under colonialism. They had not yet lost any of their land to force, intimidation, or chicanery; there are few reports of English livestock wandering into their territory and destroying their corn or driving off their game animals; no colonial authorities ever seized their arms during war scares; most critically, no English magistrate had ever dared to order the Narragansetts to turn over their people for trial and punishment by colonial courts, although Atherton came close. At one point Ninigret asked Roger Williams to write a petition for him "to the high sachems of England" imploring that the Indians "might not be forced from their religion, and for not changing their religion be invaded by war," but his sense of danger appears to have originated with other Indians rather than the English.[76] Ninigret's quarrel with the United Colonies rested on their interference in his vendetta against Uncas and his attempts to reduce other area sachems to the status of tribute payers. The problem, in other words, was that they tried to manage the Indian relationships at the center of his world.

Manowêass. I feare none.
Ninigret's Campaign against Long Island

For a brief period after the war scare of 1653, driven by a series of factors related to his troubles with Uncas and the United Colonies, Ninigret focused his attention on attacking the Long Island Indians. In the long term, Ninigret and the Narragansetts had been under tremendous pressure to produce wampum for use in diplomacy with the Mohawks and Pocumtucks and as tribute and fines to the English, demands that increased in tandem. Therefore, Ninigret raided Long Island to obtain the wampum that funded his political ambitions.[77] He might also have been trying to intimidate the Long Island Indians to join him in arms against the Mohegans, judging from his rough diplomacy with other area Indians. Around this very same time, the Nipmuck sachem of Quinabaag (modern-day Dudley, Massachusetts), complained that Ninigret and Mixano had threatened him "because he will not go to war with them," meaning alongside them.[78] In the short term, Ninigret wanted the Long Island Indians to know the consequences of defying him. Several Long Island Indians had testified against Ninigret during the 1653 war scare after, they said, he had tried to recruit them to fight against the English. Additionally, Ninigret was furious at the Long Island Indians for killing one of his men following a botched attempt to assassinate Mandush, sachem of the Shinnecocks. According to the assassin's own testimony, Ninigret had sent him to live on Long Island among relatives until he had a chance to get Mandush in his sights. When the time came, he missed with a pistol shot and fell into the hands of the very man he would have murdered. Mandush, taking a page from Uncas, dragged his captive before the General Court of Connecticut for interrogation, during which he confessed to Ninigret's role. The English then returned the prisoner to his captors, who promptly executed him just outside of Hartford. It was an incident that must have conjured up Narragansett memories of Miantonomi's death.[79]

Despite the Long Island Indians' status as English protectorates, in 1653 and 1654 Ninigret launched at least three raids against them, including one that claimed the lives of thirty people and netted fourteen captives, including Wyandanch's own daughter. This attack also involved Ninigret's men burning one of their prisoners within English territory, just as the Long Island sachems had done to Ninigret's agent after the failed assassination of Mandush.[80] Ninigret's conditions for releasing these prisoners were a steep ransom in wampum, which Wyandanch quickly paid, and an annual tribute in wampum, to which Wyandanch also agreed before repudiating the deal. According to Wyandanch, he never would have met the ransom without the timely financial assistance of Lion Gardiner, who he praised "not only as a friend, but as a father" for saving the Montauketts "when we were almost swallowed up by our enemies."[81]

Another of these attacks involved warriors from the Pocumtucks and other unnamed tribes alongside Ninigret's men. Before striking against Long Island, they rendezvoused at Fisher's Island in the sound two miles from the mouth of the Pequot River, on land belonging to an unwitting John Winthrop Jr. Reportedly, they killed a number of Winthrop's livestock and stole some items from a house he kept there, perhaps as a rebuke to the English for their protection of the Montauketts, but also possibly out of the sheer unruliness of the young warriors.[82] Although the extent of the damage is unclear—Winthrop guessed that he had lost "hundreds" of head of livestock while the Indians would admit responsibility only for "3 or 4 goats which the Pocumtuck killed"—the event caused quite a stir.[83] Roger Williams heard that news of it "was read in Boston meeting house," which gave rise to fears "that Mr. Winthrop was robbed and undone and flying from the place unless succor were sent him."[84] It seemed as if Ninigret wanted to insult the English and Long Island Indians simultaneously. At least that was how the commissioners took it.

As a result of these affronts, once again Ninigret found himself on the verge of clashing with the English in September 1654. Even Massachusetts, which had opposed war against him the previous year, was now in favor of it, perhaps because peace had been declared between England and the Netherlands, thus removing the chance of the Dutch coming to Ninigret's aid. The commissioners had reached a consensus on Ninigret "that the forbearance and lenity of the colonies does but increase his insolency and our danger," particularly when it came to maintaining their legitimacy among their Indian protectorates.[85] First, however, they gave Ninigret an opportunity to redress their complaints.

Unsurprisingly, he gave them no satisfaction at all. He refused outright to pay the English anything for Pequots who lived under his rule, arguing that ten years of such extortion was enough. In any case, he denied that there were Pequots living with him any longer. Ninigret's boldest retort had to do with his attacks on Long Island. He cast his war as revenge, for not only had the Long Islanders slain his agent a few years earlier, but more recently they had surprised a body of Ninigret's men on Block Island, killing, he said, sixty warriors and a sachem (identified only as his nephew, Wepitamock's son).[86] "Wherefore should I acquaint the Commissioners with it," Ninigret asked. "I do but Right my own quarrel which the Long Islanders began with me."[87] It was a refrain that Ninigret had been making for almost twenty years.

Faced with this intransigence, the commissioners voted over the protests of Rhode Island (which had no say in their proceedings) to send forty foot soldiers and twenty horsemen against Ninigret in October 1654, only to have him slip the noose again.[88] This force, led by Simon Willard, stormed into Niantic country to find that Ninigret had already "swamped himself," which is to say, retreated to a swamp fifteen miles away. Ninigret knew that colonists feared swamps as dark, devilish places, full of disorder and camouflage for Indian ambushes, just as Indians respected them as thresholds to the underworld of Hobbomock, the spirit of the dead.[89] From this haven, Ninigret offered to have his men escort two English spokesmen plus the interpreters Thomas Stanton and Valentine Whitman into the swamp for a meeting on the condition that the English provide hostages as bond for good behavior. Having lost the initiative, Willard reluctantly agreed. In the subsequent conference, Ninigret remained as determined as ever to continue his attacks on Long Island regardless of the United Colonies' objections. Ninigret also refused to pay for the United Colonies' expedition, saying "he was not the cause of it but the Long Island Indians [for having] killed him a man at Connecticut." The only concession Willard wrested from Ninigret was a pledge to surrender all Pequots living in his country, which was basically a fait accompli given that 109 of them had already fled to Willard's camp amid these negotiations. Without the force of arms, Willard had to be satisfied with issuing Ninigret a toothless warning "not to molest them or any other of the friends of the English lest his head were set up upon an English pole." Ninigret's head was still firmly upon his shoulders as the colonial troops marched out of Niantic country.[90]

"How proudly Ninigret hath carried it"
The Renewal of Ninigret's Campaign against Uncas
and His English Protectors

It would be overstating the case to argue that Ninigret escaped this confrontation unscathed, because, after all, he lost his Pequot tribute payers. The first step in this development was the death of Ninigret's nephew, Wequashcook, who appears to have been the son of Wepitamock killed at Block Island by the Montauketts in the early fall of 1654. His loss emboldened the Pequots living under his governance to seek their independence from Ninigret, as did the Willard expedition's warning to Ninigret to leave the Pequots alone. No sooner had Ninigret emerged from the swamp than his Pequot tributaries petitioned the United Colonies for the right to "disown the jurisdiction of Ninigret over us" and "hereafter not to join in any war with Ninigret." The commissioners granted their consent the following spring, naming Wequashcook's brother, Caushawashott (or Harmon Garrett), governor of the Pequots at Pawcatuck and Weekapaug, free of any obligation to Ninigret. Likewise, the commissioners appointed Robin Cassacinamon to be the governor of the Pequots at Nameag and Noank, independent of Uncas.[91] The Pequots had risen from the ashes to become a distinct community again, ironically, under the protection of the very colonies that had devastated them in the Pequot War. It was the beginning of a new chapter of Pequot history, with Garrett's band ultimately settling on a reservation on Lantern Hill in what became North Stonington, Connecticut, and Cassacinamon's band moving to a reservation at Mashantucket (by modern Ledyard, Connecticut).[92] Before the Pequots' break from Ninigret and Uncas, Ninigret had asked John Winthrop Jr. and, by extension, the rest of the English, to pay no heed to Wequashcook and Cassacinamon, to treat them "as your little dogs but not as your confederates."[93] Now the English were allowing themselves to be used as a wedge by minor sachems seeking an end to tributary status, just as Uncas once did. One can imagine Ninigret clenching his fists at the very thought of it. His only solace was that the Pequots' restoration came at the expense of Uncas too.

Despite this setback, Ninigret remained unbowed. The commission-ers learned that as soon as Willard rode away, Ninigret "grew high and insolent in his speech and carriages and refuses to deliver the rest of his Pequots and threatens them that have left him and has again invaded the Long Island Indians."[94] Having already seen the futility of using armed force to quell Ninigret's "pride and rage," the United Colonies settled for arming the Montauketts and forming a boat patrol of Long Island Sound to prevent Ninigret's canoes from crossing.[95] Then, in the winter of 1654–55, Ninigret led over eighty armed men into Warwick, Rhode Island, to demand compensation for a colonist having robbed the grave of Pessacus's sister and defiled the body. According to Roger Williams, "The Sachems . . . were so bold as to talk often of men's lives, and of fighting with us and demanded an English child for hos-tage until satisfaction," which was promptly paid.[96] The following year, in September 1656, Ninigret once again snubbed the United Colonies by first demanding a hearing before the commissioners of his griev-ances against Wyandanch, and then failing to show up. To add insult to injury, he sent in his place none other than Newcomb, the "cunning and bold Narragansett" who the commissioners had twice specifically banned from their proceedings. No one was under any illusion that this affront was accidental.[97]

The clearest sign that Ninigret reserved the liberty to "right my own quarrel" was his renewal of the war with Uncas in 1657. Hostilities arose again as Uncas began raiding the Podunks of the Connecticut River Valley near Wethersfield, who, in turn, appealed to the Pocumtucks and Narragansetts for help. At the same time, Uncas rekindled the Narra-gansetts' ire by taunting them with the names of their dead sachems (doubtless including Miantonomi), a taboo "which he knows they can not bear."[98] Soon Uncas was facing simultaneous attacks from the Pocumtucks and Podunks to his northwest and the Narragansetts to his east, thereby forcing him to move into a walled fortress with English gunners stationed at the perimeter. Other Mohegans moved close to English homes to labor as tenants and servants rather than risk an as-sault on their own villages. But the English were no shield. After warn-ing that they would not tolerate the English alerting Uncas to their war parties and especially furnishing him with arms, the Narragansetts and Pocumtucks began pursuing the Mohegans wherever they found them, even if colonists were in the way.[99] For instance, in June 1657, John

Mason reported that an Indian woman (certainly a Mohegan) had been killed by Ninigret's men as she worked some land belonging to "Goodman Roberts . . . not many rods from Goodm[an] Prentice his house."[100] The farm and trading post of Jonathan Brewster, just outside the walls of Uncas's fort, became a frequent target during this campaign. Over the course of 1659 alone, Narragansett-Pocumtuck forces killed at least one of Brewster's Mohegan servants (who, at the time, was holding on for dear life to the waist of Brewster's wife), killed two of his hogs, forced themselves at gunpoint into his house looking for arms and Mohegan enemies, and then finally riddled his home with eleven gunshots. The Narragansetts' mistaken belief that John Mason, Connecticut's deputy governor and Uncas's primary English advocate, was visiting Brewster not only failed to dissuade them from attacking but appears to have served as additional motivation. Some reports, which galled the English, had the Narragansetts boasting that they had killed Mason, though he remained very much alive. Yet eliminating Mason would have merely been a bonus. The Narragansetts' main target was Brewster because, they said, he "did furnish Uncas with Guns, powder, and shot." Englishmen could not simultaneously claim immunity from Narragansett and Pocumtuck attack while arming their enemies.[101] Nor could Uncas claim immunity from his killing of Miantonomi by invoking the protection of the English.

Enàtch neèn ánowà. Let my word stand.
Ninigret's Principles and Politics

By attacking Uncas and his allies, Ninigret made a powerful statement about where he saw himself and the Narragansetts in New England's balance of power. He insisted that the Narragansetts ranked among the regional forces, including the United Colonies and Mohawks. Ninigret also expected the Narragansetts, under his leadership, to lord over the area's weaker peoples, including the Montauketts, Pequots, Mohegans, and Wampanoags. Ninigret viewed himself as a great sachem along the lines of Canonicus and Miantonomi, though he shared decision making for the Narragansetts with Pessacus and Mixano given their genealogical claims to status. Yet he would not brook aspirants like Uncas, Wyandanch, or Harmon Garrett rising at his expense. When they tried, he responded with force, regardless of how the United Colonies felt about it.

Ninigret could not fulfill his ambition on his own. He needed the support of power brokers at home and abroad to consolidate his following and project his strength. Locally, he and his children married high-ranking partners to carry the family's influence far and wide. Likewise, he sought political friendships with Englishmen like Roger Williams and John Winthrop Jr., who themselves were often at odds with the United Colonies. He forced lesser sachems on both sides of Long Island Sound to pay him wampum tribute, which he then used to build alliances with inland powers such as the Mohawks and Pocumtucks. He even reached across the Atlantic to seek an alliance with the English king. These relationships helped make Ninigret and his people into powers to be reckoned with, both locally and regionally.

True to his signature, Ninigret was often a war club in politics: solid, directed, and deadly. Although we will never fully know how he conducted himself at home among family, counselors, and his closest followers, we do know this: he rose to power on the strength of his pledge to make Uncas pay for Miantonomi's death, and he remained in power in part because of his refusal to compromise this goal. He permitted no one to stand in his way—not even the United Colonies—even though the English already outnumbered his people severalfold by the mid 1640s, even though they boasted ships, superior firepower, metal armor, and horses, even though they had proven themselves to be merciless in their slaughter of the Pequots. Despite all this, Ninigret's message to them was he would be their friend if they would "doe him Justice against his Enemies," that he could do business with them if they remained neutral, but that he would make their lives hell if they tried to obstruct him. These fundamental principles guided Ninigret through the endless series of emergencies that marked his political career following the death of Miantonomi.

Still, Ninigret could not simply club his way to power. One of the ironies of Ninigret's career is that he continued to accumulate power not despite but partially because of his failure to kill Uncas. Every time Ninigret made an attempt on Uncas's life, however unsuccessful, he flouted English pretensions to authority, which raised his stature among the Narragansetts. His raids against the Indians of Long Island, which generally were successful, also defied the English while showcasing his military prowess and supplying him with the wampum he needed to cultivate allies. His impressive list of friends had not yet enabled him to defeat Uncas, but he had come close, and there was every reason to believe that he would keep up the pursuit in the future. In the meantime, Ninigret drew on his allies' influence and economic resources to strengthen his hand both domestically and against the English. In a sense, Uncas was more valuable to Ninigret alive than dead, though Ninigret probably would have failed to appreciate the point. The ongoing fight against him encouraged Ninigret to broaden his base of power and keep his people focused on an external enemy.

Ninigret was blessed with the talent to rule and more than a bit of luck. It took a courageous man to lead young warriors across open water and into foreign territory to fight their indigenous enemies. It took equal confidence to march into English capitals to confront the commissioners of the United Colonies surrounded by their guards. Colonial governors never attempted the like among Indians. The fact that Ninigret and so many of his people emerged from these contests not only alive but ascendant was testimony to the sachem's charisma and skill. Other Narragansett sachems, such as Pessacus and Mixano, did not compare. Ninigret's accomplishments were also a product of good fortune, of Ninigret's uncanny ability to elude Uncas's assassins, to dodge enemy bullets and arrows, and to "swamp himself" just before English forces arrived. At so many points, a premature start or a moment's delay might have ended Ninigret's life and dramatically altered the fate of the region.

Ninigret's career mattered. By the end of the 1650s, his Narragansetts were, for all intents and purposes, the only tribe in coastal New England and Long Island Sound that the colonies had not subjected. Several times over, the Narragansetts had faced down the powerful United Colonies and emerged from the fray with their leadership, territory, and autonomy intact. But as Ninigret's career wore on, his odds in this contest shifted from bad to worse for the English population was growing quickly. Ninigret emerged from the 1659 campaign against Uncas stronger than ever in part because he had refused to allow the English to shelter his enemies. Yet he was also setting himself up for another decade of hostility with the puritan colonies, which had come to see him as their greatest enemy.

CHAPTER 4

A Time of Decision

Throughout his career as sachem, Ninigret's approach toward the English had been guided by a single principle: to keep them out of his people's affairs. In practical terms, that meant he wanted them to stop defending the Mohegans and Montauketts so the Narragansetts could revenge Miantonomi's death and assume the role once held by the Pequots as the preeminent tribute-collecting tribe on Long Island Sound. Yet neither the English nor Indians threatened by the Narragansetts would conform to Ninigret's agenda. Ever since its founding, the United Colonies had systematically extended protection to the very Indians that the Narragansetts wanted to subjugate, usually at the invitation of those communities, thus daring the Narragansetts to risk a confrontation. Ninigret answered the challenge by repeatedly attacking the Mohegans, Montauketts, and other Long Island Indians, boasting that the English were "no matter" and would "do nothing." Basically he had been right. To be sure, colonial support had enabled Uncas to foil several Narragansett attempts on his life. However, English retaliation against the Narragansetts had amounted to little more than minor military expeditions, which the sachems repeatedly deflected by promising to pay steep fines of wampum and behave peacefully. They never made good on these pledges, at least not to the United Colonies' satisfaction. When the Narragansetts launched their offensive against Uncas in 1659 they had every reason to believe that this pattern would continue.

It did not. The United Colonies responded to the Narragansetts' attacks on English homesteads (albeit ones that were sheltering and arming Mohegans) not only by issuing a new series of fines but threatening to seize Narragansett land if the tribe failed to pay. In this, the United Colonies hoped to deal a simultaneous blow to the Narragansetts and the dissident colony of Rhode Island, whose fortunes were hitched. It also hoped to give English land speculators, including some of the commissioners, title to some of the richest pasture in the region. For decades the Narragansetts had managed to keep English encroachment at bay, quite literally, as the only place they would allow colonists to settle was along the islands and peninsulas of Narragansett Bay. Now, for the very first time, the heart of Narragansett country was at risk. Another ominous sign was that the Narragansetts needed royal authority to answer this threat. The United Colonies' designs on Narragansett land, and the Narragansetts' reliance on English power to counter English power, signaled that they had entered a perilous new era.

By the mid to late 1660s, Ninigret faced a new challenge from within the Indian ranks, the rise of Metacom, or Philip, of the Wampanoags, who was calling for an intertribal resistance movement. Philip's status as an ambitious young sachem and a Wampanoag automatically made him something of a rival to an aging Narragansett sachem like Ninigret. Yet that does not mean that Ninigret automatically rejected Philip's politics, quite the contrary. In the first half of 1669, Ninigret and rival sachems from throughout the region held an unprecedented series of meetings to discuss what, if anything, they could and should do to keep the colonies from displacing them all. This reckoning was personal as well as political. Ninigret had to take stock of everything he had built and what the future might hold for his successors. Still a robust man but entering his 70s, he was forced to consider whether to continue in his longstanding role of warrior-chief or make the transition to elder statesman. For Ninigret, indeed for all of native New England, it was a time of decision.

Ni'ttauke or Nissawna'wkamuck. My Land.
The Narragansetts Confront English Land Sharks

Unlike so many other Indians in southern New England, the Narragansetts had controlled English expansion into their territory and tailored it to their own needs up to the late 1650s. In the mid 1630s, Miantonomi and Canonicus granted Roger Williams use of the head of Narragansett Bay (modern Providence) plus Prudence Island and Aquidneck Island (modern Portsmouth and Newport). By placing colonists in those locations, the Narragansetts could use them as a shield against Wampanoag

attacks and a source of trade. In subsequent years, they permitted religious dissidents from Massachusetts and Plymouth to settle in these
areas and Williams and then Richard Smith to run a trading post at
Cocumscussoc, in what became the town of Wickford. However, the
vast majority of Narragansett land remained in Narragansett hands. As
late as the 1660s, Rhode Island still consisted of just its original four
towns—Providence, Warwick, Newport, and Portsmouth, and contained
only about fifteen hundred people, which was about a tenth the size of
the Narragansett population. The Narragansetts had managed to direct
early English settlement in Rhode Island in accordance with Narragansett priorities.[1]

It is easy to jump to the conclusion that the Narragansetts lost control
during a spate of land sales between 1657 and 1660 in which they alienated the core of their country. Early in 1657, the sachem, Cojonoquant, a
brother of Pessacus, sold a group of Rhode Island speculators his rights
around Pettaquamscutt Hill, near Point Judith on the southwest side of
Narragansett Bay. He quickly followed up this transaction with additional sales of Conanicut Island (modern-day Jamestown) and other
small islands in Narragansett Bay. The Narragansetts had long used
these areas for fishing, shellfishing, and reed gathering, but colonists
wanted them for livestock grazing. Then, in January and March 1658,
five Narragansett sachems, including Pessacus, sold a group of Rhode
Island speculators some twelve square miles of land surrounding Point
Judith, thus confirming and enlarging Cojonoquant's earlier deals.
Ninigret sold his own claims to this Pettaquamscutt Purchase, as it became known, plus additional acreage that stretched into the eastern part
of his dominion. The following year the Narragansett land market
heated up again. In the summer of 1659, a corporation from Massachusetts known as the Atherton Company acquired two tracts from Cojonoquant, one north and another south of modern Wickford. Finally, in
June 1660, another group of speculators from Newport bargained with
Sosoa for a tract called Misquamicut, running along the east side of the
Pawcatuck River northward for twenty miles and eastward to the mid-
point of Quonochontaug Pond, just a few miles from Ninigret's fort. In
sum, the Narragansetts had sold claims that extended all along the western edge of Narragansett Bay and the southern seashore bordering
Block Island Sound, preserving only the area around Ninigret Pond,
which constituted the base of Ninigret's territory.[2]

Historians, building on charges of underhanded dealing leveled by Rhode Island against the Atherton Company, have widely concluded that these land sales were fraudulent, that they involved Englishmen getting the Narragansett sachems, particularly Cojonoquant, drunk and then convincing them to sign land deeds they barely understood.[3] Yet this interpretation flattens a dynamic, politically charged process. Rhode Island's criticism of the Atherton Company extended from legitimate concerns that the company's purchases were a Trojan horse for Massachusetts and Connecticut to subjugate Rhode Island. Rhode Island's rationale for the Misquamicut Purchase, and its rush to organize the new town of Westerly out of this land, was to strengthen its claims to Narragansett Country against Connecticut in the face of this threat. The fact of the matter is that Rhode Island speculators were just as active as the Atherton Company (which itself included some Rhode Islanders) in Narragansett country, and that the full roster of Narragansett sachems, not just Cojonoquant, participated in these transactions. These sachems included Ninigret, and Ninigret was no drunk. All of which is to say, it is historical caricature to portray the sale of Narragansett country as the destructive wake of a drinking binge by Cojonoquant.

The strongest argument against casting these land sales as simple Narragansett victimization is that they made political sense for the Narragansetts.[4] It was no coincidence that the timing overlapped with the renewed Narragansett military campaign against Uncas. The sachems needed wampum and European manufactured goods for distribution in order to rally indigenous political support. Yet wampum was probably in short supply among the Narragansetts during these years because the United Colonies obstructed their tribute-collecting raids against Long Island and siphoned off much of the wampum they did possess through fines. Selling land for wampum more than made up the difference, netting the Narragansetts more than thirty-five hundred fathoms according to one account.[5] This wampum would have allowed the Narragansetts to conduct diplomacy with other Indians, but it still would have fallen short of what they needed to buy European goods because of the rapid devaluation of wampum beads on the colonial market. Throughout the 1640s and 1650s, English and Dutch traders had eagerly purchased wampum from coastal Indians in order to exchange the beads with Indians in the interior for beaver pelts. The beaver pelts, in turn, could be sold in Europe at high prices. Thus it was the European market for fur that determined wampum's value for colonists. However, in the late 1650s, the European demand for fur began to bottom out due to a glut in supply and shifting fashion trends. With it went colonial demand for wampum. Narragansett sachems who wanted to purchase European goods, including guns, powder, and shot for their warriors, needed something else of value to trade. That something else was land.[6]

Land sales also made sense to the Narragansetts as a means to cultivate English support for their strikes against Uncas, just as Uncas had alienated land to Connecticut to encourage its backing of him. According to Roger Williams, the Narragansetts' negotiations with Rhode Island speculators included demands "that we should furnish them with poison to dispatch Uncas" and that "we should constantly send English soldiers with theirs against Uncas."[7] Likewise, shortly before the first Atherton purchase, Quequaquenuit, the son of Mixano and brother of Scuttup, had asked the Massachusetts General Court to approve a multi-tribal attack against Uncas, which the court promptly rejected.[8] The Narragansetts reasonably assumed that selling land to the Atherton Company would change the magistrates' mind because many of the company's members were connected to the United Colonies. Humphrey Atherton, the group's namesake, had served the United Colonies as a military officer during the 1650 expedition into Narragansett country. More recently, he had been Massachusetts Superintendent for the praying (or Christian) Indians. Clearly his opinion carried weight among the English when it came to Indian affairs. Another investor in the company was John Winthrop Jr., who had recently acquired the titles of governor of Connecticut and commissioner of the United Colonies. Not coincidentally, Cojonoquant framed his grants to the Atherton Company as a gesture of "consideration of that great love and affection I do have unto Englishmen, especially, Mr. John Winthrop, Governor of Connecticut, [and] Major Humphrey Atherton of the Massachusetts."[9] Cojonoquant and his fellow Narragansett sachems appear to have expected these men, in loving return, to support their attacks on Uncas or at least stay out of the way.

The Narragansetts might also have anticipated that the English would never take possession of these alienated tracts. Selling land to rival groups of Rhode Island, Massachusetts, and Connecticut speculators guaranteed a paralyzing fight for control of the purchased land. Indeed, the Atherton Company had framed Cojonoquant's grants as gifts to circumvent a 1658 Rhode Island ban on land purchases from Indians without the colony's permission. Until these matters were settled, there was no way for the speculators to sell their claims without risking that a rival colony would declare the titles null and void. The colonial market for farms in Narragansett country would remain tepid amid such uncertainly, thus allowing the Narragansetts to postpone actual English encroachment until they had dealt with the more pressing matter of eliminating Uncas. As ever, the Narragansetts were more concerned with the rivalries of Indian country than the threat of colonialism.

It is an open question as to what the Narragansetts understood these land sales to mean, for in the mid seventeenth century Indians and Englishmen were still battling to define what a land sale was and what it was not. The English preference was to interpret these transactions as the transfer of fee-simple title, which is to say, the exclusive right of use and alienation. Additionally, they wanted land sales to convey jurisdiction over the land and the people on it from Indian to colonial authorities. Early in the colonial period, few Indians understood their cessions to Englishmen in these terms at all. Typically they saw a land sale as a conditional gift, as a gesture of friendship that remained valid only as long as the two parties remained friends. Indians expected that giving Englishmen the right to use the land obliged the English to the sellers in a number of respects. The Indian assumption was that the English would extend hospitality to Indian visitors, tolerate the Indians' continued use of the land, and pay tokens of respect (or tribute) to the Indians' sachems. In Plymouth and Massachusetts, unlike in Narragansett country, steady English pressure on Indian territory had already brought these conflicting understandings to the fore. The result was joint-use agreements that specified who would use what parts of the land, for what purpose, and when. For instance, Indians might retain the right to raise crops on a particular tract of land between May and October, whereupon Englishmen would have the right to put their cattle to graze in the Indians' harvested corn fields. Likewise, Indians might retain the right of access to prime fishing or gathering spots otherwise surrounded by English planting lands and livestock pastures. Though these agreements rarely addressed the problem of jurisdiction, it is telling that Indian sachems often retained the right to beached whales and other sea treasure, which for them was an important symbol of sovereignty. Moreover, some agreements required English buyers to pay sachems gifts on a regular basis. In theory, these arrangements balanced the needs of each party, but in reality Indians and Englishmen were still testing how they would play out over time.[10]

It would have been reasonable for the Narragansett sachems to assume that their people's superior strength meant their interpretations of land sales would prevail. After all, the Narragansett population of perhaps ten to fifteen thousand people was still much larger than that of Rhode Island (which stood at less than fifteen hundred in 1660) and Connecticut (some eight thousand). Even Massachusetts, which boasted a population of more than twenty thousand, was reluctant to war with the tribe.[11] It seemed unlikely that the Narragansetts were about to suffer waves of Englishmen washing over their country. We know from the perspective of hindsight that land sales were a major step in the process of colonists displacing Indians from their own country. The Narragansetts do not seem to have shared that perspective in the late 1650s. To them, land sales were a means toward accomplishing their major foreign policy goal: revenging themselves on Uncas.

"They wonder that such hard things should be required of them" The Politics of the Atherton Mortgage

The Narragansett sachems made a serious misjudgment if they expected their land deals to curry favor with the United Colonies. Rather, the commissioners decided it was high time to ratchet up their pressure on the tribe. After all, amid these sales the Narragansetts had not only attacked Uncas in violation of the commissioners' longstanding orders, but they had done so in league with the Pocumtucks and nearly killed several Englishmen along the way. As if to trump themselves, the Narragansetts had also renewed their attacks on the Montauketts. Colonist Antipas Newman wrote an urgent letter to his father-in-law John Winthrop Jr. in July 1660 exclaiming that during a recent stop at the Cocumscussoc trading post, he and his family had witnessed a party of Narragansetts beheading nine captive Long Island Indians. Lest the commissioners remain unmoved, Newman added that this "sad sight was so dreadful to my sister that she had much ado to get over it for a good space."[12] The commissioners did not need the prodding. They could plainly see that their decades-old effort to rein in the Narragansetts had been ineffective. Their dilemma was how to resolve this problem short of war.

The commissioners knew full well that the Narragansetts would never meet their first two conditions of peace, to pay a fine of ninety-five fathoms of wampum and surrender the four men who had shot up Brewster's house. In the hope of converting the Narragansetts' failure or refusal to comply into English profit, they added the unprecedented requirement that the Narragansetts take out a mortgage of land as a bond for their performance. Past experience also taught the commissioners that if they called Ninigret to one of their meetings to receive these demands, he would fail to show, sending either a deputy or nobody at all. He would then stall until the emergency passed. Consequently, in September 1660 the United Colonies sent veteran interpreter Thomas Stanton and George Denison to deliver the message directly. The commissioners were not going to let Ninigret slip their grasp again.

Still, Ninigret and his fellow sachems did everything they could to buy themselves some time. Protesting that "these things are very hard which are required, and they wonder that such hard things should be required of them," they convinced the commissioners to grant them six months instead of four to pay the fine. As for the men who had attacked Brewster's farmstead, the commissioners could not have been surprised to learn that they had taken an opportune hunting trip in the direction of Pocumtuck and thus could not be found. Ninigret agreed to suspend his attacks on the Montauketts, but only until he could acquaint the commissioners "with their reasons and of the justice of that war." Such delay and obfuscation was part of a familiar script. The new feature was Stanton and Denison returning from their mission with a mortgage, signed on September 29, in which Ninigret, Pessacus, and Scuttup agreed to forfeit "all our whole country with all our rights and titles thereunto" if they fell short of meeting the United Colonies' demands.

Given the severity of these terms, the nagging question is why the sachems would have signed such an agreement. After all, there was no English army at their doorstep. There is no way to know for sure, but in all likelihood they judged that, as in the past, the commissioners' threats would come to nothing. Ninigret had a successful record of taking such calculated risks and Pessacus and Scuttup were probably banking on his savvy to pull them through again. As Ninigret once put it, the English "talked much but do little."[13]

It took only two weeks for the sachems to hit on a strategy to postpone reckoning with the commissioners, albeit at the cost of a new risk to their territory. It came in the form of the Atherton Company, which offered to pay the Narragansetts' fine to the United Colonies in exchange for the sachems agreeing to a new mortgage, payable to the corporation. Ninigret Pessacus, Scuttup, and Ninigret's deputy Newcomb all complied, signing a mortgage for "all their country for the payment of . . . [wampum] again within five months."[14] If the Narragansetts somehow managed to raise this amount, the Atherton Company would still gain the preemptive right to Narragansett country, meaning the exclusive privilege to buy Narragansett land in the future.

There are a host of possible explanations for why the Narragansetts signed on to this agreement. For one, the Atherton mortgage offered the Narragansetts better conditions than the United Colonies' deal. It gave them five or six years to remove their homes from the land if the English foreclosed on it. Even then, the Narragansetts would retain their right to "royalties," meaning the tribute customarily paid to sachems, and to "competency of planting ground for them and their successors forever."[15] The mortgage contained a statement from the Narragansetts that they put a "great deal of trust in the said Major [Atherton] and expect kindness from him." It also included a promise from the company that it would "use the Indians with all courtesy." These words do not appear to have been merely perfunctory. No sooner had the Narragansetts signed the Atherton mortgage than the company assisted Ninigret in dealing with the commissioners over an incident in which some Narragansetts plundered a ship that had stranded off Point Judith.[16] The Narragansetts appear to have expected such services from the Atherton Company to continue well into the future.

Yet the driving force of the Atherton mortgage seems to have been an undocumented quid pro quo involving the Narragansetts, the Atherton Company, and the commissioners of the United Colonies. Conspicuously, after the Narragansetts signed the Atherton mortgage and the Atherton Company paid the Narragansetts' wampum fine to the United Colonies, the commissioners quietly dropped their demand for the Narragansett sachems to turn over the four gunmen who had shot up Brewster's house. The commissioners must have known the dire consequences of pressing the Narragansetts to surrender their men, for the Pequot War and Kieft's War had proven that Indians would rather risk their lives than suffer the indignity of having their people arrested, judged, and executed by colonial authorities. Simple considerations of profit also seem to have been at play. By the time the Atherton Company made its offer to the Narragansetts, four of the eight commissioners of the United Colonies—John Winthrop Jr., Josiah Winslow, Simon Bradstreet, and Daniel Denison—were among its investors. Other commissioners would follow them into the Atherton ranks. Making the Narragansetts' fine or mortgage payable to the Atherton Company allowed these commissioners to gain personally from the transaction.[17]

The sachems had good reason to doubt that the company would ever be able to collect on its mortgage. After all, Rhode Island had already declared any land transactions in Narragansett country without its permission to be null and void. For the company to overcome the opposition of Rhode Island and the Narragansetts, it would have to enlist the military support of the United Colonies, which had already received its fine. All this was enough to encourage the Narragansetts that they would retain their land for the foreseeable future.

There is still another explanation for the Atherton mortgage, for just as the commissioners and the company were scheming to seize Narragansett country, the tribe's old allies, the royal Stuarts, were reclaiming their throne after years in exile. News of the Stuart Restoration reached New England just as the mortgage issue was taking shape, and rumors of Charles II's return had already been circulating for a year.[18] The commissioners must have anticipated that Whitehall would not respond favorably to its exploitation of a tribe that had subjected itself to the crown back in the 1640s. In fact, the crown was likely to question the legitimacy of the United Colonies in general, for it was an extralegal, puritan governmental institution that had routinely trod on the rights of the king's subjects, English and indigenous alike. Not the least of all, one of the organization's members, New Haven, reportedly harbored some of the judges who had presided over the execution of the Stuarts' father. Fear of royal authority was likely an impetus to the commissioners' approval of the Atherton mortgage, their hope being that a private organization would be less likely to draw the crown's scrutiny. Rhode Island certainly anticipated royal assistance in fending off its puritan neighbors, which influenced its vote to proclaim Charles II and issue all writs in his name as early as October 1660.[19] It was a wise decision. The newly restored king and his brother, James, Duke of York, were nearly as determined to revenge themselves on the puritans for the execution of their father as the Narragansetts were to kill Uncas. Together, they would form the greatest single obstacle to the Atherton Company and the United Colonies fulfilling their designs on Narragansett land.

Keén nétop. Is it you friend?
The Narragansetts' Restoration

The restoration of crown authority in New England helped the Narragansetts to address the loss of three of their other allies, the Dutch, Pocumtucks, and Mohawks. In North America, the fall of New Netherland was one of the main consequences of the Stuart Restoration. Shortly after reclaiming the throne, Charles II issued his brother James, the Duke of York, a proprietary grant, including the right of governance, to all of the territory between the Delaware River on the south and west, and the Connecticut River on the north and east. This grant also included Long Island, Martha's Vineyard, Nantucket, the Elizabeth Islands, and the northern portion of Maine. Conspicuously, these claims surrounded the puritan colonies of New England. York's first move to fulfill this grant came in 1664 when he sent an English fleet to conquer New Netherland, which it accomplished without firing a shot. Dutch colonists would remain in the new English colony of New York, but Dutch authority was over. To Ninigret and the Narragansetts, who relied on the Dutch for trade, especially munitions, and who on at least one occasion had used the threat of a Dutch alliance as a military counterweight to the English, the fall of New Netherland was a substantial blow.[20]

The loss of the Dutch was even more troubling because it coincided with the decline of the Narragansetts' alliances with the Pocumtucks and Mohawks. As York's fleet was crossing the Atlantic to seize New Netherland, the Pocumtucks and Mohawks were descending into war with each other. The break occurred following the Pocumtucks' rash decision to murder a visiting Mohawk delegation, probably as a show of support for the Sokokis, who were engaged in their own conflict with the Mohawks. The Mohawks responded with a furious offensive that forced the Pocumtucks to abandon their Connecticut Valley stronghold and scatter throughout the Northeast. It was the end of their status as a distinct group. The Narragansett-Mohawk alliance suffered in kind, as the Pocumtucks had long served as bridge between their peoples. The ascension of New York made things even worse. The Mohawks had been willing to risk antagonizing the New England colonies by supporting Ninigret as long as their main trading partner was the Dutch. With the English now in control of the Hudson River colony, that calculus shifted. The Iroquois, generally, and the Mohawks, in particular, were already at war with Indian nations ranging from the Abenakis of Maine to the Ottawas of the Great Lakes and many other groups in between. Their relations with the French were equally hostile. In September 1666, a French force of a thousand men invaded Mohawk country and torched scores of homes and enough crops "to nourish all Canada for two entire years." Given these pressures, the Mohawks were not about to imperil their relationship with New York for the mere sake of the Narragansetts. Attacking the New England colonies, or even just threatening to do so, would accomplish just that, for though the Duke of York was no friend of the puritans, as their future sovereign he was not about to sanction violence against them by an Indian nation. For years Ninigret and the Narragansetts had used Mohawk, Pocumtuck, and Dutch alliances to answer the collective power of the United Colonies. Those options were now gone.[21]

The Narragansetts turned to the crown instead before the Atherton Company could secure its hold over their land. As the due date for the Narragansett mortgage approached, the sachems sent two English agents to London to present their case to the king. These agents must have been supplied by Rhode Island, which was engaged in its own lobbying campaign to have its colony charter, issued by Parliament during the Interregnum, recognized by the new royal authority. The Atherton Company responded by taking formal possession of Narragansett territory in the spring of 1662 with a Livery of seisin ceremony, a medieval English ritual in which the grantor, in this case, Scuttup, presented company men with a piece of turf and a twig from the land being transferred. Yet even the Atherton investors were unconvinced by this theater of their own making. As Edward Hutchinson wrote after hearing that the Narragansetts were appealing to the king, "If the purchase from the chief sagamors [sachems] be not good, it overthrows all the purchases in the country."[22] That was the Narragansetts' hope.

The crown, it turned out, was eager to receive the Narragansetts' petition as one in a series of complaints against New England authorities. These grievances included Boston's persecution of Quakers, Baptists, and even Anglicans; strong-arm attempts by Massachusetts to extend its jurisdiction over Maine, New Hampshire, and Rhode Island; and the trade of New England merchants with the Dutch even during war between their countries. Such behavior convinced Whitehall that the puritan colonies, foremost Massachusetts, thought of themselves as independent republics rather than subordinates of the mother country. In 1664 the crown appointed four men as royal commissioners to investigate these charges. Not coincidentally, Ninigret and Pessacus were among the first to welcome them to New England. Thanks to the farsighted record keeping of Samuel Gorton, they presented a copy of their 1644 submission to King Charles I and then "gave a long petition to the Commissioners complaining of many acts of violence and injustice, which the Massachusetts had done to them."[23] Clearly the Narragansetts associated the Atherton Company with the Massachusetts Bay colony. If the royal commissioners did the same, it would not bode well for the company's designs.[24]

The following spring the royal commissioners confirmed what the Narragansetts had known all along: the Narragansett country belonged neither to the Atherton Company nor the Massachusetts Bay Colony.[25] Moreover, the king's agents promised Pessacus and Ninigret "protection from all injustice and violence from any of the King's subjects, and defense against their Indian enemies."[26] This protection included invalidating the Atherton mortgage plus all the land sales made in 1659 by Cojonoquant. The few colonists residing in Narragansett country based on titles from the Atherton Company or Massachusetts were to quit the place, taking with them "any Cattle of any sort" (a decision the royal commissioners would later reverse). To help ensure compliance, the royal commissioners renamed Narragansett country "the King's Province" and placed the area under their supervision. In return, the Narragansetts pledged the king an annual symbolic tribute of just two wolf skins and a promise "neither to make war nor sell land, nor do anything of great consequence without acquainting the King's Commissioners or such as he shall appoint for that purpose."[27] These were relatively minor concessions given the unlikelihood that crown officers were actually going to pay close attention to the Narragansetts' internal affairs or diplomacy with other Indians.

To celebrate these developments, the Narragansetts held a ritual renewal of their friendship with the crown.[28] Narragansett dignitaries laid down their arms at the feet of the royal commissioners and presented them with "two caps of peag [wampum] and two clubs inlaid with peag for a present to the King, and a feather mantle and a porcupine bag for a present to the king." The king's officers, in turn, gave the Narragansetts two fine coats as gifts. One can only wonder if henceforth Ninigret made it a point to wear one of these coats whenever he met with colonial authorities. After all, the Narragansetts and Rhode Island had outmaneuvered the United Colonies and its shadow organization, the Atherton Company, and brought the king into their corner. For now, at least, their land remained safely in their possession.[29]

Sekinneauhettúock, Maninnewahettúock. They hate each other.
The Burgeoning Rivalry between Ninigret and Philip

As the mortgage crisis ended, Ninigret discovered a new threat emerging from Wampanoag country in the form of the young sachem Metacom, or Philip, the son of Massasoit. In many ways, Philip resembled Ninigret back in the 1630s and 1640s. Just as Ninigret had ascended to power by exploiting Narragansett resentment over the execution of Miantonomi, so too did Philip assume leadership after the untimely death of his brother Wamsutta in 1662, which many Wampanoags attributed to English poisoning.[30] Philip also earned respect by striking against external enemies, entering strategic marriages, and engaging in regional diplomacy. Ninigret knew a rival when he saw one, for there was only so much room at the top of the hierarchy of sachems. Philip's alliance-building involved drawing off disenchanted tribute payers from the Narragansetts and cultivating relationships with the eastern Narragansett sachems, whose power had declined as Ninigret's rose. Additionally, Philip followed a policy of confrontation with the English, one that Ninigret was gradually abandoning as he entered old age and witnessed the colonists' growing strength.

By attempting to draw the Narragansetts into his orbit, Philip was ushering in a new era of Wampanoag-Narragansett relations. Back in

the late 1610s and 1620s, the Narragansetts under Canonicus and Miantonomi had tried to dominate Wampanoags communities decimated by
the plague. Narragansett aggression drove Massasoit's Wampanoags
from the head of Narragansett Bay eastward onto the Mount Hope
Peninsula and ultimately into a defensive alliance with the newly established colony of Plymouth. The alliance between Massasoit and Plymouth, in which Plymouth and the Wampanoags protected each other
against the Narragansetts, and Plymouth supported Massasoit among
the Wampanoags, held for nearly forty years, until the death of the great
sachem in 1660. Yet there was a dark side to the relationship. Throughout Massasoit's lifetime, the English bought hundreds of square miles
of Wampanoag land, allowed their livestock to trespass on Wampanoag territory, and sponsored Christian missions that eventually cleaved
off Wampanoags from Massasoit's tribute network. As Wamsutta and
Metacom rose to power in the 1660s, they were determined to reverse
these losses by building an alliance of disaffected Indian nations, including the Narragansetts. First, however, Philip had to establish himself as
regional power. His initial step was to offer protection to the very communities the Narragansetts exploited.[31]

One of the first Narragansett tribute payers to whom Philip reached
out was Pomham, the sachem of Shawomet, or, as the English were by
then calling it, Warwick. Back in the 1640s, Pomham had clashed with
the Narragansetts when Miantonomi tried to deed Pomham's territory
to Samuel Gorton. Now, twenty years later, Pomham found himself
fending off a new attempt by another high-ranking Narragansett sachem, Pessacus, to sell the ground from under him. The issue was that
colonist Robert Carr, having found Pomham unwilling to part with Warwick Neck, had instead bought the title from Pessacus, however tenuous
his claim.[32] Pomham refused to recognize this sale, first by swearing off
Pessacus's authority and then refusing to quit the land. Philip pounced
on this opportunity to win Pomham as an ally, offering him military
support in the event that Pessacus or Ninigret tried to drive him off.[33]
Philip was announcing that his ambitions extended into Narragansett
country.

Philip's subsequent moves directly challenged the interests of Ninigret and his family. First, in May 1666 Philip reached out to the Montauketts of Long Island, who Ninigret had been fighting for years to keep in
tributary status. Philip, through his English-educated, Wampanoag scribe,

John Sassamon, sent the Montauketts an English-language letter encouraging them to halt their tribute payments to Ninigret and to "strengthen yourselves and prepare against [Ninigret's] coming."[34] Philip then appears to have begun maneuvering to free the Nipmuck community of Quantisset in the Quinebaug River Valley from its tributary status to Ninigret's sister, Quaiapen (or Matantuck), the widow of Mixano and a Narragansett sunksquaw (or female sachem) in her own right. Philip had learned a valuable lesson by watching Ninigret over the years, namely that terrorizing a community into paying tribute risked driving them into the arms of the English. Seemingly, Philip's plan to recruit allies against the English was to offer them tribute-free support against their Narragansett oppressors. Once their loyalty was secure, Philip planned to direct them toward his ends.

Ninigret and his sister struck back with a double-pronged campaign in the summer of 1667. Quaiapen's move was to send hundreds of warriors against Quantisset in a bloodless but nevertheless destructive raid that warned the Nipmucks never to test her again. These warriors, who might very well have included some of Ninigret's own men, destroyed the Nipmucks' houses and plundered clothes, kettles, wampum, guns, deerskins, pigs, and "other such like treasures" estimated to be worth £130.[35] Quaiapen's explanation for this raid to the Massachusetts General Court was that the Nipmucks had been "formerly my husband's and son's men . . . time out of mind."[36] The Nipmucks retorted that they were a "free people" who had never paid tribute to the Narragansetts, and called on Philip, a supposedly "uninterested" party, to support their claim.[37] To keep Philip from responding, Ninigret created a minor crisis between the Wampanoag sachem and Plymouth. Ninigret charged that Philip was conspiring with the French to war against the English, "and so not only to recover their lands sold to the English, but to enrich themselves with their [the colonists'] goods." The possibility of such a scenario was slim, given the remoteness of the French and their historic lack of contact with Indians in southern New England. Nevertheless, Plymouth did its due diligence and called Philip to account, only to have Philip protest his innocence. He charged Ninigret with dissembling, explaining "that Ninigret, a Narragansett sachem, had hired this Indian to accuse him to us," just as Ninigret had so often accused Uncas in the past. Ultimately, Plymouth authorities concluded that "there was great probability that [Philip's] tongue had been running out." However, lacking concrete evidence of a plot, they decided only "to keep a watchful eye over him." That was precisely as Ninigret hoped.[38]

At the end of the day, Philip, Quaiapen, and Ninigret all lost in this affair. Tired of being treated like pawns in the rivalries of coastal sachems, in May 1668 eight Nipmuck sachems, representing Quintisset and six other communities, submitted themselves to the protection of Massachusetts and expressed a willingness "to pray to God," which is to say, to host a mission. Implicitly, the sachems also intended to cut off their tribute payments to sachems such as Quaiapen, in the case of Quintisset, and Uncas, in the case of the Nipmuck community of Wabquissett.[39] This was no empty threat. No sooner had the sachems made their submission than John Eliot, the primary missionary in Massachusetts, and Daniel Gookin, the colony's superintendent for Christian Indians, began making plans to designate seven communities in Nipmuck country as praying towns, with organized Christian meetings and an English presence that would protect them from the coastal sachems' raids. Collectively, the Wampanoags, Narragansetts, and Mohegans were discovering the twofold threat of the mission in which God's word and English jurisdiction marched hand in hand.

There is no mistaking the shared anger among coastal sachems about the mission's expansion. As early as 1652, Eliot wrote that "there be two Great Sachems in the Country that are open & professed enemies against praying to God, namely Uncas and Ninigret, and whenever the Lord removes them, there will be a door open for the preaching of the Gospel in those parts."[40] The sachems grew more hostile to the mission in subsequent years. Uncas repeatedly obstructed missionaries from preaching at Mohegan, though, as a diplomatic nicety, he briefly tolerated the largely ineffective attempt of the Reverend James Fitch to attract Mohegans to services at Norwich, Connecticut.[41] Uncas was less politic when it came to missionary activity among his tributaries. During a visit by John Eliot to Wabquissit, Uncas sent warning that he "is not well pleased that the English should pass over Mohegan River, to call his Indians to pray to God."[42] He also suddenly began opposing the Reverend Fitch.[43] It was enough to make Gookin denounce Uncas as "an old and wicked, willful man, a drunkard and otherwise very vicious, who has always been an opposer and underminer of Praying to God." Likewise, Philip was said to have responded to Eliot's encouragement to host a mission by pulling a button off of Eliot's coat and proclaiming "that he cared for his gospel, just as much as he cared for that button."⁴⁴ Ninigret's disdain for the mission was so well known that missionaries never even bothered to approach him or his followers. The Narragansetts, Gookin complained, "are more indisposed to embrace religion, than any Indians in the country," largely because of "the averseness of their sachems."⁴⁵

Clearly, between the growing jurisdiction of the United Colonies, English landed expansion, and now the spread of the mission, the coastal sachems had much to talk about.

Awaun mesh kupp'itouwaw? Of whom did you hear it?
The Great War Scare of 1669

What a sight to behold. There, seated together in the wétu of the Pequot sachem, Robin Cassacinamon, were Ninigret and Uncas, who for the better part of thirty years had talked endlessly of killing each other. The season was *pap sap quoho*, or mid winter, when the Pleiades anticipated spring's return by reaching their zenith.⁴⁶ Typically, New England Indians gathered together on pap sap quoho to feast and dance, but bringing these men together signaled a celestial realignment of an entirely different order. Indians attending this historic event—Pequots, Narragansetts, Mohegans, and probably Montauketts and Wampanoags as well—must have crackled with nervous excitement.

The English reaction to the unexpected news of this meeting was nothing short of alarm. Their unidentified sources said that the dance was part of a multitribal plot, headed by Ninigret, involving not just local tribes, but "northern Indians" connected to the French on the St. Lawrence River. Supposedly, vast sums of wampum had been changing hands, "some say Frenchmen's wampum." The nightmarish prospect of an alliance between the northeastern tribes and the French was enough to keep colonial New Englanders awake at night. The puritans had always suspected that their Catholic rivals far to the north would stop at nothing to reestablish Rome in Protestant dominions, including encouraging Indians to put fellow Christians to the knife.⁴⁷ Unwilling to leave this matter to chance, Connecticut dispatched interpreters Thomas Stanton and Thomas Minor at the head of a group of soldiers to arrest Ninigret at Cassacinamon's town and bring him in for questioning.

They arrived to have their worst fears confirmed. It "was matter of wonderment to me," Stanton wrote later, "that they who durst not look each upon [the] other this 20 years but at the muzzle of a gun or at the pile of an arrow" were now gathered in discussion of something they did not want the English to hear.[48] Yet to arrest Ninigret in this setting risked precipitating the very war the English claimed they wanted to prevent. When Stanton and his men burst into the meeting and ordered the Pequots to seize Ninigret, Ninigret's men brandished their clubs, which the English answered by unsheathing their swords. Fortunately for everyone, Cassacinamon's cool leadership tempered Stanton's rashness. Though Cassacinamon had been at odds with Ninigret for years, he stepped forward as host and offered to pay whatever amount of wampum it would take for Stanton to abort his mission, reasoning "that wampum was like the grass, when it was gone, it would come again, but if men be once killed they will live no more." Seeing an opportunity to save face, and perhaps his head as well, Stanton gave his price, forty pounds worth, and then returned home without Ninigret, richer in wampum, but none the wiser about what he had just seen.[49]

Stanton's raid did nothing to slow the conversation between sachems. Rather, Indian polities throughout the region appeared to be setting aside their historic differences to coordinate a grand confrontation with the English. Ninigret was said to have presented the Montauketts, his longstanding enemies, with arms and wampum in order to recruit them into a design involving "as many of the Indians as he could in all parts" to "kill all the English . . . that they might get their lands again from the English." It was as if the ghost of Miantonomi had arisen to reignite his multitribal uprising. Reportedly, the Montauketts reciprocated with their own present of two or three hundred fathoms of wampum to signal their acceptance, and then began storing arms and hosting Indian ambassadors from Block Island, Narragansett, and Pequot.[50] Other rumors had Cassacinamon petitioning the Mohawks to open their country as a retreat for the coastal Indians in the event of war.[51] In July 1669 Ninigret was supposedly preparing for "the greatest dance . . . that ever was in the Narragansett," to which he sent invitations to "Nipmuck and Long Island and to the Pequots and to Uncas."[52] Ninigret's daughter (probably Weunquesh) was an agent in this diplomacy, signaling her preparations to succeed her father once he was gone. Given the possibility of war, it was prudent for Ninigret to make such arrangements.

There is no record of what the Indians said at their meetings or who led the proceedings, and though the English believed that Ninigret was the driving force, circumstantial evidence suggests it was Philip. Colonial authorities had questioned Philip in 1662 and 1667 about such plotting based on accusations that he was stockpiling arms and hosting foreign dignitaries. They would confront him again in 1671, extracting a confession that he possessed a "naughty [or wicked] heart," after which they confiscated his guns and forced him to submit to Plymouth.[53] Four years later, he would take up arms against Plymouth after the colony arrested, tried, and executed three of his men on the charge of murdering a Wampanoag, John Sassamon, in Wampanoag country. To be sure, evidence of Philip's designs is circumstantial, and the fact that he eventually struck against the English can be seen as the result of an self-fulfilling English prophesy in which the colonists' repeated persecution of him on flimsy charges finally convinced him to fight. Yet, by most appearances, Philip had been working to build an anti-English coalition well before 1669 and continued this campaign for years afterward.

Of course, Ninigret, in his younger days, had often been implicated in such plots, which raises the question of whether he had rediscovered his will to lead a grand resistance in the wake of increasing English pressure on Narragansett land and the expansion of the mission into Nipmuck country. There is no way to tell for sure, but a probable scenario is that Philip was the spark for this conversation and that he saw Ninigret as an essential ally. Ninigret had risen to the highest ranks of Narragansett sachems during his forty-year career. He also dominated the Indians of Block Island and Long Island. Without Ninigret, Philip could not hope to recruit the Pequots and Mohegans, and vice versa, for none of them would dare to fight against the English while simultaneously guarding against attacks by their closest Indian neighbors. Yet perhaps the most important role for Ninigret in a proposed multitribal uprising was his diplomatic connections to the Indians of the upper Connecticut River Valley (the so called "northern" or "French Indians") and the Mohawks. Those groups were essential to Philip's plans as connections to the gun markets of Albany and Montreal and hosts of possible places to retreat. The coastal Indians also needed assurance that the Mohawks would not suddenly throw their support to the English. Though John Mason was given to exaggeration, he was veteran of Indian politics and probably had it right when he wrote, "I verily believe the plot is deferred only until they have overtopped [or convinced] the Mohawks."[54]

If the sachems were indeed contemplating a war against the English, these meetings would have focused on how to conduct such a campaign. The details would have been endless. In all likelihood they would have favored carefully timed, surprise attacks on multiple English locations, if one is to judge from other large-scale Indian uprisings against colonial oppression, such as the Powhatan-English Wars of 1622 and 1644, the Pueblo Revolt of 1680, the Tuscarora War of 1711, and the Yamasee War of 1715–16.[55] Ambassadors would have to meet with the Mohicans and Mohawks along the Hudson River and the "northern Indians" near the French to negotiate safe havens for noncombatants. Warriors needed guns, powder, and shot, so the people would have to stockpile what they could and open up trading lines through the Mohicans to Dutch merchants in Albany (now living under English rule) and through the Sokokis to the French on the St. Lawrence. The women would need to raise extra crops for the campaign and the men to construct new, hidden, underground pits in which to store the harvest. No one—*no one*—could be allowed to reveal these plans to the English without suffering the wrath of the group. Throughout these discussions, everyone would have realized that such plotting required mutual trust of the sort that the sachems had rarely displayed toward one other.

This also would have been a time for the sachems to reflect on the state of their personal careers. A young sachem like Philip, who had already lost most of his territory and many of his tribute payers to the English, increasingly had little to lose and a great deal to gain by leading a resistance movement. Older sachems, like Ninigret and Uncas, had reason to be more cautious. The problems of land loss and the mission were still relatively minor for them compared to the Wampanoags. The English were more of a source of power for Uncas than a threat to him. Equally to the point, Ninigret and Uncas had reached an age at which sachems promoted peace rather than clamored for war, at which they focused on maintaining their authority rather than expanding it. Personal rivalries also would have crossed their minds. Could Ninigret really trust Uncas in an emergency, and vice versa? And what if the people somehow managed to roll the English back to the outskirts of Boston, or even into the sea? What then? Philip would be ascendant, and his rise could only come at their expense and that of their heirs. The structure of Indian politics, which pitted older sachem incumbents against young aspirants, militated against the kind of unity preached by Philip.

The older sachems also had a broader view of how the balance of power had shifted over the years. By 1670, southern New England's fifty thousand or so colonists outnumbered its estimated thirty thousand Indians by a significant factor.[56] The English had vast military advantages over Indians particularly when it came to fighting along the coast, where both the English and Indian populations were concentrated. English ships could ferry troops and supplies almost anywhere along New England's numerous bays, inlets, and river mouths. These shoreline areas also had the most developed pathways, which gave the English another advantage because of their draft animals and wagons. Indians held the upper hand in the forested interior. There English supply lines would become stretched and Indian warriors would have camouflage for ambush and retreat. Yet moving the fight inland required them to evacuate their coastal homes along with their planting fields, fishing places, and shellfish beds. Even under the best of circumstances, therefore, the people were going to suffer.

Rumors filled the vacuum caused by the secrecy of these meetings, sending the English into a panic. Authorities in Connecticut, Rhode Island, Plymouth, and New York wrote furiously to each other to share their suspicions and solicit other news. Sources from Long Island said that the Indians' ambition was to "kill all the English" and, in the meantime, "lay in the woods, and take opportunity to do mischief when the English were about."[57] Some Connecticut officials feared "it's not far from as great a hazard as ever New England yet saw."[58]

The English got their information and misinformation from Indians, especially those disaffected with Ninigret, which probably had something to do with the placement of him at the center of the conspiracy. For instance, one source was Harmon Garrett, sachem of the Pawcatuck Pequot community. Garrett had once lived near Weekapaug Brook within Niantic country, but he clashed with Ninigret over his lukewarm support of the campaign against Uncas and attempts to free himself from tributary status. Another reason for Garrett to spread the rumor would have been to call attention to his people's anger over English encroachment on Pequot land at Causattuck, near the growing town of Stonington, Connecticut. Back in 1666, Connecticut had forced the Pawcatuck

Pequots off of this track, and yet that very same year the commissioners had awarded Cassacinamon's Pequots two thousand acres at Mashantucket, ten miles inland from Noank.[59] Three years later, the Pawcatucks' anger continued to simmer. Some of the first news of the dance at Nameag had come from a Pequot woman who told a twelve-year-old English boy that the Pequots "hated [the English] for living on Causattuck Land" and that "the Indians would run down out of the woods and would first knock them [the English] of the head with their tomahawks."[60] Garrett's warnings in 1669 might have been his way of protesting this encroachment without having to issue a threat himself. Ninigret became his scapegoat.

However, clearly there was far more behind the 1669 affair than rumor mongering spawned by the petty rivalries of local sachems. The great Indian leaders of the coast were talking to each other, exchanging presents, dancing together, and contriving plans that they did not want to share with the English. The United Colonies' divide and conquer strategy against Indians, which had worked so effectively for years, was clearly in peril if the likes of Ninigret and Uncas were making common cause. The issue was how to force the sachems to come clean without forcing them to arms.

Ninigret was not going to talk to the commissioners of the United Colonies, for he had lost whatever fear he once had of them. Lion Gardiner, writing in 1660, complained that the Indians "say to our faces that our commissioners meeting once a year, and speak a great deal, or write a letter, and there's all, for they dare not fight."[61] Additionally, what little trust Ninigret had once placed in the commissioners was now gone too, sacrificed on their altar of land speculation. Connecticut summoned Ninigret to Hartford for questioning, but he refused to comply, responding that the magistrates could come to him if they wanted to talk. Wait Winthrop and James Avery led a party of thirteen to Niantic country in July 1669 to do just that, but Ninigret appears to have given them no satisfaction.[62] The United Colonies, founded to coordinate the Indian policies of its members, seemed incapable of managing a crisis of this magnitude.

Tiny Rhode Island was better positioned than the United Colonies to handle negotiations with Ninigret. Over the years, Rhode Island had built a constructive relationship with the Narragansetts out of recognition that the colony's independence was hinged to the tribe's ability to

fend off Massachusetts and Connecticut. Twice Rhode Island had de-
fended Narragansett land and jurisdiction against the United Colonies by enlisting the protection of the crown. Never had Rhode Islanders dared to take up arms against the Narragansetts. Though the colony
had its share of land speculators, including members of the Atherton
Company, it also possessed Roger Williams and Samuel Gorton, two of
the most trustworthy English friends the Narragansetts had. Rhode Island took the lead in investigating the 1669 war scare on the strength of
this history, and out of fear that the United Colonies might use the crisis
to renew its encroachment on the dissenting colony. A group of Rhode
Island men had tried unsuccessfully to prevent the Connecticut party
under Winthrop and Avery from reaching Ninigret precisely with this
threat in mind. To take control of the investigation, Rhode Island sent
out some "discreet persons," as opposed to an armed party, to meet with
Ninigret about the rumors.[63] He did little to allay their fears, responding
enigmatically "with a laugh" to the question of why he had met with
Philip's men.[64] Judging this to be "further cause for suspicion," the
Rhode Island Council issued Ninigret a summons to appear at a hearing
in Newport.[65] The fact that he accepted this call after rebuffing the
United Colonies testifies to the strength of the Rhode Island–Narragansett
relationship.

Anyone who had followed Ninigret's career knew that he attended
English meetings only if it served his purposes. He understood that
Rhode Island wanted him to affirm the peace as much as explain the
1669 rumors. True enough, the colony treated Ninigret like an honored
guest rather than a prisoner, making arrangements to feed and lodge
the sachem and two of his men at Thomas Waterman's inn, with the
colony picking up all of the expenses.[66] There were no signs that Rhode
Island considered Ninigret to be an enemy.

Still, the magistrates had questions they wanted Ninigret to answer.
In particular, they wanted Ninigret to explain what he was doing with
the Indians of Long Island and the Wampanoags, and to answer a charge
that he was harboring two runaway Indian servants from Block Island.[67]
Ninigret had responses for everything. He said his diplomacy with the
Long Island Indians had to do with peace, not war, that they had been
negotiating an end to their historic differences. The gifts they had exchanged sealed a friendship rather than a joint commitment to fight
against the English. Ninigret said that he had told the Montauketts that

"he did forgive them all their offenses, and gave them their lives also, and would look upon them as his friends and subjects."[68] As to the reports of Philip's men attending Ninigret's great dance, Ninigret insisted there was no harm intended or done. He had hosted only seven Wampanoags, some to view the dance, and others to teach the Niantics how to "make bark houses." Finally, on the issue of the runaway servants, Ninigret refused to budge. The servants, just children, had been wrongfully forced into bondage. They were now under his protection.

Like a courtroom veteran, Ninigret closed the meeting by turning the question from his loyalty to the reliability of the colonists' informants. He declared himself to be a loyal subject of King Charles II, but wondered who was the original source of the charges against him.[69] The court either could not or would not say, to which Ninigret responded "that since you cannot inform me who raised this report, I will tell you who it was."[70] Ninigret blamed a Long Island Indian named Nonaconapoonog for the panic, accusing him of manufacturing the story about the conspiracy to scuttle peace between the Narragansetts and Montauketts. All of the Indians knew this to be true, and so "Nonaconapoonog is forsaken of [by] all his kindred, and his in a very sad condition, laying his hand over his face" in shame. As ever, Ninigret concluded, the English had overreacted to Indian trickery. He gave a convincing performance. Rhode Island let the matter drop and then wrote to authorities in the neighboring colonies that it "saw no just ground of jealousy as to [Ninigret's] intentions." It failed to mention that Ninigret had said nothing about his discussions with Uncas, Cassacinamon, and the northern Indians. For now, New England's great hazard was over.

Tocketántam? What do you think?
Interpreting 1669

Though it is possible that everything Ninigret said was true—that his negotiations with other Indians had been nothing more than peaceful diplomacy—there is another potential explanation for why the crisis of 1669 gradually petered out. John Mason was the only Englishman to hit on the reason. He had sent a communiqué to the Mohawks in the spring of 1669 imploring them not to give the coastal Indians any support, and their response shored up his flagging confidence. Mason reported, "They have, as they say, forborn to meddle with these [matters], they say, for fear displeasing the English."[71] The Mohawks explained that their main concern was defending themselves against the French, who in 1666 had launched an invasion of Mohawk country that resulted in the destruction of massive amounts of property, if few lives.[72] The Mohawks also had to defend themselves on the eastern front, for in 1669 the Pocumtucks and Sokokis had recruited Indians from the Massachusetts praying towns to join them in an assault on the fortified Mohawk village of Ganda-ouagué, an attack that led to the deaths of some fifty Algonquians and forty Mohawks.[73] With them died any possibility of a grand alliance, at least in the short term. The loss of the Dutch authority meant that the Mohawks' defense of their homeland against these French and Indian enemies depended on the supply of guns, powder, and shot from English jurisdiction. Their friendship with the Narragansetts just was not worth the loss of this trade. The Mohawks, Mason wrote with a sigh of relief, "say they will prove our real friends."

There could be no coastal Indian uprising against the English without Mohawk support, never mind in the face of Mohawk opposition, as King Philip's War would prove in spades. No one understood this fact more than Ninigret, who had always seen the Mohawks as his counterweight to colonial strength. Thus, while on the surface it might appear that English investigations of the 1669 plot brought an end to the sachems' proceedings, the more likely factor was the sachems' inability to draw in the Mohawks. It could not have been an easy decision for Ninigret to give up the cause, for his seasoned judgment was matched by his unyielding determination to defend Narragansett sovereignty against English encroachment. Yet he could plainly see that this was a pointless fight. Philip did not agree, which meant that from this point on, these would-be allies treated each other as enemies. Their rivalry would have deep implications for the future of Indians and colonists alike in southern New England.

Ninigret's Narragansett War

The great clash pitting a broad coalition of New England Indian peoples against the English and their Indian allies burst forth in 1675–76 after decades of festering tension. Nowadays we refer to this bloodbath as King Philip's War, but some English contemporaries had a different name for it: they called it the Narragansett War.[1] Given Ninigret's track record of leading Narragansett confrontations with the English, and the English image of Ninigret as the ringleader of a number of failed multi-tribal uprisings, it is easy to imagine him being the one to raise the banner of Indian resistance. Yet that is not what happened. Ninigret did not want his people, neither the Niantics nor the Narragansetts, involved in this war. He wanted King Philip's War to remain just that, a fight between Philip's Wampanoags and the English. Many Narragansetts, particularly young men among the eastern sachemships on Narragansett Bay, disagreed with this policy. Residing as they did on the frontline of colonial expansion, they clamored to join the Wampanoags in arms, thus forcing their sachems into the choice of leading them in battle or stepping aside. Ninigret carved out an equally perilous third option. After failing to persuade the Narragansetts to stay out of the fray, he guided his Niantics out of the Narragansetts and into an untested alliance with the English. Certainly Ninigret pursued this course with the best interests of himself, his heirs, and the Niantics in mind. He probably considered the Narragansetts too, anticipating they would benefit from having a friend within the English fold and place of refuge if the English won the war. It is also likely that Ninigret's Narragansett contemporaries would have found this subtle reasoning insulting given their dire need for allies. In this sense, the Narragansett War involved more than just a contest between the Narragansetts and English; it involved the Narragansetts struggling among themselves. Ninigret's role in this crisis would become his most significant legacy. It would also be his last act.

Wepe kukkemineantin, You are the murtherer.
Jurisdictional Disputes over Murder and the Coming of King Philip's War

The internal Narragansett war had been developing for years as Philip and the eastern Narragansetts consolidated their alliance against the English while Ninigret distanced himself from their plans. In the spring and summer of 1671, just two years after the war scare of 1669, another alarm sounded that Philip was plotting a general Indian strike against the colonies. In the spring of that year, English sources reported Philip's men preparing their arms and hosting Indians from abroad, including Narragansetts. Ninigret's sister, Quaiapen, was said to be among the most active players, having settled her earlier differences with Philip and accepted wampum from him to promote his cause. At the same time, Narragansetts began making "warlike preparations" toward colonists who remained in the Pettaquamscutt Purchase. One source had Narragansetts threatening colonists "to be gone else they would slay them as they do cattle," adding that they would "kill the men first & then flay the women alive."[2] Plymouth responded by demanding Philip to turn over his guns, but he surrendered only a token amount and then returned to his military preparations. Throughout the spring and summer he held additional dances with the Narragansetts and continued to stockpile arms. If the English harbored any doubts about Philip's intentions, they were erased when he greeted an embassy from Plymouth to Pokanoket by knocking the hat from the head of councilman, James Brown. Apparently, Philip wanted these dignitaries to acknowledge that he was entitled to their respect, including the doffing of hats. Instead, Plymouth convened a war council and ordered its towns to ready their defenses. It took the joint pressure of Massachusetts, Connecticut, and Plymouth to finally bring Philip to conference in September of 1671, producing a treaty in which he submitted himself to Plymouth and not just the crown and agreed to pay a one-hundred-pound fine, among other concessions. Philip had no intention of living up to these pledges. Signing the treaty was a delaying tactic to allow him to strengthen his coalition with the Narragansetts and other neighboring Indians.[3]

Ninigret was not among them. He had emerged from the frenetic diplomacy of 1669 as an opponent of Philip's plans, which appears to have made the two sachems enemies. During the opening stages of King Philip's War in the summer of 1675, Ninigret reported that Philip's Wampanoags had killed eleven of his men, probably in the context of discussions over whether the Niantics would join other Narragansetts in supporting the cause.[4] Once hostilities began, Ninigret claimed that Philip had neglected to send him an ambassador to plead for help, whereas he did send a representative to Uncas.[5] Ninigret's word against Uncas was as untrustworthy as Uncas's was against him, but his point about being at odds with Philip rings true. No one ever mentioned Ninigret attending one of Philip's dances. After 1669, no one reported Wampanoags diplomats in Niantic country. Ninigret had made his position clear: he was not a supporter of Philip's campaign.

Yet Ninigret's policy was not set in stone, for it also required the English to ease their historic pressure on him and his people. Consider, for instance, how various English responses to three separate murder cases involving Indians affected the wartime allegiances of sachems, including Ninigret. The first case is the most widely known of the group. Sometime in the winter of 1674–75, John Sassamon, the English-educated, Christian Wampanoag who had served as Philip's scribe in the 1660s, warned Plymouth's governor that Philip was organizing the region's Indians against the English. Sassamon also predicted that Philip would take his life for revealing the plot. Just as he foretold, Sassamon went missing shortly after this meeting. Eventually Sassamon's body was found interred under the ice of Assawompsett Pond in modern-day Middleboro, Massachusetts, and everyone suspected foul play. Indian testimony, both eyewitness and hearsay, plus an autopsy, pointed to Sassamon's death as murder, not drowning, and to three of Philip's men as the perpetrators. Plymouth's next move sent the region spiraling into war. In June 1675, English authorities arrested, tried, and then executed three Wampanoag men for the murder of Sassamon, a Wampanoag in Wampanoag country, whereupon Philip's enraged people urged the sachem to lead them into war earlier than he probably would have liked.[6] As in the events leading to the Pequot War, the breaking point for Indians in their relations with colonists was the colonists' assumption of the right to pass capital sentences on Indians according to colonial jurisprudence. Plymouth's strong-armed prosecution of the Sassamon murder all but required Philip to strike, but only Philip and his home community of Pokanoket; his would-be allies, including Wampanoags in communities outside Pokanoket, were still uncommitted to war against the English. Given the slow-churning of Indian politics, King Philip's War might never have happened if Plymouth had left the matter alone.[7]

Another, more obscure, murder case also shaped King Philip's War. In April 1671, the English arrested, tried, and executed a Nipmuck Indian named Ascooke (or Nehehmiah) on the charge of having shot down and robbed an Englishman, Zachary Smith, outside the town of Dedham, Massachusetts. Not only did English authorities hang Ascooke for the crime, they severed the head from his dead body and left it on the gallows to rot in public. This execution was a devastating blow to Ascooke's father, a Nipmuck sachem named Matoonas. In the months leading up the murder, Matoonas had aligned his community Pakachoog (near modern day Worcester, Massachusetts) with the English by agreeing to host a mission and adopting the title of Christian constable, with the responsibility of upholding biblical law. Matoonas no longer wanted to work with the English after the execution of his son; he wanted revenge on them. Not coincidentally, the Nipmucks would become the Wampanoags' first allies in King Philip's War, with Matoonas as one of their foremost war leaders. By executing his son, the English had made an enemy of their former friend Matoonas.[8]

Ninigret was also involved in a murder case on the eve of King Philip's War, but his experience tempered his relations with the English. In the winter of 1671–72, Robin Cassacinamon's Pequots were appalled to discover that someone had murdered their powwow's daughter. Never one to act rashly, Cassacinamon built on the spirit of dialogue that had characterized the Indian diplomacy of 1669 to call for a great meeting at Quackatauge, near the town of Stonington, to discuss the case. Thomas Stanton and Thomas Minor arrived on the scene to find "some hundred of Indians of which [were] some of the chief of Ninigret's councilors, and Owaneco, Uncas's son, with other Narragansetts, Mohegans, and Pequot chief men of all sorts."[9] The consensus was that the murderer was Moweam, a man from "Ninigret's country but [who] hath lived much amongst the Pequots," which probably indicates that he was a

Pawcatuck.[10] Connecticut arrested and jailed Moweam in preparation for trial, but that was no long-term solution.[11] Moweam escaped and fled not to Pawcatuck but to Ninigret. In May 1672, Hartford threatened Ninigret to return Moweam to English custody or else it would be "ill taken," only to have Moweam disappear again.[12] Searches for him proved futile, but Cassacinamon charged that Ninigret knew where he was hiding. Richard Smith Jr., a longtime resident in Narragansett country, agreed, adding that Ninigret was "of an obstinate temper" and that he might prove more compliant "if he were humbled a little."[13] Unwilling to provoke a confrontation, Connecticut allowed the issue to pass. While it is unlikely that the colony would have showed such restraint if the murder victim had been an English girl instead of Pequot one or a praying Indian instead of a so-called pagan, the legacy of this case was that it contributed to keeping Ninigret out of Philip's alliance at a critical juncture. If the English had pressed this issue too far, forcing Ninigret to choose between handing over one of his people and taking up arms against colonial authorities, he might very well have picked the latter.

Wunnetu nta. My heart is true.
Tests of Loyalty in the Early Stages of King Philip's War

King Philip's War expanded so quickly in the summer and fall of 1675 that it seemed as if the entire region was descending into a general Indian-English war. It nearly became just that, mostly because of English violations of Indian neutrality. In late June 1675, just a few weeks after the executions of Sassamon's supposed killers, the Pokanoket Wampanoags attacked the nearby English towns of Swansea, Rehoboth, and Taunton. Pursued by English forces, Philip's people fled into the peninsular territory of the neighboring Saconnet Wampanoags under the sunksquaw (or female sachem) Awashunks, and the Pocasset Wampanoags under the sunksquaw Weetamoo. Plymouth could have halted its chase there and entered negotiations. Instead, its troops forced their way into Saconnet and Pocasset territory and drove the Wampanoags of those places into Philip's ranks. By mid July, a party of Nipmucks had attacked the Massachusetts town of Mendon, followed quickly by the Wampanoags fleeing northward to join the Nipmucks in assaults on the small, exposed towns of Brookfield and Lancaster. The English, fearing that they were witnessing the emergence of a pan-Indian uprising, scrambled to contain the violence, only to unleash it by treating Indian allies and noncombatants like enemies. Indians had to think twice about trusting the English after Plymouth enslaved more than two hundred Wampanoags noncombatants who had turned themselves in to colonial authorities. Thus, in the fall of 1675, when colonists in the upper Connecticut River Valley demanded the local "River Indians" or "Friend Indians" to hand over their guns, even though they had previously joined the English in expeditions against the Nipmucks, those Indians instead resolved to join the resistance. On October 5, 1675, the night before the colonists' deadline for the surrender of weapons, the River Indians put Springfield to the torch. To English authorities, this attack proved that the River Indians had supported Philip all along, which might have been true, but the weight of evidence suggests that this was a self-fulfilling prophesy. The colonists' strong-armed tactics, fueled by dread of "savages" and the Indians' recent multitribal diplomacy, was what turned English nightmares into reality.[14]

The English feared no group of Indians in southern New England more than the Narragansetts, for good reason, and thus focused on securing their neutrality.[15] Leading Narragansetts had participated in several of Philip's dances in recent years, and in 1671 Narragansett warriors had risen up simultaneously with Philip's men to intimidate colonists in the Pettaquamscutt Purchase. Shortly after hostilities began in the summer of 1675, Quaiapen had reportedly accepted three English heads sent to her from Philip, which in Indian diplomacy represented sympathy and even support for the cause.[16] Pessacus was said to have rejected those trophies, but it is conspicuous that on the eve of the war he changed his name to Canonicus, after his deceased uncle, one of the greatest sachems in Narragansett history. The name change signaled that he saw this war as a defining moment for him and his people. So did Massachusetts, which in late June 1675 wisely handed negotiations with the Narragansetts over to Roger Williams, by then in his early seventies, out of respect for his longstanding friendship with those people and the fragility of the situation.

Things did not go smoothly but, from Williams's perspective, they did go well. The Narragansett sachems, especially Quaiapen, refused to meet at Smith's trading house near Warwick, probably out of fear of being ambushed by the English. So instead the meeting took place ten miles west of Smith's, somewhere in the vicinity of modern day Worden Pond, securely in Narragansett territory. Ninigret was in attendance and, under his influence, no doubt, the Narragansetts unequivocally "professed to hold no agreement with Philip in this his rising against the English."[17] Yet the English wanted more, a pledge that the Narragansetts would hand over any Wampanoags who fled to them for refuge. Reluctantly, the Narragansetts agreed. Little did anyone know that this would become the key issue in the Narragansetts' entry into the war.

The Narragansetts had their own agenda to pursue at this council which, as usual, pivoted on redirecting colonial scrutiny away from them and toward Uncas. The sachems asked, though they probably already understood, why Massachusetts and Rhode Island "left not Philip and Plymouth to fight it out." Williams's answer, "that all the colonies were subject to one King Charles," conveniently overlooked that the Wampanoags were royal subjects too and, for that matter, so were the Narragansetts, which might have been the subtext of the sachems' question. The sachems also tried to convince Williams that Uncas, unlike them, was playing a double game, secretly providing Philip with twenty warriors while at the same time volunteering men to support the English. Additionally, Uncas's son Owaneco (or Tatuphosuwit) had recently murdered one of the Narragansetts' leading men, and they wanted justice done on him, the implicit criticism being that the lives of their people were just as valuable as that of the Christian, John Sassamon. In short, the Narragansetts were trying to turn this crisis in English-Indian affairs into an opportunity to commit revenge on Uncas. They were also subtly warning the English that they refused to be treated as unworthy subordinates.[18] Williams did not relay the message, even if he grasped it.

This conference gave a false impression of Narragansett unity when in fact there was none. Rather, there was a range of Narragansett opinion on the war and no one sachem had the power to contain it, not even Ninigret. At one end of the spectrum were Quaiapen and the majority of Narragansett young men, who seemed eager to join the Wampanoags and Nipmucks in arms. This group also included Narragansetts married or otherwise related to Wampanoags. They were unwilling to sacrifice their kin to the English regardless of the consequences. At the other end of the spectrum was Ninigret, who considered this campaign to be futile and saw no point in allowing a fiery Wampanoag sachem to determine the fate of his people. Caught in the middle was Canonicus (or Pessacus), who preferred peace while heading a community clamoring for war. Later that fall he would tell messengers from Boston and Newport that he was "sorrowed for the English" but could not help them. "He could not rule the youth & common people," he complained, "nor persuade others, chief amongst them, except his brother Miantonomi's son Nananautunu [Canonchet]." All he could do was advise "the English at Narragansett to stand upon their guard, to keep strict watch, and, if they could, to fortify one or more houses strongly, which if they could not do, then to fly."[19] The warriors, it seemed to Canonicus, had taken the lead over their sachems.

Indeed they had, at least among the eastern Narragansetts. No sooner had the sachems finished their meeting with Williams than one hundred Narragansetts in arms marched toward the town of Warwick, which had long been a sore point in Narragansett-English affairs.[20] They did no harm, but obviously intended to send a threat, like the martial displays that Philip's Wampanoags had made against Swansea back in June, just days before they attacked that village. This event, combined with intelligence that "canoes passed to and again (day and night) between Philip and the Narragansetts," and that "the Narragansett Indians have committed many robberies on English houses," was enough to make Williams and his English neighbors "suspect that all the fine words from the Indian sachems to us were but words of policy, falsehood & treachery."[21] The English also began to doubt Ninigret. In early July, Massachusetts sent a force under Benjamin Batten to order Ninigret to surrender his guns or else face attack. There is no record of what happened next, but it appears that no disarmament took place. It is difficult to imagine Ninigret, given his decades of experience at rebuffing such demands, caving in to the twenty-five-year-old Batten, particularly in light that disarming his people would render them vulnerable to Uncas.[22] At the same time, Ninigret must have realized that keeping his people out of this war was going to be as difficult as any challenge he had ever faced.

Whereas Uncas distanced himself from Philip by making dramatic gestures of allegiance to the English—such as raising fifty warriors for the English cause, handing over two of his sons as hostages, and surrendering a cache of arms—Ninigret had to be more cautious. After all, many of his Niantics were sympathetic to Philip and reluctant to separate themselves from the other Narragansetts.[23] He held at least three meetings with English representatives in the early days of the war, all of them in Narragansett territory, in which he repeatedly emphasized his loyalty to King Charles II and the royal commissioners and his hostility toward Philip. In one of these meetings, he wore the coat from King Charles II to accentuate that he "had engaged his heart to the English."[24] In another, he told Connecticut's Tobias Saunders that "he cannot forget the kindness that he received from King Charles, and the commissioners when they were in these parts . . . he saith it again & again."[25] As for his relationship with Philip, Ninigret pointed to recent bloodshed between their men, including a shadowy incident in which Philip's Wampanoags killed some Niantics "driven amongst them in a boat by storm from Block Island."[26] For these reasons and certainly others, Ninigret reasserted his willingness to turn over any Wampanoags on whom he could lay his hands. It is testimony to the quality of Ninigret's performance that his longtime English rivals believed him.

Yet as the war spread the pressure mounted on Ninigret to make concessions beyond fine speeches. Whereas the Narragansett sachems had initially rejected English demands for hostages, a week later, on July 15, they agreed to surrender four of their people as bonds.[27] Then Narragansett sachems began to deliver to the English the heads of Wampanoag warriors. In late July, Ninigret sent his first head to John Winthrop Jr.'s son, Fitz-John, with the hope that "the English will take notice of his fidelity." In exchange, he received some English coats, to "his great satisfaction." Ninigret presented Richard Smith Jr. with another two heads in September. Even Canonicus rendered a remarkable fourteen Wampanoag heads over the course of July and August in the dwindling hope that he could keep his people out of this war.[28] He had another motivation too. With every conveyance the Narragansetts asked for the release of their hostages, "they having they say proved themselves loyal by bringing in of heads."[29]

Sacrificing Wampanoag warriors was one thing for the Narragansetts, but turning over Wampanoag noncombatants seeking refuge, some of them kin, was another matter entirely. Contrary to their treaty with the English, in early August the eastern Narragansetts took in the sunksquaw Weetamoo and approximately one hundred of her people, either closely preceded or closely followed by Weetamoo's marriage to the Narragansett sachem Quinnapen, the nephew of Canonicus and son of the deceased Cojonoquant.[30] Given Weetamoo's status as the widow of Philip's late brother, Wamsutta, or Alexander, and as a powerful Wampanoag leader in her own right, this marriage signaled the Narragansetts' commitment to defend her people. No one was under any illusion that the English would tolerate this impasse for long.

With the war having spread from Wampanoag country to Nipmuck country and then the upper Connecticut River Valley, and with the Narragansetts standing at the brink, Ninigret hatched a ambitious proposal to end the bloody cycle. He presented his idea to Thomas Stanton, the veteran interpreter and go-between.[31] These men knew each other well and, insofar as their negotiations had brought New England to the edge of war and back again several times in the past, there was a certain amount of respect between them. Judging from the detail with which Stanton recalled this meeting, he gave Ninigret his rapt attention, and Ninigret gave him something worthy of it. Ninigret knew that the future of this war hinged on two questions: the fate of the Wampanoags among the Narragansetts, and, in the long run, the role of Indian powers on the margins of New England, like the Mohawks and Sokokis. To break the stalemate between the Narragansetts and the English, Ninigret proposed handing over nine Wampanoags in his possession, whereupon the English would return them to his governance with the charge to "use them kindly." Ninigret believed this theater would convince the Narragansetts and Wampanoags alike that the English were merciful, whereupon the Wampanoags would begin surrendering. As further encouragement for the Wampanoags to lay down their arms, Ninigret advised circulating a message reminding Indians that the English had restored the Pequots under Robin Cassacinamon to a portion of their ancestral country. Once the Wampanoags were in custody, the English could "carry them where they will and dispose of them." By this, Ninigret probably envisioned something like the settlement of the Pequot War, in which the Narragansetts obtained a portion of the war captives. After all, the Wampanoags were not his concern, the Narragansetts were.

Ninigret's strategy to prevent other Indian powers from joining Philip was equally bold. He volunteered to undertake a wide-ranging diplomatic mission despite his advanced years alongside Fitz-John Winthrop "or some other gentleman of quality." He would visit the Sokokis of the upper Connecticut River Valley, the Esopus, Wappingers, and Mohicans of the Hudson River Valley, and the Mohawks of the Iroquois League, to counsel them to reject any appeals for aid from the warring Indians. Ninigret knew that the warring Indians would ultimately turn to Albany and New France for guns, powder, and shot, using local Indians as middlemen in the trade. He also knew that they would petition distant Indian powers to open their countries for refuge and retreat. In the best of circumstances, the Indians in arms hoped to recruit foreign warriors to join their campaign. Ninigret believed his reputation and wampum could head off such support. "He can and will," Stanton wrote, "put out this fire that Philip has kindled." Given the Indians' customary use of such metaphors, these were likely Ninigret's own words.

Stanton was taken by this plan and believed that it deserved urgent consideration and action. Any delay, he and Ninigret agreed, would only allow "the fire [to] break out farther and farther [and] it will be harder to quench than now it is." Yet English authorities paid no heed to Ninigret's proposal, even though Stanton relayed it to John Winthrop Jr. and Fitz-John Winthrop in Connecticut, and to Richard Smith Jr. in Rhode Island. Perhaps colonial leaders were too distracted by the endless details and drama of their multifront war. Perhaps they found it laughable to put their confidence in a figure like Ninigret with a history of double-crossing them. Perhaps they actually relished the idea of finally attacking the Narragansetts in order to reduce them to slavery and seize their land. Whatever the case—and perhaps it was all this and more—Ninigret's strategy to end the war amounted to nothing more than a tantalizing conversation between him and Stanton.

Except for this: simply by designing this proposal and offering to set it motion, Ninigret distanced his people from the Narragansetts' impending clash with the English and further convinced powerful colonists that he could be trusted. Smith was surprised to find that "Ninigret doth show himself faithful," while Daniel Gookin, no friend of Ninigret given the sachem's opposition to missionary work, even had to admit, "there is good reason he should be distinguished from the rest of the Narragansetts."[32] Massachusetts and Connecticut wrote the sachem to assure him that "we take knowledge of his friendship and tender him ours."[33] Hartford went so far as to release one of two hostages that Ninigret had sent as a bond for his faithfulness, the other hostage having already escaped.[34] To be sure, the colonies made these gestures out of sheer political calculation. Connecticut, for instance, must have worried that if Ninigret entered the war the colony might suffer the loss of Stonington and New London and the services of the Mohegans and Pequots, who would have to defend their home fronts. Yet historically the colonies had shown their fear of Ninigret by trying to subordinate him, always unsuccessfully. Now they were putting stock in his professions of friendship because he had convinced them that this was a good gamble.

Stanton was the essential English player in this high-stakes diplomacy with Ninigret. His house in Stonington, perhaps a half day's journey west from Niantic country, became Ninigret's embassy to the rest of the colonial world when it was just too dangerous for the sachem to venture any farther abroad. In the early days of the war, Ninigret refused to have English officials meet with him at his headquarters out of concern that "his women and children should be affrighted and damage be done in his corn fields," presumably from the colonists' horses. Instead, he proposed meeting at the edge of Stanton's farm, where Niantic civilians would be at a safe distance and English soldiers were less likely to be trigger happy.[35] Thereafter, whenever Ninigret or colonial officials had a message to communicate to each other, they ran it through Stanton. Ninigret's lead advisor, Cornman, sometimes even lodged at Stanton's house during these councils. Stanton's place also became the site for the exchange of diplomatic gifts. It was where Ninigret delivered Wampanoags his people had captured. In return, Stanton gave Ninigret trade coats, cloth, kettles, pots, "a pair of women's stockings for his wife," and sometimes even powder and shot, occasionally at his own expense.[36] Such gestures developed into a relationship of genuine goodwill. For instance, in September 1675, Stanton handed one of his own sons over to Ninigret to serve as a hostage so the sachem would send his representatives, Cornman and Harry, to a meeting between the Narragansetts and the commissioners of the United Colonies held at Wickford.[37] Ninigret reciprocated by giving Stanton a large gift of wampum, believing, as Stanton put it, that this would "wipe of[f] what . . . prejudice, he thought might be in my breast."[38] The sachem also ended a longstanding dispute when he compensated Stanton for having harbored two of Stanton's runaway Indian servants and for Niantic men having killed a number of Stanton's horses.[39] The irony, of course, was that before King Philip's War, Ninigret and Stanton had dealt with each other mostly as adversaries. Now these men were entrusting each other with the lives of their kindred and the security of their prized possessions. That kind of faith, so rare in Indian-English relations during this perilous time, translated into peace between their peoples.

Ninigret might have gone further still to ingratiate himself to the English and distance himself from the Narragansetts in arms. In 1685, nearly a decade after King Philip's War, John Stanton, the son of Thomas, wrote to Fitz-John Winthrop with some supposed testimony from Wonkow, who he identified as Ninigret's former "Viceroy," about Ninigret's activities during the war. According to Stanton, Wonkow testified that shortly after hostilities began, Ninigret had instructed him and Cornman to approach Fitz-John with an offer to give John Winthrop Jr., Fitz-John's father, guardianship over Ninigret's children, "they to live where he should appoint them, in manner and form as he should judge meet." Moreover, Ninigret was said to have granted John Winthrop Jr. "his right of inheritance," meaning land, and a confirmatory gift of a brass gun, a Spanish gun, and a girdle of wampum. Ninigret trusted Winthrop Jr., Wonkow recalled, "in consideration of his former kindness and lenity toward him, and in special in not taking advantage of him for the wrongs and injuries done unto him at Fisher's Island in the time of their war with the Long Islanders," back in 1654.[40] Yet the late timing of this account's appearance calls its veracity into question. By the 1680s, Fitz-John Winthrop was a shareholder in the "Narragansett Company," successor to the Atherton Company, which continued the effort to capitalize on the old Atherton grants and bring the Narragansett country into Connecticut's jurisdiction. The company's hope was to gather enough "evidence" to persuade the crown to favor its claims. With Ninigret and John Winthrop Jr. dead there was no one but Wonkow to contest the story. Regardless, neither the Winthrops nor Connecticut ultimately received title to Niantic lands—never mind control over the upbringing of Ninigret's children.[41]

The rapprochement of Ninigret and the English would be sorely tested as the colonies' standoff with the Narragansetts built toward a climax. One of the challenges to their relationship was that for every Thomas Stanton who recognized the difference between Ninigret and the Narragansetts, and between allied Indians and enemy Indians generally, there were numerous other colonists who judged such distinctions to be false and dangerous. If any of the Niantics had doubted this point, the message rang through loud and clear during a visit by Ninigret's deputy, Cornman, to Boston in late September of 1675. Although Cornman, "an old Indian," was there on a peace mission, out of nowhere an English bystander seized him by the neck and threw him to the ground. The man was arrested and fined, with Cornman receiving part of the proceeds, but the attack must have come as a jolt to all Niantics. Clearly their friendship with the English was only as stable as the people's tempers would allow. The Narragansetts were not the only ones with unruly young men.[42]

The most fundamental challenge to Ninigret's accord with the English was the ongoing dispute about the fate of the Wampanoag refugees. The agreement that Cornman negotiated, and which was subsequently signed by Indian representatives of the Narragansett sachems in Boston on October 18, set October 28 as the deadline for the Narragansetts to hand over their Wampanoag guests, but it passed unmet.[43] Canonchet, the rising leader of Narragansett militants and the son of Miantonomi, had reportedly reached the point where he declared, "No, not a Wampanoag, nor the paring of a Wampanoag's nail."[44] Both sides began girding for war, with the Narragansetts readying their arms and building fortifications, and the commissioners, after an acrimonious debate, ordering the colonies to raise a thousand men and supplies for a December campaign. They even asked for Rhode Island's assistance in providing transport and provisions for the troops and use of Wickford as the expedition's advance base. It is telling of how fearful Rhode Island had grown of the Narragansetts that the colony granted these requests. Colonial leaders would have preferred to wait until the spring thaw to send their men out on the march, but time seemed short. Indian sources warned that the Narragansetts were resolved to join the war in the spring, when their men would have the benefit of leaf cover in setting forest ambushes. This intelligence also held that some Narragansetts had already fallen in with Philip's warriors. Though attacking the Narragansetts risked driving them into the hands of the enemy, the commissioners concluded that the tribe had already made that choice.[45] The English strategy was to strike first.

Ninigret kept assurances of his loyalty fresh in English ears as this crisis built to a head. In early November, Stanton returned home after a day abroad to find Ninigret waiting for him. The sachem wanted to cash in nine Wampanoag captives for an assortment of English goods, and, more important, to tell Stanton that he had ordered all of his followers to return home from other Narragansett communities.[46] A month later he had gone a step farther, moving his people inland toward his "old fort" and away from the road running along the north side of Ninigret

Pond (today's Route 1), the better to avoid contact with any fighters crossing Niantic country. He had also reissued the warning to Niantics abroad to return home immediately if they wanted his protection because "when the war is once begun then it will be too late." As for what he would do once the shooting began, Ninigret pledged that he was "resolved to stand upon his defense against the rest of the Narragansett Indians if any [came] to oppose him," which was an unlikely scenario, and that "if the English shall desire him he will be ready to assist them to the utmost of his abilities," which was a far stronger possibility. Ninigret's overall point was this: he was not going to come to the Narragansetts' aid over the fate of the Wampanoags. Those who would not follow him were on their own.

When the fight finally came, English soldiers unleashed their decades of fear and loathing for the Narragansetts in a slaughter comparable only to the massacre at Mystic Fort forty years earlier. The campaign began in mid December with five hundred men from Massachusetts and Plymouth rendezvousing at Wickford and then destroying two Narragansett settlements, including Quaiapen's stronghold, a stone fort atop a steep hill in modern day Exeter, Rhode Island. Then, reinforced by more than 300 militia from Connecticut and 150 Mohegans and Pequots, they shifted to their main target, a stoutly palisaded, bastioned fortress in the so-called Great Swamp in modern-day West Kingston. Unfortunately for the Narragansetts, one of the colonists' captives, a Narragansett they called Peter, offered to lead English forces through the dark bogs and dense forest to the fort in exchange for his life. The frigid weather took a heavy toll on colonial troops, but it also froze the swamp water, thereby allowing them to advance on the fort from several directions instead of from a single, ambush-prone pathway. The Narragansett defenders knew an attack was coming at some point, however they did not expect the English to find their hideaway so quickly, and thus they still had not completed one corner of their palisade, rendering their stronghold vulnerable. When the battle ensued in the early afternoon of December 19, Narragansetts managed to repulse the first English assault on the opening with a volley of lead, but the soldiers proved too numerous to resist. Gradually, inexorably, they forced their way into opening of the palisade and then began torching the enclosed wétus to force the inhabitants out. The result was a massacre of mostly women, children, and the elderly, numbering in the hundreds. English losses amounted to twenty dead and some two hundred wounded. By any measure, it was a resounding English victory and a traumatic Narragansett defeat. Indeed, the Narragansetts were forced to flee their country and join the Wampanoags, Nipmucks, and Connecticut River tribes on the move. King Philip's War had now become theirs.

It must have taken every bit of influence Ninigret could muster to keep his men from rushing to defend the Narragansetts at the Great Swamp Fight. Aside from the basic unfairness of a thousand-man force marching against a civilian community half that size, the Niantics would have seethed that the attackers included Mohegans. Yet Ninigret's pledge of friendship held firm, if only out of fear that battling the colonies was futile. None of the English involved in that bloody affair accused the Niantics of coming to the Narragansetts' defense, and they would have been on the lookout. Nevertheless, there is little question that the Niantics' sympathies lay with their Narragansett kin. Once the slaughter was over, Ninigret's men moved in to bury the Narragansett and English dead with dignity. Narragansetts believed that the souls of their dead would fail to reach the afterlife at Cautantowwit's House if their remains did not receive proper treatment. It is uncertain whether this gesture earned Ninigret some forgiveness from the surviving Narragansetts for abandoning them in their time of need, or whether it just came as cold comfort. Perhaps no incident so crystallizes the dilemma in which Ninigret and the Niantics found themselves.

Cowaúnckamish. My service to you. Netompaûg? Friends? Ninigret's Uneasy Alliance with the English during King Philip's War

The wisdom of Ninigret's policy depended on the fortunes of the war, which remained in question for nearly a year. From the late fall of 1675 until March of 1676, the English proved utterly incompetent at countering the guerrilla tactics of their Indian enemies, unless they happened to have the benefit of Mohegan and Pequot allies. English forces repeatedly wandered into ambushes at bridge crossings, bends in the road, and trails flanked by reeds, forest, or high ground. Hundreds of English militiamen perished in these attacks. Over and over again, Indian warriors surprised sleepy English towns with dawn-light attacks in which they pinned down the defenders in blockhouses while burning everything else. Within the span of just three months, from January to March 1676, such tactics led to the destruction of Medfield, Weymouth, Warwick, Marlborough, Rehoboth, Swansea, Providence, and Groton.[47] By the end of the war, Indian forces had taken the lives of some eight hundred Englishmen and eight thousand head of cattle, destroyed sixteen colonial towns and severely damaged twenty-five others, and pushed the line of Massachusetts settlement back to the ring of towns around Boston.[48] Particularly in the early months of 1676, it seemed possible that the warring Wampanoags, Nipmucks, River Indians, and Narragansetts would be able to claim victory.

Yet during this same period, the Indian resistance experienced major setbacks that crippled its long-term prospects. Foremost among them was the loss of supply lines to guns, powder, and shot. In the first months of fighting, Philip boasted that he was on the verge of securing French material support, but for unknown reasons his plans came to naught.[49] Philip and his allies certainly acquired gunpowder and shot from the Dutch in Albany, whether directly or through Indian middlemen.[50] By the winter of 1676, however, even that supply was no longer available. In February, the Mohawks fell on Philip's men a short distance outside of Albany, forcing them to retreat eastward away from Dutch and Indian traders and into the teeth of English forces. New York governor Edmund Andros had encouraged the Mohawks to drive Philip away, but one source suggests that Philip brought this disaster on himself by murdering two Mohawks and trying unsuccessfully to pin it on the English.[51] Instead of drawing the Mohawks over to his side, he had made them enemies. Worse yet for the warring Indians, in May 1676, English forces surprised one of their camps at Turner's Falls on the Connecticut River, destroying two gunsmith forges, other smithing tools, and large amounts of raw lead, which had given the Indians some self-sufficiency in the maintenance of their arms and manufacture of shot.[52] With their guns in disrepair after months of itinerant living, and gunpowder and shot in short supply, the Indians were losing their capacity to wage war. These developments, combined with the ravages of camp diseases, malnutrition, and psychological stress, dampened the prospects of Indian forces translating their short-term military victories into permanent gains.

The Mohawks' pivotal repulse of Philip confirmed Ninigret's doubts about the Indian resistance movement from its very beginning. Ninigret knew from his long and frustrating pursuit of Uncas that the Mohawks were essential to offsetting the United Colonies and their Indian allies. Without Mohawk neutrality, Indian combatants would lack access to the gun trade at Albany and the ability to retreat to the Hudson or Mohawk rivers. Without active Mohawk support, the possibility of Indians forcing an English surrender was quite remote, given the colonists' superior numbers and material resources. The Mohawks' close alliance with English New York made both prospects unlikely. Ninigret understood these basic facts even before Philip began organizing his anticolonial bloc. If Philip brashly thought he could address the problem of a Mohawk alliance once the war was underway, he was dead wrong. By the spring of 1676, he must have come to appreciate Ninigret's perspective that the Mohawks were one of the keys to the balance of power in southern New England. Ninigret's followers understood that point too, which encouraged them to adhere to his policy of concord with the English.

Ironically, Ninigret's control of his men might also have stemmed from their hope of giving the Narragansetts clandestine support in the form of intelligence, materials, and refuge. The historical record is full of other cases in which Indian communities divided by colonial wars did everything they could to assist their kin on the other side.[53] Some Englishmen suggested that the Niantics were among this group. A number of colonists, including Roger Williams, accused unidentified Indians serving alongside the English of aiming high when firing at other Indians.[54] Another English source charged that the colonists' Indian allies "sometimes obtained gunpowder and gave or sold it to the enemy Indians, or threw it under trees for the enemy to take."[55] It would have been relatively easy for the Niantics to pass on intelligence about English and Mohegan troop movements, or to take in small numbers of Narragansett noncombatants. After all, the decision to move the Niantic settlement away from the road made it difficult for outsiders to monitor Niantic behavior. There is no way to know for certain whether such things occurred, but given the close ties between the Niantics and Narragansetts, it is equally difficult to conclude that they did not.

Ninigret was reluctant to send his men into service alongside colonial troops, not only out of concern about clashing with fellow Narragansetts, but out of the revulsion of sharing the field with Mohegans and Pequots. Uncas and Robin Cassacinamon had recruited dozens of their men to fight alongside the English from the very onset of the war, and by most accounts they performed invaluable service as scouts and trackers.[56] Ninigret could not have cared less. After forty years, he still counted Uncas as his archenemy. Cassacinamon was somewhat more tolerable, but Ninigret never considered him as more than a "little dog" unworthy of sachem status. In January 1676, the Reverend James Noyes, the minister of New London, tried to heal Ninigret's breach with the Pequots as a step toward bringing the Niantics into military service. He encouraged Ninigret to send a present to the Pequot sachems Momaho and Cassacinamon as a "sign of his willingness to forget past wrongs."[57] Not surprisingly, Ninigret was "cool towards the proposal" but he offered to relent on one condition: Noyes and Thomas Stanton had to tell the Pequots that the gift was from the English, not him. Framed this way, Ninigret turned the conciliatory gesture dictated to him by the English into a theatrical display of his authority in which the English were willing to give presents to reconcile others to him. Momaho, unwilling to act a bit part in this power play, refused the gift, and then Cassacinamon did too, citing the insult of Momaho having been offered the gift first. Even amid New England's greatest crisis, local sachem rivalries continued to shape Indian decisions.

As the war dragged on, pressure mounted on the Niantics to prove themselves in battle alongside the English, to which they responded by offering up a token force. In the early spring of 1676, twenty of Ninigret's men joined sixty Pequots and Mohegans on an expedition led by George Denison.[58] In exchange, Connecticut provided the Niantic warriors with powder and shot.[59] The small size of the Niantic band seems to have been designed to minimize their risk and their impact on the outcome of the campaign. Unfortunately for them, on April 11, 1676, somewhere along the Pawtuxet River northwest of Warwick, they met up with a large Narragansett force that had just finished sacking Providence, Rehoboth, and Swansea, inflicting major losses on English troops along the way. The fighting was vicious and the results, from the perspective of the Niantics, were mixed. On the one hand, their side clearly won the fight, with few to no Niantic losses. On the other hand, they were forced to deal with the capture of Canonchet, perhaps the most important leader of the Narragansett resistance. Now the Niantics confronted their greatest horror: the execution of one of their own kin.

By any measure, this was a torturous moment for the Niantics, but they turned it into an honoring of their relationship to the Narragansetts.

The company marched Canonchet to the west bank of the Pawcatuck River, near the English town of Stonington, and sentenced him to death. At this, a number of the Indians (doubtlessly Niantics) "with uplifted hands and other indication of lamentation, showed their regret that such a great man was fallen into the hands of his enemies."[60] Some sources, none of which were eyewitnesses, held that Owaneco, Uncas's son, led the execution. If true, the symbolism would not have been lost on any of the Indians in attendance. Thirty years earlier, Uncas had executed Canonchet's father, Miantonomi, also with the encouragement of the English. Now, if these sources are correct, the scenario was playing out again with the sons. However, another account of these events, by a purported eyewitness, James Noyes, identified Canonchet's executioner as "a relation of his."[61] In this telling, the executioner took Canonchet by the head and said to him " 'farewell cousin I must now kill you' " before shooting him dead. This executioner might very well have been a Niantic. There is just no way to tell.[62]

Another account of Canonchet's execution, by the Boston merchant Nathaniel Saltonstall, has the Niantics burning his remains, which rings true as a sign of respect.[63] After all, Canonchet was their relative. They did not agree with his policies toward the English and the Wampanoags, but that did not make him an enemy. On the contrary, Canonchet must have embodied the desire of so many Niantics, including Ninigret, to lash out against the English. Thus, he deserved their reverence, and burning his body was one way to communicate that sentiment. Ritual destruction by fire was spiritually powerful for the Narragansetts as a step toward renewal.[64] Under normal circumstances, the Narragansetts used fire to destroy a dead sachem's possessions, not his corpse, which would have been buried. Yet this was not a typical case. The Niantics chose cremation instead of leaving Canonchet's remains to rot above ground, with his head likely set atop a pole. They chose, in other words, to release his soul to begin its journey toward Cautantowwit's House. None of the Niantics wanted to be involved in the death of Canonchet, yet because they were there he was able to leave this world with dignity as the Narragansetts understood it.

At least some Narragansetts failed to appreciate the gesture. They were losing the war, stalked as they were by their enemies, disease, and hunger. Under these circumstances, the Narragansetts needed active support, not subtle expressions of affinity. They could understand the

Mohegans and Pequots taking up arms against them, but not the Nian-tics. Two weeks after Canonchet's execution, Canonicus (or Pessacus) sent an envoy to the English asking for peace. He explained that he did not hold colonists responsible for the death of his nephew, Canonchet, but instead blamed "Ninigret and the Indians . . . that he was killed by Ninigret's advice."[65] Put another way, whereas the Narragansetts, or at least Canonicus, were willing to concede defeat to the English, they saw their battle with Ninigret as just beginning.

Yet, symbolically, Canonchet's death was the beginning of the end of the Indian resistance. Warring Indians found themselves in a vice grip, unable to flee westward because of the Mohawks, and unable to strike eastward because of the strength of English troops reinforced by pray-ing Indians and turncoat Wampanoags, who the English wisely offered to spare in exchange for military service. Disease and starvation ran riot through Indian camps. Those with working guns had little powder and shot. As their fortunes dimmed, Wampanoags and Narragansetts began breaking into small bands to search for food and refuge. Canonicus led one body of Narragansetts northeastward to the Piscataqua River of Maine, only to be killed in May or June 1676 by Mohawk raiders ventur-ing hundreds of miles from Iroquoia.[66] Most of Canonicus's starving tribesmen met their ends closer to home, to which they had returned in the hopes of feeding themselves with hidden caches of corn and familiar fishing and gathering places. English and allied Indian forces were wait-ing for them. By July 2, Quaiapen was dead. By the end of the month, so too was Pomham. Matoonas surrendered himself at Boston on July 27 and went straight to the gallows. On August 6, Weetamoo's body was discovered drowned in the Taunton River across from her natal territory. Then, on August 12, a Christian Indian named Alderman shot Philip dead in a swamp in the heart of Wampanoag territory. Residual battles would continue in the upper Connecticut River Valley and Maine, but in southern New England the conflict was essentially over.[67]

Tellingly, Ninigret spent these critical days focused on disputes with Uncas and Robin Cassacinamon, even though his health was probably in steep decline. In May 1676, Ninigret charged Uncas with using the distracted state of the English to steal wampum belonging to his wife and brother-in-law.[68] Later that same month, Ninigret appeared before a Connecticut magistrate to answer a charge of debt filed by Cassacina-mon. The Pequot sachem wanted to recoup the wampum he had paid to

Thomas Stanton at the 1669 dance to prevent Ninigret's arrest. The justice found no grounds for intervening and counseled the sachems to set aside their differences and attend to more important matters, like the war.[69] The English still did not appreciate that the reputations of sachems were at the heart of the region's Indian politics.

This court session might have been the last time that anyone aside from the Niantics saw Ninigret alive, for by the fall of 1676 the great sachem lay dead. A petition by Nowwaquanu, Ninigret's brother-in-law, dated October 7, 1676, made mention of "his sister, the widow: Ninigret's wife."[70] It is the only reference to Ninigret's death on record. His health must have been waning for some time. Earlier, in the spring of 1676, English sources were already referring to the Niantics as "Ninigret's or Ninigret's daughter's men," which suggests that Weunquesh was preparing to assume the mantle of leadership upon the death of her father.[71] Ninigret managed to hold on until the end of the Narragansett War, as if out of desperation to see his people through the crisis. It was testimony to his savvy, thick-skinned decisions during an impossibly difficult time that he had a sachemship left to pass down to his heir.

The Small Matter of Eltwood
Pomeroy's Mare

Ninigret's political career was filled with so many crises that it is easy to overlook a less dramatic issue that dogged him throughout most of his life: compensating colonist Eltwood Pomeroy for the death of his mare. This seemingly minor affair testifies to Ninigret's skill at acquiring and managing power during an era that undermined so many of his sachem peers, and reveals his management of the multipolar politics of seventeenth-century New England. It also shows that our tendency to characterize Indian leaders as either militant resisters of colonialism or colonial lackeys fails to capture the complexity of figures like Ninigret. His dealings with colonial authorities mixed strategic concessions with forceful stands of principle, usually with an eye toward how those positions would play among Native people.

The problem of Indians killing colonial-owned livestock plagued Indian-European relations throughout colonial America. One reason for this issue was that Indians initially did not understand the colonists' notion of a property right in animals, particularly animals that wandered beyond the bounds of English settlements. Indians were even more puzzled when colonists protested their killing of livestock that had ventured into Indian cornfields looking for an easy meal. Their mystification turned to anger when the English insisted that it was the Indians' responsibility to fence out livestock from their communities rather than the colonists' responsibility to fence them in. In this context, sometimes Indians killed livestock out of hostility toward colonists, not just their animals, particularly once they understood how much the English valued these beasts. Such problems led Miantonomi to approach Massachusetts in the early stages of the Pequot War with a proposal that "if any of theirs should kill our cattle, that we would not kill them, but cause them to make satisfaction," which is to say, seek compensation for the damages from the sachems rather than punish their followers.[1] The sachem must have had in mind the colonists' furious response to the murders of John Stone and John Oldham.

No sooner was this compact reached than it had its first case. During the Pequot War, Ninigret's brother or brother-in-law, Poquium, killed a mare belonging to Eltwood Pomeroy of Windsor, Connecticut.[2] Three years later, Pomeroy went to Connecticut to ask the colony to help him seek restitution, a request that worked its way up to the commissioners of the United Colonies.[3] The sources disagree on what happened next. Thomas Stanton's recollection was that Miantonomi promised to compensate Pomeroy forty pounds for the loss of his mare, which was at the high end of the market rate.[4] John Mason's understanding was that at negotiations surrounding Treaty of Hartford of 1638, the commissioners agreed that Ninigret was entitled to take in twenty Pequots but only on the condition that "he should satisfy for a Mare of Edward Pomeroy's killed by his men."[5] Surviving copies of the treaty say nothing of this sort. Whatever informal terms had been reached, neither Miantonomi nor Ninigret paid Pomeroy for his damages and Ninigret kept his Pequots.[6]

Even after the death of Miantonomi the commissioners would not let this matter go, for they saw it as a wedge issue to use against Ninigret. Already, Ninigret had emerged as their foremost Indian enemy through his role in the murder of Oldham, his lackluster support of the English during the Pequot War, and his raids against the colonies' Mohegan and Long Island Indian protectorates. By 1650, English frustration with the Niantic sachem had reached a boiling point. In a prelude to the Humphrey Atherton expedition, the commissioners threatened Ninigret with war if he would not give them satisfaction for his many offenses. Included in their list was a demand for twenty-nine pounds in retribution for Pomeroy's mare or the extradition of Poquium to English authorities.[7]

Ninigret's response to this order, as in so many of his disputes with the English, was to ignore it. Even if Ninigret had wanted to hand over Poquium, seizing him would have required bloodshed and surrendering him would have compromised Ninigret's standing among his own people. Paying compensation would have had a like effect by humiliating the

Niantics and emboldening the English. There was also the flimsy basis on which the English held Ninigret responsible for the mare. It was Miantonomi, not Ninigret, who had promised to handle the colonists' charges against Narragansetts who killed their animals. Ninigret's refusal to abide by this agreement was a way of saying that he was nobody's man. In short, Ninigret took positions toward the English based largely on how he thought those policies would be received by other Indians. The English were a secondary concern.

Nevertheless, the English kept this issue smoldering for years as a symbol of their authority and Indian subjugation, only to have Ninigret make them appear toothless. In October 1651 the United Colonies sent Thomas Stanton to Ninigret to revive their demand.[8] Stanton returned with nothing more than an empty promise. Eight years later the commissioners reopened the case, with Walter Phyler, a veteran lieutenant from the Pequot War, giving testimony.[9] The timing was not coincidental, for the commissioners were determined to use every tool at their disposal to pressure Ninigret in light of his renewed war with Uncas and the attack on Jonathan Brewster's home. Yet Thomas Stanton advised them to drop the matter. By this time, Poquium was dead and clearly Ninigret was not going to pay voluntarily. Unwilling to resort to blows, the commissioners threw up a white flag and advised Hartford to pay for the loss of Pomeroy's mare. As if to save face, the colony drew the funds out of the store of wampum that it had collected in fines from the Narragansetts.[10]

It is too easy and even lazy to use Ninigret's behavior during King Philip's War to cast him as weak or timid. As the case of Eltwood Pomeroy's mare captures, Ninigret never shied from a fight that he had a reasonable chance of winning. He raided the Mohegans and Montauketts even though they were English protectorates. He warned English messengers, even men in arms, that he would hunt them while they pissed and slaughter their cattle in heaps if they obstructed his affairs. As the colonists' population and military might grew, Ninigret adopted a pattern of promising concessions to the English and then failing to honor the terms, as if daring the English to force him. To have done otherwise would have diminished his bold reputation in Indian country, which was one of the pillars of his leadership. These characteristics were on display in Ninigret's handling of the issue of Eltwood Pomeroy's mare. They were also evident in the way he managed the challenges of King Philip's War.

Posterity loves the Indian chief who sacrifices himself and his people in a noble but losing cause. Live Indians tended to be less supportive of such tragic endings. During King Philip's War, Ninigret acted for them. He could plainly see that the chances of a successful Indian resistance were slim to none. Yes, the full participation of his Niantics would have improved the warring Indians' fortunes, but what then? Indians were not going to roll back the English into the sea, not without the Mohawks and French on their side. Whatever losses the English suffered, they were going to return a hundredfold, drawing on a supply chain of men and resources that reached from New England all the way down the coast into Virginia, to the Caribbean, and across the Atlantic to England proper. Ninigret was probably in his seventies at the start of King Philip's War and had grown to respect English resources. He knew the odds. So rather than make a disastrous choice, he first tried to orchestrate an end to the burgeoning conflict. When that imaginative effort failed, he made the heart-wrenching decision to separate from the warring Narragansetts and do what he could to ensure the safety of his followers. Lesser Indian leaders tried to do the same only to have their young men, the English, or both, draw them into the conflict. By contrast, Ninigret kept his people under his influence. None of them were charged with running away to fight alongside Philip or even fellow Narragansetts. None of them responded to Uncas's provocations during the war, lest the English interpret their retaliation as hostility. Ninigret provided the English with some measure of military support, but it appears to have been half-hearted. The sum of these efforts constitutes one of the great ironies of seventeenth-century New England: Ninigret, who teetered on the edge of war with the United Colonies throughout his entire political career, managed to secure his people and their land during the penultimate Indian-English conflict when so many other Indians lost all. This was the record of a wise, strong, and tactful leader.

Surviving the war was just the first challenge for Ninigret's Narragansett cousins who had taken up arms alongside Philip. They then had to survive the peace, for colonial authorities were determined to execute any Indian associated in the killing of Englishmen. Suffice it to say, the magistrates were not inclined to err on the side of caution when making these determinations. English townspeople did their part, killing a number of Narragansetts summarily when they straggled into colonial settlements starving and injured. When the English did spare Narragansett survivors of the war it was usually with the intent of forcing them into servitude, even lifetime slavery. They sold hundreds of them, and perhaps even more, to toil in the fields of Caribbean plantations. Even Roger Williams participated in these sales, having given up his friendship toward the Narragansetts after watching his colony, including his home town of Providence, torched by Indians during the war. Not surprisingly, some Narragansetts preferred to take their chances elsewhere, joining other New England Indians who scatted to the edges of the region. Some of them went to the refugee community of Schagticoke just outside of Albany, and others to Abenaki missions among the French in the St. Lawrence River Valley. A few might have retreated to the Wabenakis of Maine, the Mohicans of the Hudson River Valley, or even the Delawares of New Jersey and Pennsylvania, but if so they eluded the keepers of the written record, which is just as they would have wanted it.[11]

At least some Narragansetts took refuge with Ninigret's Niantics, but here too the historical record is silent. We know nothing about the terms, and nothing about how these survivors felt about having to join a community led by a man who had refused to defend them. We know nothing about whether they enjoyed full or second-class status among the Niantics. What we do know is this: whereas Ninigret and his people had formerly been known to the English sometimes as Niantics and at other times as Narragansetts, soon after the war they became known solely as Narragansetts.

The Ninigret family name has not aged well since the great sachem's death. Following the rule of his daughter, the sunksquaw Weunquesh, who died in the mid 1680s, most of his successors were, by practically any measure, incompetent and venal, even allowing for the straightened circumstances in which they operated. They included the great sachem's son, Ninigret II (who died in 1723), his grandson Charles Augustus Ninigret (d. 1735), another grandson George Augustus Ninigret (d. 1746), great grandson Tom Ninigret (d. 1769), great granddaughter Esther Ninigret (d. 1777), and great great grandson George Ninigret. Their main legacy was presiding over one fire sale of Narragansett land after another, usually to pay debts they had accumulated by providing their close kin with the best that colonial society offered. In fairness, there was little these men and women could have done to resist colonial pressure to part with their people's land—the English were a clear majority of the population of Narragansett country within a few decades of the end of

King Philip's War—but it is nevertheless also true that they seemed to put up little fight. All the while, their followers struggled to make do with ever less territory, even eventually losing their access to the seashore and coastal ponds that had been the staff of their existence. Predictably, they suffered poverty and sometimes servitude as a result. Fed up, in the 1770s a sizable minority of Narragansetts left the coast for Oneida country in what is now upstate New York alongside Mohegans, Pequots, Montauketts, and other Long Island Sound Indians, to create the new community of Brothertown. Within a few decades, white pressure on their land forced them to move again to Wisconsin. As for the Narragansetts who stayed back home, they abandoned the office of sachem after the death of George Ninigret and then dug in to make ends meet and defend their rights against a much larger white population insistent that they disappear. That battle has lasted to this very day.[12]

Ninigret might have fallen short when it came to preparing his son, Ninigret II, to defend the sachemship amidst the crush of colonial expansion, but there is no denying the effectiveness of his leadership during his own lifetime. His ability to confront the English and escape the consequences raised his profile among the Narragansetts and other surrounding Indians even as it made him the colonists' primary Indian enemy in the years preceding King Philip's War. If the United Colonies had their way after the Pequot War, they would have quickly reduced the Narragansetts just like they did the Pequots, the better to seize their rich land, subjugate Rhode Island, and intimidate the region's other Indians. That they did not testifies to the force of Ninigret's alliances. His relationships with the Mohawks, Pocumtucks, Dutch, and even the English king convinced the United Colonies that warring against him would carry great costs for them as well. Consequently, the Narragansetts remained a regional power throughout Ninigret's lifetime. Their strength was partly a creation and very much a reflection of Ninigret, the man who signed his name as a war club.

That is why Eltwood Pomeroy never received satisfaction from Ninigret for the loss of his mare.

Acknowledgments

Throughout the writing of this book, we have tried to avoid the "biographer's disease" of identifying too closely with our subject. Yet we have been unable to avoid the parallel risk of growing closer with a circle of valued friends and colleagues. Of that we gladly plead guilty.

A number of scholars read our manuscript in full and offered invaluable, often lengthy critiques that demanded much of their time. We offer particular thanks to Michael Zuckerman, Michael Oberg, and an anonymous reader for Cornell University Press, all of whom produced penetrating reader's reports, and to our editor, Michael McGandy, for helping us to sort out the comments (and more). We are humbled to have our work taken so seriously by such leading lights. Friends and fellow historians George Boudreau, Cathy Matson, John Murrin, Philip Seitz, and Greg Ablavsky joined us for a festive and yet marvelously productive dinner at our home in Mount Airy centered around discussion of the manuscript. Not the least of all, we profited from the comments of two of David's undergraduate classes and a graduate seminar at George Washington University, both of which read the manuscript in full. Thank you all.

A number of scholars generously answered questions, shared documents, and pointed us toward sources we otherwise would have missed. These include Paul Costa of the Yale Indian Papers Project, Charlotte Taylor of the Rhode Island Historical Preservation and Heritage Commission, Kevin McBride and Ashley Bissonnette of the Mashantucket Pequot Museum and Research Center, and Ann Woosley of the Rhode Island School of Design. We also had the benefit of archivists and librarians at a number of institutions, including the American Antiquarian Society, Library Company of Philadelphia, Massachusetts Historical Society, Massachusetts State Archives, Connecticut State Archives, Rhode

Island Historical Society, Newport Historical Society, Westerly (R.I.) Town Clerk's Office, East Hampton (N.Y.) Town Clerk's' Office, and the libraries of the University of Delaware, George Washington University, and the University of Pennsylvania.

The Department of History at George Washington University funded a number of research trips and production costs related to this project. We extend special gratitude to the department chair, William Becker, and department administrator, Michael Weeks, for their advocacy and consistent professionalism.

Last but not least, we thank our parents, Dennis and Mary Fisher, and Richard and Julia Silverman, and our children and stepchildren, Aquinnah and Bela Silverman, for their unwavering support during what was supposed to be a side project for both authors but turned into something more. It is with great joy that we dedicate this book to them. If good history is about recovering people long-since gone, good history writing is about rediscovering the people in one's own life.

Notes

Abbreviations Used in the Notes

Connecticut Records	Hoadly, Charles J., ed. *The Public Records of the Colony of Connecticut.* 15 vols. Hartford, 1850–90.
CSP	Colonial State Papers Online. Available at http://colonial.chadwyck.com.
DRCHNY	O'Callaghan, E. B., ed. *Documents Relative to the Colonial History of the State of New York.* 3 vols. Albany, 1856–83.
Massachusetts Records	Shurtleff, Nathaniel B., ed. *Records of the Governor and Company of the Massachusetts Bay in New England.* 5 vols. Boston, 1853–54.
MHSC	Massachusetts Historical Society, Collections.
NYCD	O'Callaghan, E. B., and Berthod Fernow, comps. and eds. *Documents Relative to the Colonial History of the State of New York.* 14 vols. Albany, 1856–83.
Plymouth Records	Shurtleff, Nathaniel B., and David Pulsifer, eds. *Records of the Colony of New Plymouth.* 12 vols. Boston, 1855.
Rhode Island Records	Bartlet, John R. ed. *Records of the Colony of Rhode Island and Providence Plantations in New England.* 10 vols. Providence, R.I., 1856–65.
RIHSC	*Collections of the Rhode Island Historical Society.*

United Colonies Records	Acts of the Commissioners of the United Colonies of New England. Vols. 9 and 10 of Plymouth Records.
Williams Correspondence	The Correspondence of Roger Williams. Edited by Glenn LaFantasie. 2 vols. Hanover, N.H.: University Press of New England for the Rhode Island Historical Society, 1988.
Williams, Key into the Language	Williams, Roger. A Key into the Language of America [1643]. Eds. John J. Teunissen and Evelyn J. Hinz. Detroit: Wayne State University Press, 1973.
Winthrop Family Papers	Winthrop Family Papers, microfilm, Ms. N-262, 62 document boxes, 121 volumes, 5 extra-tall volumes, and 6 oversize boxes, Massachusetts Historical Society, Boston, Mass. Organized chronologically unless noted otherwise.
Winthrop Family Transcripts	Winthrop Family Papers, Transcripts, Ms. N-2211, 10 boxes, Massachusetts Historical Society, Boston, Mass.
Winthrop Journal	Winthop, John. The Journal of John Winthrop, 1630–1649. Eds. Richard S. Dunn, James Savage, and Laeititia Yeandle. Cambridge, Mass.: Belknap Press of Harvard University Press, 1996.
Winthrop Papers	Forbes, Allyn B., ed. Winthrop Papers. 5 vols. Boston: Massachusetts Historical Society, 1929–45.
Yale Indian Papers	Yale Indian Papers Project, Yale Library. Available at http://www.library.yale.edu/yipp, last accessed September 27, 2012.

Preface

1. On indigenous forms of literacy, see Kristina Bross and Hillary Wyss, eds., *Early Native Literacies in New England: A Documentary and Critical Anthology* (Amherst, Mass., 2008).

2. Williams, *Key into the Language*, 213–14.

3. *Massachusetts Records*, 4:53–54 ("insolent"); Increase Mather, *A Brief History of the Warr with the Indians in New-England* [Boston, 1676], in Richard Slotkin and James K. Folsom, eds., *So Dreadfull a Judgment: Puritan Responses*

to *King Philip's War, 1676–1677* (Middletown, Conn., 1978), 107 ("crafty"); *Rhode Island Records*, 1:297 ("proud and fierce"); John Eliot to New England Company, October 10, 1652, *New England Historic Genealogical Register* 65 (1882): 294–95 ("professed enemies").

4. Elisha R. Potter Jr., *The Early History of Narragansett* (Providence, R.I., 1835), 47; Federic Denison, *Westerly (Rhode Island) and Its Witnesses* (Providence, R.I., 1878), 22; "The Ninigret Portrait," *RIHSC* 18, no. 3 (July 1925): 99–100.

5. *United Colonies Records*, 1:86–89.

6. On Winthrop's alchemical science, see Walter W. Woodward, *Prospero's America: John Winthrop, Jr., Alchemy, and the Creation of New England Culture, 1606–1676* (Chapel Hill, N.C., 2010). Generally on natural science collecting in this era, see Henry Lowood, "The New World and the European Catalog of Nature"; and Christian Feest, "The Collecting of American Indian Artifacts in Europe," in Karen Ordahl Kupperman, ed., *America in European Consciousness, 1493–1750* (Chapel Hill, N.C., 1995), 295–323, 324, 360; Karen Ordahl Kupperman, "A Cabinet of Curiosities," *Common-Place* 4, no. 2 (January 2004), accessed April 29, 2013, http://www.common-place.org/vol-04/no-02/kupperman/; Joyce Chaplin, *Subject Matter: Technology, the Body, and Science on the Anglo-American Frontier, 1500–1676* (Cambridge, Mass., 2001), 232–35.

7. James Axtell, "The First Consumer Revolution," in his *Beyond 1492: Encounters in Colonial North America* (New York, 1992), 136–39.

8. William Wood, *New England's Prospect* [1634], ed. Alden T. Vaughan (Amherst, Mass., 1977), 84.

9. That copy can be viewed at http://www.masshist.org/database/1700. Last accessed May 31, 2013.

10. Williams, *Key into the Language*, 214.

11. There is no systematic study of New England Indian dress after King Philip's War, but the following works inform this analysis: William S. Simmons, "The Earliest Prints and Paintings of New England Indians," *Rhode Island History* 41, no. 3 (1982): 72–85; Ann M. Little, " 'Shoot That Rogue, for He Hath an Englishman's Coat On!': Cultural Cross-Dressing on the New England Frontier, 1620–1760," *New England Quarterly* 74, no. 2 (2001): 238–73; Timothy J. Shannon, "Dressing for Success on the Mohawk Frontier: Hendrick, William Johnson, and the Indian Fashion," *William and Mary Quarterly*, 3rd ser., 53 (2000): 733–60.

12. On English and Dutch portraiture of the period, see Louisa Dresser, ed., *XVIIth Century Painting in New England* (Worcester, Mass., 1935); Abbott Lowell Cummings, "Seventeenth-Century Boston Portraiture: Profile of the Establishment," in Peter Benes, ed., *Painting and Portrait Making in the American Northeast* (Boston, 1995), 17–29; Arthur K. Wheelock Jr., *Dutch Paintings of the Seventeenth Century* (New York, 1995); Wayne Frantis, *Looking at Seventeenth-*

Century Dutch Art: Realism Reconsidered (New York, 1997). On Dutch colonial painters active during Ninigret's era, see Louisa Wood Ruby, "Dutch Art and the Hudson Valley Patroon Painters," in Joyce D. Goodfriend, Benjamin Schmidt, and Annette Scott, eds., Going Dutch: The Dutch Presence in America, 1609–2009 (Leiden, 2008), 27–58; Charles X. Harris, "Jacobus Gerritsen Strycker (c. 1619–1687): An Artist of New Amsterdam," New York Historical Society Quarterly Bulletin (October 1926), 83–91. This discussion is also informed by personal correspondence with Ann Woolsey, Museum of Art, Rhode Island School of Design, April 16, 2013; personal correspondence with Kevin McBride, Mashantucket Pequot Museum and Research Center, April 20 and April 22, 2013; and personal correspondence with Ashley Bissonnette, Mashantucket Pequot Museum and Research Center, May 3, 2013.

13. Douglas Edward Leach, Flintlock and Tomahawk: New England in King Philip's War (New York, 1958); James David Drake, King Philip's War: Civil War in New England (Amherst, Mass., 1999); Jill Lepore, King Philip's War and the Origins of American Identity (New York, 1998); Jenny Hale Pulsipher, Subjects unto the Same King: Indians, English, and the Contest for Authority in Colonial New England (Philadelphia, 2005); Patrick M. Malone, The Skulking Way of War: Technology and Tactics among the New England Indians (Baltimore, 1991); Russell Bourne, The Red King's Rebellion: Racial Politics in New England, 1675–1678 (New York, 1991).

14. On the notion that colonial America was a "new world" for Indians too, see James H. Merrell, The Indians' New World: Catawbas and Their Neighbors from European Contact through the Era of Removal (Chapel Hill, N.C., 1989). On colonialism shaping the lives of Indians at a remove from the colonies, see Kathleen DuVal, The Native Ground: Indians and Colonists in the Heart of the Continent (Philadelphia, 2006); Ned Blackhawk, Violence over the Land: Indians and Empires in the Early American West (Cambridge, Mass., 2006); and Pekka Hämäläinen, The Comanche Empire (New Haven, Conn., 2008). For a recent statement about the mutual influences of Indians and colonists, see Daniel K. Richter, Before the Revolution: America's Ancient Pasts (Cambridge, Mass., 2011).

15. Ola Elizabeth Winslow, Master Roger Williams, a Biography (New York, 1957).

16. This is not to say that Williams's relationship with Narragansett leaders lacked problems. For a careful consideration of his relationship with Miantonomi, see Paul A. Robinson, "Lost Opportunities: Miantonomi and the English in Seventeenth-Century Narragansett Country," in Northeastern Indian Lives, 1632–1816, ed. Robert Grumet (Amherst, Mass., 1996), 13–28.

17. Patricia Rubertone, Grave Undertakings: An Archaeology of Roger Williams and the Narragansett Indians (Washington, D.C., 2001).

18. Williams, Key into the Language, 83–84.

19. Models for our approach include Laurel Thatcher Ulrich, *A Midwife's Tale: The Life of Martha Ballard, Based on Her Diary, 1785–1812* (New York, 1991); Michael Leroy Oberg, *The Head in Walter Nugent's Hand: Roanoke's Forgotten Indians* (Philadelphia, 2007); and Camilla Townshend, *Pocahontas and the Powhatan Dilemma* (New York, 2004).

1. Being and Becoming a Sachem

1. Williams, *Key into the Language*, 203; William Wood, *New England's Prospect* [1634], ed. Alden T. Vaughan (Amherst, Mass., 1977), 98–99; Edward Winslow, *Good News from New England* [London, 1624], in Edward Arber, ed., *The Story of the Pilgrim Fathers, 1616–1623 A.D., as Told by Themselves, Their Friends, and Their Enemies* (London, 1897), 590.

2. Increase Mather, *Early History of New England* [1677], ed. Samuel G. Drake (Boston, 1864), 182.

3. Generally on New England Indian clubs, see Patrick M. Malone, *The Skulking Way of War: Technology and Tactics among the New England Indians* (Lanham, Md., 1991), 23–24.

4. Bert Salwen, "Indians of Southern New England and Long Island: Early Period," and William S. Simmons, "Narragansett," in *Handbook of North American Indians, Northeast*, vol. 15, Bruce G. Trigger, ed., William C. Sturtevant, genl. ed. (Washington, D.C., 1978), 167, 193; Simmons and George F. Aubin, "Narragansett Kinship," *Man in the Northeast* 9 (1975): 21–32; Kathleen J. Bragdon, *Native People of Southern New England, 1500–1650* (Norman, Okla., 1996), 157–63, 179, 186.

5. Williams, *Key into the Language*, 138.

6. Ibid., 118.

7. Bragdon, *Native People of Southern New England, 1650–1775*, 104–7; Howard S. Russell, *Indian New England before the Mayflower* (Hanover, N.H., 1980), 51–57.

8. Williams, *Key into the Language*, 134.

9. Bragdon, *Native People of Southern New England, 1500–1650*, 116–19.

10. Williams, *Key into the Language*, 190.

11. Ibid.

12. "Isaack de Rasiers to Samuel Blommaert (1628)," in Sydney V. James Jr., ed. *Three Visitors to Early Plymouth* (Plymouth, Mass., 1963), 78–79; Williams, *Key into the Language*, 193–94; Paul J. Lindholdt, ed., *John Josselyn, Colonial Traveler: A Critical Edition of "Two Voyages to New-England"* [1674] (Hanover, N.H., 1988), 95–96; Bragdon, *Native Peoples of Southeastern New England, 1650–1775*, 170; Patricia E. Rubertone, *Grave Undertakings: An Archaeology of Roger Williams and the Narragansett Indians* (Washington, D.C., 2002), 148; R. Todd Romero, *Making War and Minting Christians: Masculinity, Religion, and Colonialism in Early*

New England (Amherst, Mass., 2011), 25–27. Generally, see Åke Hultkrantz, *The Religions of the American Indians*, trans. Monica Setterwall (Berkeley, Cal., 1979), 66–83.

13. Ives Goddard and Kathleen J. Bragdon, *Native Writings in Massachusetts*, 2 vols. (Philadelphia, 1988), 1:216–19.

14. On New England Indian naming practices, see Bragdon, *Native People of Southern New England, 1500–1650*, 170; Romero, *Making War and Minting Christians*, 47. On private names among the Powhatans, a Virginia Algonquian people, see Helen C. Rountree, *Pocahontas, Powhatan, Opechancanough: Three Indian Lives Changed by Jamestown* (Charlottesville, Va., 2005), 166–67; Camilla Townsend, *Pocahontas and the Powhatan Dilemma* (New York, 2004), 13–14.

15. Williams, *Key into the Language*, 93.

16. Matthew Mayhew, *A Brief Narrative of the Success which the Gospel Hath Had, among the Indians of Martha's Vineyard (and the Places Adjacent) in New-England* (Boston, 1694), 7.

17. Williams, *Key into the Language*, 202.

18. Wood, *New England's Prospect*, 85 ("courtly"); Mayhew, *Brief Narrative*, 7 ("majestic").

19. *Winthrop Journal*, 83. Generally on English impressions of Indian polities, see Karen Ordahl Kupperman, *Indians and English: Facing Off in Early America* (Ithaca, N.Y., 2000), 76–109.

20. Bragdon, *Native People of Southern New England, 1650–1775* (Norman, Okla., 2009), 55–62; Bragdon, "'Emphatical Speech and Great Action': An Analysis of Seventeenth-Century Native Speech Events Described in Early Sources," *Man in the Northeast* 33 (1987): 101–11.

21. Howard W. Chapin, *Sachems of the Narragansetts* (Providence, R.I., 1931), 5; Ann Marie Plane, *Colonial Intimacies: Indian Marriage in Early New England* (Ithaca, N.Y., 2000), 21–22. Generally, see William Burton and Richard Lowenthal, "The First of the Mohegans," *American Ethnologist* 1, no. 4 (November 1974): 589–99; Bragdon, *Native People of Southern New England, 1500–1650*, 158–61; Michael S. Nassaney, "Native American Gender Politics and Material Culture in Seventeenth-Century Southeastern New England," *Journal of Social Archaeology* 4, no. 3 (2004): 335–67; Eric S. Johnson, "'Some by Flatteries and Others by Threatenings': Political Strategies among Native Americans of Seventeenth-Century New England (Ph.D., diss., University of Massachusetts, 1993), 164–87.

22. Chapin, *Sachems of the Narragansetts*, 92–93, 104–5.

23. Williams, *Key into the Language*, 116.

24. On Anglo-American childrearing, see Philip J. Greven, *The Protestant Temperment: Patterns of Child-Rearing, Religious Experience, and the Self in Early America* (Chicago, 1977); David Hackett Fischer, *Albion's Seed: Four British Folk-*

ways in America (New York, 1989), 97–102. On Indian practices, see James L. Axtell, ed., *The Indian Peoples of America: A Documentary History of the Sexes* (New York, 1981), 31–43; R. Todd Romero, "Colonizing Childhood: Religion, Gender, and Indian Children in New England, 1620–1720," in James Marten, ed., *Children in Colonial America* (New York, 2007), 33–47.

25. Williams, *Key into the Language*, 125.

26. Ibid., 115–16.

27. Ibid., 115.

28. Constance A. Crosby, "From Myth to History, or Why King Philip's Ghost Walks Abroad," in Mark P. Leone and Parker Potter Jr., eds., *The Recovery of Meaning: Historical Archaeology in the Eastern United States* (Washington, D.C., 1988), 190–91; Bragdon, *Native People of Southern New England, 1650–1750*, 197–98. For closely related beliefs among the Iroquois, see Daniel K. Richter, "War and Culture: The Iroquois Experience," *William and Mary Quarterly*, 3rd ser., 40 (1983): 528–59.

29. Wood, *New England's Prospect*, 85.

30. Joan M. Vastokas and Roman K. Vastokas, *Sacred Art of the Algonkians* (Petersborough, Ont., 1973), 93–94; Bragdon, *Native People of Southern New England, 1500–1650*, 187–88, 212.

31. This discussion is informed by Christopher L. Miller and George R. Hamell, "A New Perspective on Indian-White Contact: Cultural Symbols and Colonial Trade," *Journal of American History* 73, no. 2 (1986): 311–28; Hammell, "Mythical Realities and European Contact in the Northeast during the Sixteenth and Seventeenth Centuries," *Man in the Northeast* 33 (1987): 63–87; William A. Turnbaugh, "Post-Contact Smoking Pipe Development: The Narragansett Example," in Charles F. Hayes III, ed., *Proceedings of the 1989 Smoking Pipe Conference* (Rochester, N.Y., 1992), 113–24; Bragdon, *Native People of Southern New England, 1500–1650*, 185–89.

32. Wood, *New England's Prospect*, 85 ("humbird"); Lindholdt, ed., *John Josselyn*, 68 ("accounted of worth").

33. Bragdon, *Native People of Southern New England, 1650–1775*, 30.

34. Williams, *Key into the Language*, 249.

35. Winslow, *Good News from New England*, 588.

36. Williams, *Key into the Language*, 249.

37. William S. Simmons, *Cautantowwit's House: An Indian Burial Ground on the Island of Conanicut in Narragansett Bay* (Providence, R.I., 1970), 82–89; William Turnbaugh, "Community, Commodities, and the Concept of Property in Seventeenth-Century Narragansett Society," in James B. Stoltman, ed., *Archaeology of Eastern North America: Papers in Honor of Stephen Williams* (Jackson, Miss., 1993), 285–96; Paul Robinson, "The Struggle Within: The Indian Debate in Seventeenth-Century Narragansett Country" (Ph.D. diss., State

University of New York at Binghamton, 1990), 178–79, 232–39; Patricia E. Rubertone, "Archaeology, Colonialism, and 17th Century Native America: Towards an Alternative Interpretation," in Robert Layton, ed., *Conflict in the Archaeology of Living Traditions* (London, 1989), 41; Susan G. Gibson, ed., *Burr's Hill: A 17th Century Wampanoag Burial Ground in Warren, Rhode Island* (Providence, R.I., 1980). Generally on the ideological use of material objects to support chiefly power, see Timothy Earle, *Chiefdoms: Power, Economy, and Ideology* (New York, 1991), and *How Chiefs Come to Power: The Political Economy of Prehistory* (Stanford, Cal., 1997).

38. Williams, *Key into the Language*, 164.

39. Winslow, *Good News from New England*, 585.

40. Franklin Bowditch Dexter, ed., *The Literary Diary of Ezra Stiles, D.D., LL.D.*, 3 vols. (New York, 1901), 1:385–86. Generally, see Bragdon, *Native People of Southern New England, 1500–1650*, 184–90.

41. Williams, *Key into the Language*, 86.

42. William S. Simmons, *Spirit of the New England Tribes: Indian History and Folklore, 1620–1984* (Hanover, N.H., 1986), 235–46.

43. Williams, *Key into the Language*, 173.

44. On powwows, see William S. Simmons, "Southern New England Shamanism: An Ethnographic Reconstruction," in William Cowan, ed., *Papers of the Seventh Algonquian Conference* (Ottawa, 1976), 218–53; and Bragdon, *Native People of Southern New England, 1500–1650*, 203–14. On their connections to sachems, see Bragdon, ibid., 200–201, 227–28.

45. This discussion is informed by David Bernstein, *Prehistoric Subsistence on the Southern New England Coast: The Record from Narragansett Bay* (New York, 1993); Kevin A. McBride, "Native American Cultures in Transition: The Eastern Long Island Sound Culture Area in the Prehistoric and Contact Period," *Connecticut History* 55, no. 1 (spring 1994): 10–12; Bragdon, *Native People of Southern New England, 1500–1650*, 55–101; William Cronon, *Changes in the Land: Indians, Colonists, and the Ecology of New England* (New York, 1983); Shepard Krech III, *The Ecological Indian: Myth and History* (New York, 1999), 101–22; Russell, *Indian New England before the Mayflower*.

46. Williams, *Key into the Language*, 150.

47. Ibid., 182.

48. Ibid., 85.

49. Ibid., 128.

50. Ibid., 85.

51. See the debate, "Where Are the Woodland Villages?" in *Bulletin of the Massachusetts Archaeological Society* 49, no. 2 (1988): Peter F. Thorbahn, "Where Are the Woodland Villages in Southern New England?" 46–57; Barbara E. Luedtke, "Where Are the Woodland Villages in Eastern Massachusetts?"

58–65; Jordan E. Kerber, "Where Are the Woodland Villages in the Narragansett Bay Region?" 66–71; and Elizabeth A. Little, "Where Are the Woodland Villages on Cape Cod and the Islands?" 72–82; followed by Alan Leveille, Joseph Waller Jr., and Donna Ingham, "Dispersed Villages in Late Woodland Period South-Coastal Rhode Island," *Archaeology of Eastern North America* 34 (2006): 71–89. See also Robert J. Hasenstab, "Fishing, Farming, and Finding the Village Sites: Centering Late Woodland New England Algonquians," in Mary Ann Levine, Kenneth E. Sassaman, and Michael S. Nassaney, eds., *The Archaeological Northeast* (Westport, Conn., 1999), 139–53.

52. Charlotte C. Taylor, "The History and Archaeology of Fort Ninigret," in Gaynell Stone, ed., *Native Forts of the Long Island Sound Area*, Readings in Long Island Archaeology and Ethnohistory, vol. 8 (Stony Brook, N.Y., 2006), 277–86; Susan N. Meyer, Fort Ninigret site report, ms. provided courtesy of Charlotte Taylor, Rhode Island Historic Preservation and Heritage Commission; Christopher Jazwa, "Temporal Changes in a Precontact and Contact Period Cultural Landscape along the Southern Rhode Island Coast," in Ben Ford, ed., *Where the Land Meets the Sea: The Archaeology of Maritime Landscapes* (New York, 2011), 133.

53. Williams, *Key into the Language*, 167; Bragdon, *Native People of Southern New England*, 1500–1650, 66–71, 77–79.

54. Elizabeth A. Little, "Three Kinds of Indian Land Deeds at Nantucket, Massachusetts," in William Cowan, ed., *Papers of the 11th Algonquian Conference* (Ottawa, 1980), 61–70; Bragdon, *Native People of Southern New England, 1500–1650*, 143–47.

55. Williams, *Key into the Language*, 224.

56. Winslow, *Good News from New England*, 587.

57. Williams, *Key into the Language*, 181, 227; Bragdon, *Native People of Southern New England, 1500–1650*, 145–46; Elizabeth A. Little and J. Chilton Andrews, "Drift Whales on Nantucket: The Kindness of Moshup," *Man in the Northeast* 23 (1982): 17–38.

58. Williams, *Key into the Language*, 115 (quote), 193, 231; Bragdon, *Native People of Southern New England, 1500–1650*, 227–28.

59. Williams, *Key into the Language*, 203 (quote); Winslow, *Good News from New England*, 590.

60. Williams, *Key into the Language*, 235. See also accounts of the visits of Massasoit to Martha's Vineyard and Philip to Nantucket in David J. Silverman, *Faith and Boundaries: Colonists, Christianity, and Community among the Wampanoag Indians of Martha's Vineyard, 1600–1871* (New York, 2005), 39, 92–93.

61. Eric S. Johnson, "Released from Thraldom by the Stroke of War: Coercion and Warfare in Native Politics of Seventeenth-Century Southern New England," *Northeast Anthropology* 55 (1998): 1–13.

62. Bragdon, *Native People of Southern New England, 1500–1650*, 43, 145–48, 227–28. The material inequality in coastal sachemships can be seen in Simmons, *Cautantowwit's House*; William A. Turnbaugh, *The Material Culture of RI-1000: A Mid-17th Century Narragansett Indian Burial Site in North Kingstown, Rhode Island* (Kingston, R.I., 1984); and Gibson, ed., *Burr's Hill*.

63. Williams, *Key into the Language*, 203.

64. Bragdon, *Native People of Southern New England, 1500–1650*, 146–48.

65. Daniel Gookin, "Historical Collections of the Indians in New England," MHSC, 1st ser., 1 (1792): 148.

66. Gookin, "Historical Collections," 147, 148; Wood, *New England's Prospect*, 80–81.

67. *Winthrop Journal*, 408–12. See also *Massachusett Records*, 2:24–25; William Hubbard, *A General History of New England, from the Discovery to 1680*, 2nd ed. [Boston, 1848], MHSC, 2nd ser., 5 and 6 (Boston, 1848): 447–48.

68. Chapin, *Sachems of the Narragansetts*, 92–93; 104–5; Bragdon, *Native People of Southern New England, 1500–1650*, 181.

69. The best case study is Margaret Holmes Williamson, *Powhatan Lords of Life and Death: Command and Consent in Seventeenth-Century Virginia* (Lincoln, Neb., 2003).

70. Chapin, *Sachems of the Narragansetts*, 13; Editorial note in *Williams Correspondence*, 95, notes 5 and 6.

71. Testimony of Nathanial Waterman, February 6, 1705/6, vault A, box 60, folder 8, Indians in Rhode Island Collection, Newport Historical Society, Newport, R.I.

72. Franklin Bowditch Dexter, ed., *Extracts from the Itineraries and Other Miscellanies of Ezra Stiles, D.D., LL.D., 1755–1794* (New York, 1916), 28.

73. Eric S. Johnson, "Community and Confederation: A Political Geography of Contact-Period Southern New England," in Levine, Sassaman, and Nassaney, eds., *The Archaeological Northeast*, 155–68; Bragdon, *Native People of New England, 1500–1650*, 140–55; Simmons, "Narragansett," 193.

74. Chapin, *Sachems of the Narrgansetts*, 93–94; *Williams Correspondence*, 77 (note 17), 100 (note 3).

75. The best discussion of the multiple and sometimes fluid political identities of southern New England Indians during this era is Johnson, "Community and Confederation," 155–68.

76. Neal Salisbury, *Manitou and Providence: Indians, Europeans, and the Making of New England, 1500–1643* (New York, 1982), 147–48; Robinson, "Struggle Within," 81–87.

77. Salisbury, *Manitou and Providence*, 210; Alfred A. Cave, *The Pequot War* (Amherst, Mass., 1996), 50, 58, 65, 135.

78. Lynn Ceci, "Tracing Wampum's Origins: The Shell Bead Evidence from Archaeological Sites in Western and Coastal New York," in Charles Hayes III, ed., *Proceedings of the 1986 Shell Bead Conference* (Rochester, N.Y., 1983), 63–80; Kevin A. McBride, "The Source and Mother of the Fur Trade: Native-Dutch Relations in Eastern New Netherland," in Laurie Weinstein, ed., *Enduring Traditions: The Native Peoples of New England* (Westport, Conn., 1994), 41–42.

79. Salisbury, *Manitou and Providence*, 147–52; Cave, *Pequot War*, 49–68; Lynn Ceci, "Native Wampum as a Peripheral Resource in the Seventeenth Century World System," in Laurence M. Hauptman and James D. Wherry, eds., *The Pequots in Southern New England: The Fall and Rise of an American Indian Nation* (Norman, Okla., 1990), 48–64; Daniel K. Richter, *The Ordeal of the Longhouse: The Peoples of the Iroquois League in the Era of European Colonization* (Chapel Hill, N.C., 1992), 47–48, 84.

80. William B. Weeden, "Indian Money as a Factor in New England Civilization," *Johns Hopkins University Studies in Historical and Political Science*, 2nd ser., 8–9 (Baltimore, 1884); Cronon, *Changes in the Land*, 95–97; Ceci, "Native Wampum as a Peripheral Resource"; Jerry Martin, *Shell Game: A True Account of Beads and Money in North America* (San Francisco, 1996).

81. James Axtell, "At the Water's Edge: Trading in the Sixteenth Century," in his *After Columbus: Essays in the Ethnohistory of Colonial North America* (New York, 1988), 144–81; Axtell, "The First Consumer Revolution," in his *Beyond 1492: Encounters in Colonial North America* (New York, 1992), 125–51. Narragansett use of European goods can be gleaned from the collection of burial goods recovered from cemetery sites. See, for instance, Simmons, *Cautantowwit's House*; Turnbaugh, *Material Culture of RI-1000*; Turnbaugh, "Assessing the Significance of European Goods in Seventeenth-Century Narragansett Society," in J. Daniel Rogers and Samuel M. Wilson, eds., *Ethnohistory and Archaeology: Approaches to Postcontact Change in the Americas* (New York, 1993), 133–62.

82. Lawrence C. Worth, *The Voyages of Giovanni da Verrazzano, 1524–1528* (New Haven, Conn., 1970), 138.

83. Generally, see McBride, "Source and Mother of the Fur Trade," 31–52; Salisbury, *Manitou and Providence*, 85–100; David B. Quinn, *North America from Earliest Discovery to First Settlements: The Norse Voyages to 1612* (New York, 1977), 385–416; Axtell, "Consumer Revolution."

84. Among a vast literature, see Alfred W. Crosby, "Virgin Soil Epidemics as a Factor in the Aboriginal Depopulation in America," *William and Mary Quarterly*, 3rd ser., 33 (1976): 289–99; John M. Murrin, "Beneficiaries of Catastrophe: The English Colonies in America," in Eric Foner, ed., *The New American History* (Philadelphia, 1997), 3–30.

85. Thomas Morton, *New English Canaan* [1632], ed. Charles F. Adams, *Publications of the Prince Society*, vol. 14 (Boston, 1883), 132–33.

86. On the first outbreak, see Timothy Bratton, "The Identity of the New England Indian Epidemic of 1616–1619," *Bulletin of the History of Medicine* 62 (1988): 351–83; S. F. Cook, "The Significance of Disease in the Extinction of the New England Indians," *Human Biology* 45 (1973): 485–508; Dean Snow and Kim M. Lanphear, "European Contact and Indian Depopulation in the Northeast: The Timing of the First Epidemics," *Ethnohistory* 35 (1988): 15–33; Catherine C. Carlson, George L. Armelagos, and Ann Magennis, "Impact of Disease on the Precontact and Early Historic Populations of New England and the Maritimes," in John W. Verano and Douglas H. Ubelaker, eds., *Disease and Demography in the Americas* (Washington, D.C., 1992), 141–52; and Brenda J. Baker, "Pilgrim's Progress and Praying Indians: The Biocultural Consequences of Contact in Southern New England," in Clark Spencer Larsen and Geroge R. Milner, eds., *In the Wake of Contact: Biological Responses to Conquest* (New York, 1994), 35–44. On subsequent outbreaks, see Winthrop Journal, 101, 105–6, 108–10; Edward Johnson, *Johnson's Wonder-Working Providence, 1628–1651*, ed. J. Franklin Jameson (New York, 1910), 79–80; Salisbury, *Manitou and Providence*, 190–92; and William A. Starna, "The Pequots in the Early Seventeenth Century," in Hauptman and Wherry, eds., *The Pequots in Southern New England*, 46. The Bradford quotation is from William Bradford, *Of Plymouth Plantation*, ed. Samuel Eliot Morrison (New York, 1952), 271.

87. Salisbury, *Manitou and Providence*, 105–6, 109.

88. T. Morton, *New English Canaan*, 130–31; Nathaniel Morton, *New England's Memorial* [1669] (Boston, 1855), 37 (comet), 44 (curse).

89. Winslow, *Good News from New England*, 585.

90. Salisbury, "Squanto: Last of the Patuxets," David Sweet and Gary B. Nash, eds., *Survival and Struggle in Colonial America* (Berkeley, Cal., 1981), 228–46; Salisbury, *Manitou and Providence*, 110–40; Alden T. Vaughan, *New England Frontier: Puritans and Indians 1620–1675*, 3rd ed. (Norman, Okla., 1995), 64–92.

91. On the "Great Migration," see Virginia DeJohn Anderson, *New England's Generation: The Great Migration and the Formation of Society and Culture in the Seventeenth Century* (New York, 1991). On early politics between Indians and the Massachusetts Bay Colony, see Salisbury, *Manitou and Providence*, 166–202; Vaughan, *New England Frontier*, 93–121. On the trouble of livestock, see Robert E. Gradie, "New England Indians and Colonizing Pigs," in William Cowan, ed., *Papers of the Fifteenth Algonquian Conference* (Ottawa, 1984), 147–69; Virginia DeJohn Anderson, *Creatures of Empire: How Domestic Animals Transformed Early America* (New York, 2004).

92. Williams, *Key into the Language*, 210; Wood, *New England's Prospect*, 81.

93. McBride, "Source and Mother of the Fur Trade," 31–52.

94. The population figure is from W. J. Eccles, *The Canadian Frontier, 1534–1760*, rev. ed. (Albuquerque, N.M., 1983), 85.

95. Patricia Rubertone, *Grave Undertakings: An Archaeology of Roger Williams and the Narragansetts* (Washington, D.C., 2001), 159–60; Turnbaugh, *Material Culture of RI-1000*, 50–53. See also Gibson, ed., *Burr's Hill*, 111–12.

96. On Mohawk-French relations, see Richter, *Ordeal of the Longhouse*; Jon Parmenter, *Edge of the Woods: Iroquoia, 1534–1701* (Lansing, Mich., 2010); and José António Brandão, *"Your Fyre Shall Burn No More": Iroquois Policy toward New France and Its Native Allies to 1701* (Lincoln, Neb., 1997). On the Connecticut River tribes, see Peter A. Thomas, "In the Maelstrom of Change: The Indian Trade and Cultural Process in the Middle Connecticut River Valley, 1635–1665" (Ph.D., diss., University of Massachusetts at Amherst, 1979); Gordon M. Day, "The Identity of the Sokokis," in Michael K. Foster and William Cowan, eds., *In Search of New England's Native Past: Selected Essays by Gordon M. Day* (Amherst, Mass., 1998), 89–97; Colin G. Calloway, *The Western Abenakis of Vermont, 1600–1800: War, Migration, and the Survival of an Indian People* (Norman, Okla., 1990), 55–75; Richard I. Melvoin, *New England Outpost: War and Society in Colonial Deerfield* (New York, 1989), 25–48. Generally on New France, see W. J. Eccles, *The French in North America*, rev. ed. (East Lansing, Mich., 1998).

2. "To obtaine it by force"

1. The following three paragraphs draw on Neal Salisbury, *Manitou and Providence: Indians, Europeans, and the Making of New England, 1500–1643* (New York, 1982), 203–10; Michael Oberg, *Uncas: First of the Mohegans* (Ithaca, N.Y., 2003), 34–40; Eric S. Johnson, "Uncas and the Politics of Contact," in Robert S. Grumet, ed., *Northeastern Indian Lives, 1632–1816* (Amherst, Mass., 1996), 31; and Arthur A. Cave, *The Pequot War* (Amherst, Mass., 1996). Cave, *Pequot War*, is the authoritative account of the conflict. See also Vaughan, "Pequots and Puritans: The Causes of the War of 1637," in his *Roots of American Racism: Essays on the Colonial Experience* (New York, 1995), 277–321; Francis Jennings, *The Invasion of America: Indians, Colonialism, and the Cant of Conquest* (Chapel Hill, N.C., 1975), 186–27; Ronald Dale Karr, "'Why Should You Be So Furious?': The Violence of the Pequot War," *Journal of American History* 85 (1998): 876–909; Adam J. Hirsch, "The Collision of Military Cultures in Seventeenth-Century New England," *Journal of American History* 47 (1988): 1187–212; Steven T. Katz, "The Pequot War Reconsidered," *New England Quarterly* 64 (1991): 206–24; Michael Freeman, "Puritans and Pequots: The Question of Genocide," *New England Quarterly* 68 (1995): 278–93; Katz, "Pequots and the Question of Genocide: A Reply to Michael Freeman," *New England Quarterly* 68 (1995): 641–49.

2. Salisbury, *Manitou and Providence*, 205.

3. John Underhill, *Newes from America; Or, a New and Experimentall Discoverie of New England; Containing a True Relation of Their War-like Proceedings These Two*

Years Past [London, 1638], in Charles Orr, ed., *History of the Pequot War: The Contemporary Accounts of Mason, Underhill, Vincent, and Gardener* (Cleveland, Ohio, 1897), 57–58. For a compelling discussion of this issue, see Alfred A. Cave, "Who Killed John Stone: A Note on the Origins of the Pequot War," *William and Mary Quarterly*, 3rd ser., 49 (1992): 509–21.

4. On Indian land cessions and the founding of Connecticut, see Jennings, *Invasion of America*, 190–201; Cave, *Pequot War*, 76, 83, 87.

5. The best account of this event is Andrew Lipman, "Murder on the Saltwater Frontier: The Death of John Oldham," *Early American Studies* 9, no. 2 (May 2011): 268–94. The essential primary sources are *Winthrop Journal*, 179–83; Roger Williams to John Winthrop, September 9, 1637, *Williams Correspondence*, 117; Thomas Cobbet, "A Relation of New England's Deliverances," *New England Historical and Genealogical Register* 7 (1853): 209–19; William Hubbard, *A General History of New England, from the Discovery to 1680*, 2nd ed. [Boston, 1848], MHSC, 2nd ser., 5 and 6 (Boston, 1848): 250–51.

6. *Winthrop Journal*, 180.

7. The testimony is described in ibid., 180–82.

8. Ibid., 181.

9. Roger Williams to John Winthrop, October 28, 1637, *Williams Correspondence*, 130.

10. Salisbury, *Manitou and Providence*, 215–16.

11. On Plymouth, see Alden T. Vaughan, *New England Frontier: Puritans and Indians 1620–1675*, 3rd ed. (Norman, Okla., 1995), 97; George D. Langdon Jr., *Pilgrim Colony: A History of New Plymouth, 1620–1691* (New Haven, Conn., 1966), 82–83. On Connecticut, Salisbury, *Manitou and Providence*, 216.

12. *Winthrop Journal*, 181.

13. Hubbard, *General History*, 250.

14. Ibid., 250–51.

15. *Winthrop Journal*, 99.

16. The figure of seven hundred comes from *Winthrop Journal*, 109. Kevin A. McBride, "Fort Island: Conflict and Trade in Long Island Sound," in Gaynell Stone, ed., *Native Forts of the Long Island Sound Area*, Readings in Ethnohistory and Archaeology, vol. 8 (Stony Brook, N.Y. 2006), 255, favors this explanation for the murder of Oldham.

17. R. Williams to John Winthrop, September 9, 1637, and R. Williams to John Winthrop, October 26, 1637, *Williams Correspondence*, 117, 127.

18. R. Williams to Governor Henry Vane or Deputy Gov. John Winthrop, May 13, 1637, *Williams Correspondence*, 79. An October 1637 letter from Roger Williams to John Winthrop suggests that the Block Islanders themselves killed Adussah. It says that Canonicus and Miantonmi claimed to have had

no contact with the Manisees since "the getting of the head of Adussah the chiefe murtherer." See *Williams Correspondence*, 126.

19. John Mason, *A Brief History of the Pequot War* (Boston, 1736), and Underhill, *Newes from America*, 17–19, 50–63.

20. Cave, *Pequot War*, 145.

21. William Bradford, *Of Plymouth Plantation*, ed. Samuel Eliot Morison (New York, 1971), 296 (quote); Philip Vincent, *A True Relation of the Late Battell Fought in NewEngland, between the English, and the Salvages: With the Present State of Things There* [London, 1637], in Orr, ed., *History of the Pequot War*, 101; William Hubbard, *A Narrative of the Troubles with the Indians in New England* [Boston, 1677], in Samuel G. Drake, ed., *The History of the Indian Wars in New England, from the First Settlement to the Termination of the War with King Philip, in 1677*, 2 vols. (Roxbury, Mass., 1865), 52.

22. This fort might have been "Fort Ninigret," a palisaded area of 152 feet long by 137 feet wide at the head of modern-day Fort Neck Cove on Ninigret Pond. See Charlotte C. Taylor, "The History and Archaeology of Fort Ninigret," in Stone, ed., *Native Forts of the Long Island Sound Area*, 277–86; Susan N. Meyer, Fort Ninigret site report, ms. provided courtesy of Charlotte Taylor, Rhode Island Historic Preservation and Heritage Commission.

23. Mason, *Brief History of the Pequot War*, 4.

24. Ibid.; Hubbard, *Narrative of the Troubles*, 47.

25. Vincent, *True Relation*, 8.

26. Cave, *Pequot War*, 122–67; Jennings, *Invasion of America*, 202–27; Vaughan, *New England Frontier*, 122–54.

27. Johnson, "Uncas and the Politics of Contact," 31–33; Oberg, *Uncas*, 48–51.

28. The treaty appears in full in Vaughan, *New England Frontier*, 340–41.

29. Two of the best statements on this point are Robert A. Williams Jr., *Linking Arms Together: American Indian Treaty Visions of Law and Peace, 1600–1800* (New York, 1987); and Russel L. Barsh, "The Nature and Spirit of North American Political Systems," *American Indian Quarterly* 10 (1986): 181–98.

30. Paul Robinson, "The Struggle Within: The Indian Debate in Seventeenth-Century Narragansett Country" (Ph.D. diss., State University of New York at Binghamton, 1990), 123.

31. John A. Strong, *The Montaukett Indians of Eastern Long Island* (Syracuse, N.Y., 2001); Strong, "Wyandanch: Sachem of the Montauks," in Grumet, ed., *Northeastern Indian Lives*, 48–73. The best contemporary account of Wyandanch as a friend to the English is Lion Gardiner, "Relation of the Pequot Warres" [1660], in Orr, ed., *History of the Pequot War*, 140–48.

32. Jenny Hale Pulsipher, *Subjects unto the Same King: Indians, English, and the Contest for Authority in Colonial New England* (Philadelphia, 2005), 25–28; Jennings, *Invasion of America*, 264; Joshua Micah Marshall, "'A Melancholy People': Anglo-Indian Relations in Early Warwick, Rhode Island, 1642–1675," *New England Quarterly* 68 (1995): 402–28; Eric Hinderaker, "Diplomacy between Britons and Native Americans, c. 1600–1830," in H. V. Bowen, Elizabeth Mancke, and John G. Reid, eds., *Britain's Oceanic Empire: Atlantic and Indian Ocean Worlds, c. 1550–1850* (New York, 2012), 224–28.

33. The following two paragraphs draw on Roger Ludlow to John Winthrop, July 3, 1638, *Winthrop Papers*, 4:44–45 (all quotes); *Winthrop Journal*, 259–60. See also Leicester Bradner, "Ninigret's Naval Campaigns against the Montauks," *Rhode Island Historical Society Collections* 18 (1925): 14–19; Timothy J. Sehr, "Ninigret's Tactics of Accommodation: Indian Diplomacy in New England, 1637–1675," *Rhode Island History* 36 (1977): 43–53.

34. Roger Ludlow to John Winthrop, July 3, 1638, *Winthrop Papers*, 4:44–45.

35. Roger Williams to John Winthrop, May 27, 1638, *Williams Correspondence*, 157–58.

36. Roger Williams to John Winthrop, August 14, 1638, *Williams Correspondence*, 176; *Winthrop Journal*, 259–60.

37. *The First Book of Records of the Town of Southampton, with Other Ancient Documents of Historic Value* (Sag Harbor, N.Y., 1874), 12–13.

38. Israel Stoughton to John Winthrop, July 6, 1637, *Winthrop Papers*, 3:442.

39. Daniel Patrick to Increase Nowell, July 6, 1637, and Israel Stoughton to John Winthrop, July 6, 1637, *Winthrop Papers*, 3:440–41, 442.

40. R. Williams to J. Winthrop, July 21, 1640, *Williams Correspondence*, 202; Johnson, "Uncas and the Politics of Contact," 40.

41. Hubbard, *General History*, 254–55.

42. Mason, *Brief History of the Pequot War*, 18–20 (all quotes); Increase Mather, *A Relation of the Troubles which Have Hapned [sic] in New-England by Reason of the Indians There from the Year 1614 to the Year 1675* (Boston, 1677), 39–41; *Connecticut Records*, 1:32; R. Williams to J. Winthrop, September 10, 1638, *Williams Correspondence*, 179–82.

43. Generally, see Oberg, *Uncas*, 110–38.

44. Wood, *New England's Prospect*, 75 ("cruel"); Williams, *Key into the Language*, 102 ("Men-eaters" and "terror").

45. Generally on relations between the Mohawks and coastal Indians, see Neal Salisbury, "Toward the Covenant Chain: Iroquois and Southern New England Algonquians, 1637–1684," in Daniel K. Richter and James H. Merrell, eds., *Beyond the Covenant Chain: The Iroquois and Their Neighbors in Indian North America* (Syracuse, N.Y., 1987), 61–73.

46. *Winthrop Journal*, 329 (quote); Oberg, "'We Are All Sachems from East to West': A New Look at Miantonomi's Campaign of Resistance," *New England Quarterly* 77 (2004): 478–99.

47. *Winthrop Journal*, 406.

48. Journal of New Netherland, Written in the Years 1641, 1642, 1643, 1644, 1645, and 1646, DRCHNY, 1:183.

49. On this conflict, see Evan Haefeli, "Kieft's War and the Systems of Violence in Colonial America," in Michael A. Bellesiles, ed., *Lethal Imagination: Violence and Brutality in American History* (New York, 1999), 17–40; Paul Otto, *The Dutch-Munsee Encounter in America: The Struggle for Sovereignty in the Hudson Valley* (New York, 2006), 113–26.

50. Gardiner, "Relation of the Pequot Warres," 142–43.

51. *Winthrop Journal*, 408.

52. *Winthrop Journal*, 408–12. See also *Massachusetts Records*, 2:24–25; Hubbard, *General History*, 447–48

53. Oberg, *Uncas*, 100–101.

54. *Winthrop Journal*, 468.

55. *United Colonies Records*, 1:10–11; *Winthrop Journal*, 471–73; Vaughan, *New England Frontier*, 163–66; Jennings, *Invasion of America*, 266–68; Salisbury, *Manitou and Providence*, 234–35.

56. Ives Goddard and Kathleen Bragdon translate *nannogquit* as "the southwest," based on a critical reading of Roger Williams, *Key into the Language of America*, as well as some Native language land deeds. See their *Native Writings in Massachusetts*, 2 vols. (Philadelphia, 1988), 2:657–58 (entry for *nannogquit*).

3. "I doe but Right my owne quarrell"

1. Memorandum, ca. 1645, *Winthrop Papers*, 5:17–18.

2. On Gorton and spectrum of puritan dissent, see Philip F. Gura, *A Glimpse of Sion's Glory: Puritan Radicalism in New England* (Middletown, Conn., 1984). From among an enormous literature addressing other issues raised in this paragraph, see Stephen Foster, *The Long Argument: English Puritanism and the Shaping of New England Culture, 1570–1700* (Chapel Hill, N.C., 1991); Michael P. Winship, *Making Heretics: Militant Protestantism and Free Grace in Massachusetts, 1636–1641* (Princeton, N.J., 2002); Darren Staloff, *The Making of an American Thinking Class: Intellectuals and Intelligentsia in Puritan Massachusetts* (New York, 1998); Edmund S. Morgan, *Roger Williams: The Church and State* (New York, 1967); Carla Gardina Prestana, *Quakers and Baptists in Colonial Massachusetts* (New York, 1991); Philip Ranlet, *Enemies of the Bay Colony: Puritan Massachusetts and Its Foes*, 2nd ed. (Lanham, Md., 2006); Perry Miller, "Thomas Hooker and the Democracy of Connecticut," in his *Errand into the*

Wilderness (Cambridge, Mass., 1956), 16–47; John M. Murrin, "Magistrates, Sinners, and a Precarious Liberty: Trial by Jury in Seventeenth-Century New England," in David D. Hall, John M. Murrin, and Thad Tate, eds., *Saints and Revolutionaries: Essays on Early American History* (New York, 1984), 152–206; Francis J. Bremer, *The Puritan Experiment: New England Society from Bradford to Edwards* (New York, 1976), 77–88; Jane Kamensky, *Governing the Tongue: The Politics of Speech in Early New England* (New York, 1997). Gura, *Glimpse of Sion's Glory*, 276–303, provides a critical assessment of Perry Miller's argument that Gorton belonged to the "lunatic fringe" of reformed Protestantism (quote on 276).

3. Samuel Gorton, *Simplicity's Defence against Seven-Headed Policy* [London, 1646], RIHSC 2 (Providence, 1835): 156–57 (quote on 157); Francis Jennings, *The Invasion of America: Indians, Colonialism, and the Cant of Conquest* (Chapel Hill, N.C., 1975), 270–73; Paul Robinson, "The Struggle Within: The Indian Debate in Seventeenth-Century Narragansett Country" (Ph.D. diss., State University of New York at Binghamton, 1990), 150–53.

4. *United Colonies Records*, 2:416.

5. *Winthrop Journal*, 509.

6. Ibid., 481; *Connecticut Records*, 1:94; Charles J. Hodley, ed., *Records of the Colony and Plantation of New Haven, from 1638 to 1649* (Hartford, Conn., 1849), 110, 118; *United Colonies Records*, 1:28–30.

7. Thomas Peters to John Winthrop, May 1645, *Winthrop Papers*, 5:19.

8. Roger Williams to John Winthrop, June 25, 1645, *Williams Correspondence*, 225.

9. John Winthrop, *Declaration of Former Passages and Proceedings betwixt the English and the Norrowganset, with Their confederates, Wherein the Grounds and Justice of the Ensuing Warre Are Opened and Cleared* (Boston, 1645), 6.

10. The account attributing this threat to Ninigret appears in *United Colonies Records*, 1:88.

11. Ibid., 1:54.

12. Ibid., 1:33.

13. Ibid., 1:55; Winthrop, *Declaration of Former Passages*.

14. On the amount of labor required to produce wampum, see Robinson, "Struggle Within," 169–70.

15. *United Colonies Records*, 1:86.

16. Ibid., 1:42–43.

17. William Pynchon to John Winthrop, September 15, 1645, *Winthrop Papers*, 5:45.

18. For Ninigret's cultivation of this relationship, see R. Williams to J. Winthrop Jr., August 20, 1647, *Williams Correspondence*, 1:236–27.

19. Eric S. Johnson, "Uncas and the Politics of Contact," in Robert S. Grumet, ed., *Northeastern Indian Lives, 1632–1816* (Amherst, Mass., 1996), 31, 35, 39–40.

20. Walter W. Woodward, *Prospero's America: John Winthrop, Jr., Alchemy, and the Creation of New England Culture, 1606–1676* (Chapel Hill, N.C., 2010), 93–102; Harry M. Ward, *The United Colonies of New England, 1643–90* (New York, 1961), 139–41; Jennings, *Invasion of America*, 257–59; Wendy B. St. Jean, "Inventing Guardianship: The Mohegan Indians and Their 'Protectors,'" *New England Quarterly* 72 (1999): 362–87.

21. On the Pequot plight after the war, see Michael L. Fickes, "'They Could Not Endure That Yoke': The Captivity of Pequot Women and Children after the War of 1637," *New England Quarterly* 73 (2000): 58–81.

22. Woodward, *Propero's America*, 110. On Winthrop's Jr.'s home experiments, see 112; on his healing practice, see 111, 160–99; on his correspondents and use of Indian runners, see 111, 143–46, 200–209. On Winthrop's Indian messengers, see also Katherine Alysia Grandjean, "Reckoning: The Communications Frontier in Early New England (Ph.D., diss., Harvard University, 2008), 72–112.

23. Quoted in Woodward, *Prospero's America*, 131.

24. R. Williams to J. Winthrop Jr., August 20, 1647, Williams to Winthrop Jr., October 10, 1648, *Williams Correspondence*, 236–37 ("respects"), 252 ("corn").

25. For an informative discussion of the symbolic importance of corn as a gift, see Martin S. Quitt, "Trade and Acculturation at Jamestown: The Limits of Understanding," *William and Mary Quarterly*, 3rd ser., 52, no. 2 (April 1995): 247. On Winthrop's knowledge, see John Winthrop Jr., "On Indian Corn," ed. Fulmer Mood, *New England Quarterly* 10 (1937): 121–33.

26. Petition of the Inhabitants of New London to the Commissioners of the United Colonies, *Winthrop Papers*, 5:111. See also *Winthrop Papers*, 5:124; *United Colonies Records*, 1:71–73, 102; Woodward, *Prospero's America*, 115–17.

27. R. Williams to J. Winthrop Jr., December 3, 1648, *Williams Correspondence*, 260.

28. United Colonies Commissioners to J. Winthrop Jr., September 13, 1648 (quote), John Mason to J. Winthrop Jr., September 17, 1648, J. Winthrop Jr. to John Mason, September 19, 1648, John Haynes to J. Winthrop Jr., September 20, 1648, *Winthrop Papers*, 5:252, 253, 255, 256; *Williams Correspondence*, 244–48 (editor's note).

29. J. Winthrop Jr. to J. Mason, September 19, 1648, William Coddington to J. Winthrop Jr., September 31, 1648, and J. Mason to J. Winthrop Jr., October 1648, *Winthrop Papers*, 5:255, 262–63.

30. J. Winthrop Sr. to J. Winthrop Jr., March 3, 1649, *Winthrop Papers*, 5:311.

31. Ibid.

32. R. Williams to J. Winthrop Jr., January 29, 1648/49, *Williams Correspondence*, 271.

33. *Winthrop Journal*, 626. See also John Coggeshall to J. Winthrop, September 13, 1647, *Winthrop Papers*, 5:182.

34. *Winthrop Journal*, 626; John Haynes, to J. Winthrop Jr., September 20, 1648, *Winthrop Papers*, 5:256; R. Williams to J. Winthrop Jr., ca. March 20, 1648/49, *Williams Correspondence*, 273.

35. *United Colonies Records*, 1:86.

36. For a snapshot, see Darrett Rutman, *Winthrop's Boston: A Portrait of a Puritan Town, 1630–1649* (Chapel Hill, N.C., 1965), 164–201.

37. *Winthrop Journal*, 691.

38. *United Colonies Records*, 1:86–89, 106.

39. R. Williams to J. Winthrop Jr., August 20, 1647, *Williams Correspondence*, 236.

40. J. Winthrop Sr. to J. Winthrop Jr., July 3, 1648, *Winthrop Papers*, 5:235.

41. John W. DeForest, *History of the Indians of Connecticut* (Hartford, Conn., 1852), 218–22; *Williams Correspondence*, 242–43 (editor's note); Michael Oberg, *Uncas: First of the Mohegans* (Ithaca, N.Y., 2003), 125, 127.

42. *United Colonies Records*, 1:148.

43. Ibid.

44. Ibid.; J. Mason to J. Winthrop Jr., September 9, 1648, and United Colonies to J. Winthrop Jr., September 13, 1648, *Winthrop Papers*, 5:250–51, 252.

45. *United Colonies Records*, 1:143–45; R. Williams to J. Winthrop Jr., April 7, 1649, *Williams Correspondence*, 277–78.

46. Alden T. Vaughan, *New England Frontier: Puritans and Indians 1620–1675*, 3rd ed. (Norman, Okla., 1995), 341 (quote); R. Williams to J. Winthrop Jr., mid-November 1648, ca. March 20, 1648/49, May 9, 1649, and June 13, 1649, *Williams Correspondence*, 258, 272–73, 286, 290; *United Colonies Records*, 1:143–45, 2:417–18; Edward Hopkins to J. Winthrop Jr., March 20, 1648/49, *Winthrop Papers*, 5:321–22; J. Winthrop Jr. to the United Colonies, July 1649, *Winthrop Papers*, 5:354; Kevin A. McBride, "The Legacy of Robin Cassacinamon: Mashantucket Pequot Leadership in the Historic Period," in Grumet, ed., *Northeastern Indian Lives*, 85–86; Shawn G. Wiemann, "Lasting Marks: The Legacy of Robin Cassacinamon and the Survival of the Mashantucket Pequot Nation" (Ph.D., diss., University of New Mexico, 2011), 199–202.

47. *United Colonies Records*, 1:168–69.

48. Increase Mather, *A Relation of the Troubles which Have Hapned* [sic] *in New-England by Reason of the Indians There from the Year 1614 to the Year 1675* (Boston, 1677), 59–60.

49. R. Williams to J. Winthrop Jr., October 9, 1650, *Williams Correspondence*, 322–24.

50. R. Williams to J. Winthrop Jr., October 17 and October 23, 1650, *Williams Correspondence*, 325–28.

51. J. Winthrop Jr., to Atherton, November 10, 1650, *Winthrop Papers*, 6:77–78.

52. R. Williams to John Winthrop Jr., October 17, 1650, *Williams Correspondence*, 325–28.

53. *United Colonies Records*, 2:23–25.

54. Ward, *United Colonies of New England*, 157–69.

55. *United Colonies Records*, 2:28. On Dutch-English hostilities during these years, see Jonathan Israel, *The Dutch Republic: Its Rise, Greatness, and Fall, 1477–1806* (Oxford, 1995), 715–16.

56. Ninigret might have been referring to a French doctor named Shoyes who briefly resided in New Haven in 1651 after receiving medical training in the Netherlands. Shoyes left New Haven shortly thereafter, possibly relocating to New Amsterdam. John Davenport of New Haven did correspond with John Winthrop Jr. about this figure. See Francis J. Bremer, *Building a New Jerusalem: John Davenport, a Puritan in Three Worlds* (New Haven, Conn., 2012), 249–50.

57. *United Colonies Records*, 2:3–9. See also Richard Smith to J. Winthrop Jr., April 9, 1653, *Winthrop Papers*, 6:279; Thomas Minor to J. Winthrop Jr., April 2, 1653, MHSC, 5th ser., 9: 5–6; also in *Winthrop Papers* 6:275–76.

58. *United Colonies Records*, 2:23.

59. Ibid.

60. Ibid., 2:23–24. See also Thomas Stanton to J. Winthrop Jr., May 2, 1653, *Winthrop Papers*, 6:289.

61. *United Colonies Records*, 2:43.

62. Ibid., 2:43–44, 47.

63. Ibid., 1:44–45.

64. Ibid., 1:10.

65. Ibid., 1:10–11.

66. Indian New-Come to J. Winthrop Jr., December 1, 1652, *Winthrop Papers*, 6:234.

67. Ward, *United Colonies*, 178–200.

68. *United Colonies Records*, 2:374–77.

69. Oliver A. Rink, *Holland on the Hudson: An Economic and Social History of Dutch New York* (Ithaca, N.Y., 1986), 165.

70. John Grier Varner and Jeanette Johnson Varner, *Dogs of the Conquest* (Norman, Okla., 1983). We thank Marcy Norton for this citation.

71. Martin Pring, "A Voyage Set Out from the Citie of Bristoll . . . in the Yeere 1603," in David B. Quinn and Alison M. Quinn, eds., *The English New England Voyages, 1602–1608* (London, 1983), 214–28.

72. Lion Gardiner, "Relation of the Pequot Warres" [1660], in Charles Orr, ed., *History of the Pequot War: The Contemporary Accounts of Mason, Underhill, Vincent, and Gardener* (Cleveland, Ohio, 1897), 129.

73. Williams, *Key into the Language*, 173 ("cannot comprehend), 191 ("excellency").

74. *United Colonies Records*, 2:374–77.

75. Charles J. Hoadly, ed., *Records of the Colony or Jurisdiction of New Haven, from May 1653 to the Union* (Hartford, Conn., 1858), 117–18.

76. R. Williams to the General Court of Massachusetts Bay, October 5, 1654, *Williams Correspondence*, 409.

77. Robinson, "Struggle Within," 167–72.

78. John Endecott to J. Winthrop Jr., August 15, 1651, *Winthrop Papers*, 6:134–35.

79. *United Colonies Records*, 2:96–97, 98.

80. Ibid., 2:88, 98–99; J. Winthrop Jr. to Ninigret, mid-September 1653, *Winthrop Papers*, 6:339.

81. William S. Pelletreau, ed., *Records of the Town of Smithtown, Long Island, N.Y.* (Smithtown, N.Y., 1898), 3.

82. *United Colonies Records*, 2:115; R. Williams to J. Winthrop Jr., October 9, 1654, *Williams Correspondence*, 417.

83. *United Colonies Records*, 2:115 ("some hundreds"); R. Williams to J. Winthrop Jr., ca. February 15, 1654/55, *Williams Correspondence*, 426 ("3 or 4 goats");

84. R. Williams to J. Winthrop Jr., October 9, 1654, *Williams Correspondence*, 417.

85. *United Colonies Records*, 2:126.

86. Roger Williams claimed that this attack took thirty, not sixty, lives. See his letter to the General Court of Massachusetts, October 5, 1654, *Rhode Island Records*, 1:295–96, and *Williams Correspondence*, 408–15.

87. *United Colonies Records*, 1:125.

88. Rhode Island's protest can be found in Roger Williams to the General Court of Massachusetts, October 5, 1654, *Williams Correspondence*, 411.

89. Kevin A. McBride, "Prehistoric and Historic Patterns of Wetland Use in Eastern Connecticut," *Man in the Northeast* 43 (spring 1992): 10–24.

90. *United Colonies Records*, 1:145–48. The commissioners' grounds for war are listed in ibid., 2:435–37.

91. Ibid., 2:142–43; *Connecticut Records*, 1:257, 259; "The names of the Pequots that have subjected themselves under the Government of the English," October 16–17, 1654 (quotes), Simon Newman to J. Winthrop Jr., probably October 23, 1654, Winthrop Papers, MHS (quotes); Oberg, *Uncas*, 139–44; DeForest, *Indians of Connecticut*, 245–48.

92. For a historical summary, see Jack Campisi, "The Emergence of Mashantucket Pequot Tribe, 1637–1975," in Laurence M. Haputman and James D. Wherry, eds., *The Pequots in Southern New England: The Fall and Rise of an American Indian Nation* (Norman, Okla., 1990), 179–93.

93. R. Williams to J. Winthrop Jr., October 10, 1648, *Williams Correspondence*, 252.

94. *United Colonies Records*, 2:148–49.

95. Ibid., 2:149–51; Leicester Bradner, "Ninigret's Naval Campaigns against the Montauks," *RIHSC* 18, no. 1 (January 1925): 14–19.

96. R. Williams to J. Winthrop Jr., February 15, 1654/55, *Williams Correspondence*, 425.

97. *United Colonies Records*, 2:169–72.

98. Ibid., 2:172 (quote); *Massachusetts Records*, 3:436–37; Francis Newman to J. Winthrop Jr., February 17, 1658/59, Winthrop Family Papers. On Uncas's provocations to the Pocumtucks, see John Pynchon to J. Winthrop Jr., February 16, 1657/58, and May 22, 1658, Winthrop Family Papers. The Pynchon letter is also in *The Pynchon Papers*, vol. 1, *Letters of John Pynchon, 1654–1700*, ed. Carl Bridenbaugh (Boston, 1982), 21–23.

99. *Rhode Island Records*, 1:362–63; Humphrey Atherton et al. to J. Winthrop Jr., August 30, 1659, Winthrop Family Transcripts.

100. J. Mason to J. Winthrop Jr., June 1657, Winthrop Family Transcripts.

101. The attacks on Brewster and other Englishmen associated with the Mohegans can be traced in *United Colonies Records*, 2:227–28, 236–37 ("did furnish . . ."), 248–49; Thomas Welles to J. Winthrop Jr., March, 25, 1659, J. Winthrop Jr. et al. to John Endecott, March 27, 1659, John Mason to Connecticut, August 22, 1659, Newman to Winthrop, July 5, 1660, Winthrop Family Transcripts; *Connecticut Records*, 1:576–77.

4. A Time of Decision

1. Sydney V. James, *Colonial Rhode Island: A History* (New York, 1975), 8, 13, 31–32; Joshua Micah Marshall, " 'A Melancholy People': Anglo-Indian Relations in Early Warwick, Rhode Island, 1642–1675," *New England Quarterly* 68 (1995): 402–28; Paul Alden Robinson, "The Struggle Within: The Indian Debate in Seventeenth Century Narragansett Country" (Ph.D., diss., State University of New York at Binghamton, 1990), 114–15, 142–45; Daniel Berkeley

Updike, Richard Smith: First English Settler of the Narragansett Country, Rhode Island (Boston, 1937).

2. Generally on these transactions, see Richard Dunn, "John Winthrop, Jr. and the Narragansett Country," William and Mary Quarterly, 3rd ser., 13, no. 1 (January 1956): 68–86; John Frederick Martin, Profits in the Wilderness: Entrepreneurship and the Founding of New England Towns in the Seventeenth Century (Chapel Hill, N.C., 1991), 58–79; Sydney V. James, The Colonial Metamorphoses of Rhode Island (Hanover, N.H., 2000), 88–96. The Atherton Company records are contained in James N. Arnold, ed., The Records of the Proprietors of the Narragansett, Otherwise Called the Fones Record (Providence, R.I., 1984).

3. Francis Jennings, The Invasion of America: Indians, Colonialism, and the Cant of Conquest (Chapel Hill, N.C., 1975), 278–79; Howard W. Chapin, Sachems of the Narragansetts (Providence, R.I., 1931), 68–69; Williams Correspondence, 493, n. 13.

4. The only scholar to gesture in this direction is Robinson, "Struggle Within," 192–93.

5. Ibid., 193.

6. Ibid., 194–95; Peter A. Thomas, "In the Maelstrom of Change: The Indian Trade and Cultural Process in the Middle Connecticut River Valley, 1635–1665" (Ph.D. diss., University of Massachusetts Press, 1979), 300–29.

7. Williams to [General Court of Commissioners of Providence Plantations?], August 25, 1658, Williams Correspondence, 489.

8. Massachusetts Records, 3:436–47.

9. Fones Record, 1; Trumbull Papers, Connecticut State Archives, 2.

10. On evolving Indian notions of land sales, see William Cronon, Changes in the Land: Indians, Colonists, and the Ecology of New England (New York, 1983), esp. 67–81; David J. Silverman, "'Natural Inhabitants, Time out of Mind': Sachem Rights and the Struggle for Wampanoag Land in Colonial New England," Northeast Anthropology 70 (2005): 4–10; Emerson W. Baker, "'A Scratch with a Bear's Paw': Anglo-Indian Land Deeds in Early Maine," Ethnohistory 36 (1989): 235–56; Peter S. Leavenworth, "'The Best Title That Indians Can Claime': Native Agency and Consent in the Transferal of Penacook-Pawtucket Land in the Seventeenth Century," New England Quarterly 72 (1999): 275–300; Stuart Banner, How the Indians Lost Their Land: Law and Power on the Frontier (Cambridge, Mass., 2005). Cf. Elizabeth Little, "Daniel Spotso: A Sachem at Nantucket Island, Massachusetts, circa 1691–1741," in Robert S. Grumet, ed., Northeastern Indian Lives, 1632–1816 (Amherst, Mass., 1996), 193–207; John Strong, "Tribal Systems and Land Alienation: A Case Study," in William Cowan, ed., Papers of the Sixteenth Algonquian Conference (Ottawa, 1985), 183–200. On drift whales, see Elizabeth A. Little and

J. Chilton Andrews, "Drift Whales on Nantucket: The Kindness of Moshup," *Man in the Northeast* 23 (1982): 17–38.

11. William S. Simmons, "Narragansett," in Bruce G. Trigger, ed., William C. Sturtevant, genl. ed., *Handbook of North American Indians, Northeast,* vol. 15 (Washington, D.C., 1978), 196; Jack P. Greene, *Pursuits of Happiness: The Social Development of Early Modern British Colonies and the Formation of American Culture* (Chapel Hill, N.C., 1988), 178.

12. Antipas Newman to John Winthrop Jr., July 17, 1660, Winthrop Family Transcripts.

13. Roger Ludlow to John Winthrop, June 1638, *Winthrop Papers,* 4: 43–48.

14. Humphrey Atherton and Edward Hutchinson to John Winthrop Jr., October 23, 1660, Winthrop Family Transcripts.

15. *Fones Records,* 13.

16. *United Colonies Records,* 2:286.

17. The list of Atherton Company members can be found in *Proceedings of the Massachusetts Historical Society,* 2nd ser., 2 (1885–1886): 151–52; and *Fones Records,* 12–13. Profiles of United Colonies commissioners can be found in Harry M. Ward, *The United Colonies of New England, 1643–90* (New York, 1961), 400–11.

18. Carla Gardina Prestana, *The English Atlantic in an Age of Revolution, 1640–1661* (Cambridge, Mass., 2004), 214–16.

19. Ibid., 216.

20. John M. Murrin, "The New York Charter of Liberties, 1683 and 1693," in Stephen L. Schechter, ed., *Roots of the Republic: American Founding Documents Interpreted* (Madison, Wis., 1990), 47–65; Michael Kammen, *Colonial New York: A History* (New York, 1975), 71–87; Robert C. Ritchie, *The Duke's Province: A Study of New York Politics and Society, 1664–1691* (Chapel Hill, N.C., 1977), 9–46.

21. Neal Salisbury, "Toward the Covenant Chain: Iroquois and Southern New England Algonquians, 1637–1684," in Daniel K. Richter and James H. Merrell, eds., *Beyond the Covenant Chain: The Iroquois and Their Neighbors in Indian North America, 1600–1800* (Syracuse, N.Y., 1987), 66–67; Daniel K. Richter, *The Ordeal of the Longhouse: The Peoples of the Iroquois League in the Era of European Colonization* (Chapel Hill, N.C., 1992), 99–104 (quote on 104); Richard I. Melvoin, *New England Outpost: War and Society in Colonial Deerfield* (New York, 1989), 43–47; Colin G. Calloway, *The Western Abenakis of Vermont, 1600–1800: War, Migration, and the Survival of an Indian People* (Norman, Okla., 1990), 70–74.

22. Edward Hutchinson Jr. to Samuel Marverick, September 29, 1662, Winthrop Family Transcripts.

23. The King to the Commissioners of New England, December 5, 1665, CSP, CO 1/19, No. 140; *Rhode Island Records*, 2:127–28.

24. Jenny Hale Pulsipher, *Subjects unto the Same King: Indians, English, and the Contest for English Authority in Colonial New England* (Philadelphia, 2005), 37–52.

25. *Rhode Island Records*, 2:127–28.

26. Declaration of his Majesty's Commissioners to the Narragansett Indians, March 20, 1665, CSP, CO 1/19, No. 40.

27. Ibid.

28. Sir Robt. Carr, George Cartwright, and Sam. Mavericke to [Col. Nicolls], March 20, 1665, CSP, CO 1/19, No. 39.

29. Pulsipher, *Subjects unto the Same King*, 55–57 (quote on 56); Jennings, *Invasion of America*, 282–85.

30. Douglas Edward Leach, *Flintlock and Tomahawk: New England in King Philip's War* (New York, 1958), 23.

31. On the epidemic, see Timothy Bratton, "The Identity of the New England Indian Epidemic of 1616–1619," *Bulletin of the History of Medicine* 62 (1988): 351–83; Dean Snow and Kim M. Lanphear, "European Contact and Indian Depopulation in the Northeast: The Timing of the First Epidemics," *Ethnohistory* 35 (1988): 15–33; Catherine C. Carlson, George L. Armelagos, Ann Magennis, "Impact of Disease on the Precontact and Early Historic Populations of New England and the Maritimes," in John W. Verano and Douglas H. Ubelaker, eds., *Disease and Demography in the Americas* (Washington, D.C., 1992), 141–52; and Brenda J. Baker, "Pilgrim's Progress and Praying Indians: The Biocultural Consequences of Contact in Southern New England," in Clark Spencer Larsen and George R. Milner, eds., *In the Wake of Contact: Biological Responses to Conquest* (New York, 1994), 35–44. On Wampanoag-English relations, see Virginia DeJohn Anderson, "King Philip's Herds: Indians, Colonists, and the Problem of Livestock in Early New England," *William and Mary Quarterly*, 3rd ser., 51, no. 4 (October 1994): 601–24; David J. Silverman, *Faith and Boundaries: Colonists, Christianity, and Community among the Wampanoag Indians of Martha's Vineyard, 1600–1871* (New York, 2005), 39–43, 89, 100; James Drake, *King Philip's War: Civil War in New England, 1675–1676* (Amherst, Mass., 1999), 62–66; Laurie Weinstein, "Indian vs. Colonist: Competition for Land in Seventeenth-Century Plymouth Colony" (Ph.D., diss., Southern Methodist University, 1983).

32. Robert Carr to Lord Arlington, April 9, 1666, Yale Indian Papers, 1666.04.09.00.

33. Roger Williams to Sir Robert Carr, March 1, 1665/66, *Williams Correspondence*, 551.

34. King Philip to the Chief Officer of the town of Long Island, May 7, 1666, CSP, CO 1/20, no. 68. On Sassamon, see Jill Lepore, *The Name of War: King Philip's War and the Origins of American Identity* (New York, 1998), 21–47.

35. Quantisset petition to the Massachusetts General Court, September 1667, and John Eliot to the Massachusetts General Court, September 3, 1667, Misc. Ms., MHS; *Massachusetts Records*, 4:357–59, 386; Massachusetts Archives Series, 30:138, 138a, 150, 151, Massachusetts State Archives, Boston; Roger Williams to the General Court of Massachusetts Bay, May 7, 1668, *Williams Correspondence*, 576–79.

36. Minutes of the Massachusetts General Court, October 5, 1669, misc. photostats, MHS.

37. *Massachusetts Records*, 4:358.

38. *Plymouth Colony Records*, 4:164–66. See also 4:151.

39. Richard Cogley, *John Eliot's Mission to the Indians before King Philip's War* (Cambridge, Mass., 1999), 154–65.

40. John Eliot to the New England Company, October 10, 1652, *New England Historic Genealogical Register* (Boston, 1882), 294–95.

41. Michael Leroy Oberg, *Uncas: First of the Mohegans* (Ithaca, N.Y., 2003), 167–68.

42. Daniel Gookin, "Historical Collections of the Indians in New England," MHSC, 1st ser., 1 (1792): 191.

43. Oberg, *Uncas*, 169.

44. Lepore, *Name of War*, 39.

45. Gookin, "Historical Collections," 210.

46. Thomas, "Maelstrom of Change," 96; Lynn Ceci, "Watchers of the Pleiades: Ethnoastronomy among Native Cultivators in Northeastern North America," *Ethnohistory* 25 (1978): 309–10.

47. On New Englanders' anti-Catholicism and related fears of Indians during this and slightly later periods, see Carla Gardina Prestana, *Protestant Empire: Religion and the Making of a British Atlantic World* (Philadelphia, 2009); Owen Stanwood, *The Empire Reformed: English America in the Age of the Glorious Revolution* (Philadelphia, 2011); John Demos, *The Unredeemed Captive: A Family Story from Early America* (New York, 2004); Thomas S. Kidd, *The Protestant Interest: New England after Puritanism* (New Haven, Conn., 2004); Mary Beth Norton, *In the Devil's Snare: The Salem Witchcraft Crisis of 1692* (New York, 2002).

48. Thomas Stanton to John Mason, July 8, 1669, Yale Indian Papers, 1669.07.08.00.

49. John Mason to John Winthrop Jr., March 8, 1668/69, and Cassacinamon's Petition, May 6, 1669, Winthrop Family Transcripts.

50. Testimony of Thomas James, June 29, 1669, Yale Indian Papers, 1669.06.29.00; Letter from Long Island, June 30, 1669, Yale Indian Papers, 1669.06.30.00.

51. Deposition of John Gallop and Thomas Stanton, July 1669, Yale Indian Papers, 1669.07.00.01.

52. Thomas Stanton to John Mason, July 8, 1669, Yale Indian Papers, 1669.07.08.00.

53. *Plymouth Records*, 5:63.

54. John Mason to John Allyn, July 7, 1669, Yale Indian Papers, 1669.07.04.00

55. J. Frederick Fausz, "Opechancanough: Indian Resistance Leader," in David Sweet and Gary B. Nash, eds., *Struggle and Survival in Colonial America* (Berkeley, Cal., 1981), 21–37; Andrew L. Knaut, *The Pueblo Revolt of 1680: Conquest and Resistance in Seventeenth Century New Mexico* (Norman, Okla. 1995); Alan Gallay, *The Indian Slave Trade: The Rise of the English Empire in the American South, 1670–1717* (New Haven, Conn., 2002), 259–87, 315–44; William L. Ramsey, *The Yamasee War: A Study of Culture, Economy, and Conflict in the Colonial South* (Lincoln, Neb., 2008); Steven J. Oatis, *A Colonial Complex: South Carolina's Frontiers in the Era of the Yamasee War, 1680–1730* (Lincoln, Neb., 2004).

56. Indian population figures are necessarily approximate, but it is clear that most historians have underestimated the size of Indian population on the eve of King Philip's War by half by ignoring entire Indian groups (such as Wampanoags on the Cape and islands, and the Wagunks, Tunxis, and Western Niantics in Connecticut) and undercounting others. We've used the following estimates: 10,000 Narragansetts (including the Eastern Niantics), 3,000 Mohegans, 1,000 Pequots, 250 Western Niantics, 500 Tunxis and Wagunks, 2,500 "River Indians" (Norwotucks, Pocumtucks, Sokokis), 1,500 Nipmucks living outside of praying towns, 5,000 Praying Indians (Massachusetts, Cape Cod, Martha's Vineyard, and Nantucket), and 3,000 mainland Wampanoags under Philip. For some of these figures, we have drawn on English estimates of Indian fighting men in Gookin, "Historical Collections," and multiplied those numbers by five, assuming a certain amount of undercounting on the part of the English commentators. We have checked Gookin's numbers against the discussions of Indian population numbers in the following essays in *Handbook of North American Indians, Northeast*: Gordon M. Day, "Western Abenaki," 152–53; Bert Salwen, "Indians of Southern New England and Long Island: Early Period," 169; Simmons, "Narragansett," 196; Praying Indian numbers appear in Gookin, "Historical Collections." See the chart gathering his figures in Silverman, *Faith and Boundaries*, 80.

57. Letter from Long Island, June 30, 1669, Yale Indian Papers, 1669.06.30.00.

58. Letter from Thomas Stanton to John Mason, with a Postscript by Thomas Minor, July 8, 1669, Yale Indian Papers, 1669.07.08.00.

59. Shawn G. Wiemann, "Lasting Marks: The Legacy of Robin Cassacinamon and the Survival of the Mashantucket Pequot Nation" (Ph.D., diss., University of New Mexico, 2011), 207–8.

60. Relation of Goodwife Osborn, July 20, 1669, Yale Indian Papers, 1669.07.20.00.

61. Quoted in Ward, *United Colonies*, 206.

62. *Connecticut Records*, 2:548–51.

63. *Rhode Island Records*, 2:267.

64. Regarding laughter, see James H. Merrell, "'The Customs of Our Countrey': Indians and Colonists in Early America," in Bernard Bailyn and Philip D. Morgan, eds. *Strangers within the Realm: Cultural Margins of the First British Empire* (Chapel Hill, N.C., 1991), 120.

65. *Rhode Island Records*, 2:264–65, 268–69.

66. Ibid., 2:268–69.

67. Ibid., 2:269–74.

68. Ibid., 2:271.

69. Ibid., 2:270.

70. Ibid.

71. John Mason to John Allyn, July 4, 1669, Yale Indian Papers, 1669.07.04.00.

72. Richter, *Ordeal of the Longhouse*, 102–4; Jon Parmenter, *Edge of the Woods: Iroquoia, 1534–1701* (East Lansing, Mich., 2010), 122–27.

73. Gookin, "Historical Collections," 167; Reuben Gold Thwaites, ed., *The Jesuit Relations and Allied Documents*, 73 vols. (Cleveland, Ohio, 1896–1901), 53:141.

5. Ninigret's Narragansett War

1. Jenny Hale Pulsipher, *Subjects unto the Same King: Indians, English, and the Contest for Authority in Colonial New England* (Philadelphia, 2006), 128.

2. Ibid., 95 (quote).

3. On this crisis, see John Richards to John Winthrop Jr., April 18, 1671, Winthrop Family Transcripts; *Plymouth Records*, 5:63–65, 73–75, 77, 79; Francis Jennings, *The Invasion of America: Indians, Colonialism, and the Cant of Conquest* (Chapel Hill, N.C., 1975), 293–94; Pulsipher, *Subjects unto the Same King*, 94–100; Douglas Edward Leach, *Flintlock and Tomahawk: New England in King Philip's War* (New York, 1958), 26–30.

4. Tobias Sanders to Fitz John Winthrop, July 3, 1675, MHSC, 5th ser., 1 (1871), 426.

5. Roger Williams to John Winthrop Jr., June 25, 1675, *Williams Correspondence*, 693–95.

6. Leach also argued that Philip acted before he was ready or before preparations were complete. See *Flintlock and Tomahawk*, 48.

7. Josiah Winslow and Thomas Hinckley, "Narrative Shewing the Manor of the Beginning of the Present Warr with the Indians of Mount Hope and Pocassett," in Nathaniel B. Shurtleff and David Pulsifer, eds, *Records of the Colony of New Plymouth in New England*, 12 vols. (Boston, 1855–1861), 10:362–64; Jill Lepore, *The Name of War: King Philip's War and the Origins of American Identity* (New York, 1998), 21–47; James P. and Jeanne Ronda, "The Death of John Sassamon: An Exploration in Writing New England Indian History," *American Indian Quarterly* 1 (1974): 91–102; Yasuhide Kawashima, *Igniting King Philip's War: The John Sassamon Murder Trial* (Lawrence, Kans., 2001), 76–87; and James D. Drake, "Symbol of a Failed Strategy: The Sassamon Trial, Political Culture, and King Philip's War," *American Indian Culture and Research Journal* 19 (1995): 111–41.

8. William Pynchon to John Winthrop Jr., May 10, 1671, in Carl Bridenbaugh, ed., *The Pynchon Papers*, 2 vols. (Boston, 1982), 1:86–87; William Hubbard, *A Narrative of the Troubles with the Indians in New England* (Boston, 1677), in Samuel G. Drake, ed., *The History of the Indian Wars in New England, from the First Settlement to the Termination of the War with King Philip, in 1677*, 2 vols. (Roxbury, Mass., 1865), 44; Samuel G. Drake, *The Old Indian Chronicle; Being a Collection of Exceedingly Rare Tracts, Written and Published in the Time of King Philip's War* (Boston, 1836), 137–38; Katherine Alysia Grandjean, "Reckoning: The Communications Frontier in Early New England" (Ph.D., diss., Harvard University, 2008), 252–55.

9. Indian Child Murdered at Quoketaug, December 28, 1671, "Crimes and Misdemeanors Series, 1662–1789," ser. I, vol. 1, roll 22, doc. 50, Connecticut State Archives.

10. J. Winthrop Jr. to Wait Winthrop, January 25, 1672, Winthrop Family Transcripts; also in Eva Butler, "Notes on Indian Ethnology and History: The Moweam Case," *Bulletin of the Archaeological Society of Connecticut* 27 (December 1953): 36.

11. "Crimes and Misdemeanors Series, 1662–1789," ser. I, vol. 1, roll 22, doc. 51b, Connecticut State Archives; Summons of Sabyanatoosit, January 17, 1672, Yale Indian Papers, 1672.01.17.00.

12. *Connecticut Records*, 2:178–79.

13. Richard Smith Jr. to J. Winthrop Jr., June 25, 1673, Daniel Updike, *Richard Smith, First English Settler of the Narragansett Country, Rhode Island, with a Series of Letters Written by His Son, Richard Smith, Jr., to Members of the Winthrop Family and Notes on Cocumscussuc, Smith's Estate in Narragansett* (Boston, 1937), 96–97.

14. Daniel Gookin, "An Historical Account of the Doings and Sufferings of the Christian Indians in New England in the Years 1675, 1676, 1677," *Transactions and Collections of the American Antiquarian Society* 2 (1836): 434, 450,

454; Thomas Walley to John Cotton Jr., November 18, 1675, Curwen Family Papers, box 1, file 3, American Antiquarian Society (Worcester, Mass.); William Hubbard, *A Narrative of the Indian Wars in New England, from the first Planting Thereof in the Year 1607 to the Year 1677* (1677; Boston, 1775), 56; Commissioners of the United Colonies to Anonymous, November 12, 1675, *Further Letters on King Philip's War* (Providence, R.I., 1923), 18–19; William Harris, *A Rhode Islander Reports on King Philip's War: The Second William Harris Letter of August, 1676*, ed., Douglas Leach (Providence, R.I., 1963), 66; Increase Mather, *A Brief History of the Warr with the Indians in New-England* [Boston, 1676], in Richard Slotkin and James K. Folsom, eds., *So Dreadfull a Judgment: Puritan Responses to King Philip's War, 1676–1677* (Middletown, Conn., 1978), 94–99; Leach, *Flintlock and Tomahawk*, 50–102; Richard Melvoin, *New England Outpost: War and Society in Colonial Deerfield* (New York, 1989), 41–47, 97–107; James D. Drake, *King Philip's War: Civil War in New England, 1675–1676* (Amherst, Mass., 1999), 84–90, 103; Pulsipher, *Subjects unto the Same King*, 106–18, 138–41.

15. R. Smith Jr. to J. Winthrop Jr., September 3, 1675, in *Richard Smith*, 111; Yale Indian Papers, 1675.07.08.00.

16. R. Williams to J. Winthrop Jr., June 27, 1675, *Williams Correspondence*, 698–99; Andrew Lipman, "'A Meanes to Knitt Them Togeather': The Exchange of Body Parts in the Pequot War," *William and Mary Quarterly*, 3rd ser., 65, no. 1 (January 2008): 3–28.

17. R. Williams to J. Winthrop Jr., June 25, 1675, *Williams Correspondence*, 693–95 (quote on 694).

18. Ibid., 693–95.

19. R. Williams to J. Winthrop Jr., June 27 1675, *Williams Correspondence*, 698–99.

20. Joshua Micah Marshall, "'A Melancholy People': Anglo-Indian Relations in Early Warwick, Rhode Island, 1642–1675," *New England Quarterly* 68 (1995): 402–28.

21. R. Williams to J. Winthrop Jr., June 27, 1675, *Williams Correspondence*, 698.

22. CSP, CO 1/34, No. 108.

23. Michael Leroy Oberg, *Uncas. First of the Mohegans* (Ithaca, N.Y., 2003), 171–87.

24. *Connecticut Records*, 2:338.

25. Tobias Sanders to Fitz John Winthrop, July 3, 1675, MHSC, 5th ser., 1:426.

26. Ibid., 1:426–27; Thomas Stanton to John Winthrop Jr., September 22, 1675, Winthrop Family Papers.

27. *Connecticut Records*, 2:338.

28. R. Smith Jr. to J. Winthrop Jr., September 3, 1675, in *Richard Smith*, 110–11.

29. R. Smith Jr. to J. Winthrop Jr., September 12, 1675, in *Richard Smith*, 112.

30. R. Smith Jr. to J. Winthrop Jr., August 5, 1675, in *Richard Smith*, 110; Chapin, *Sachems of the Narragansetts*, 79.

31. This account, including all quotes in the following three paragraphs, are from Thomas Stanton to R. Smith Jr., September 13 and September 19, 1675, Winthrop Family Papers, reel 12, Unbound Manuscripts.

32. R. Smith Jr. to Fitz-John Winthrop, November 3, 1675, in *Richard Smith*, 114; Daniel Gookin to R. Smith Jr., November 21, 1675, Massachusetts Archives Series, 30:188, Massachusetts State Archives, Boston.

33. *Connecticut Records*, 2:368.

34. Ibid., 2:371.

35. Tobias Saunders to Wait Winthrop, July 7, 1675, Winthrop Family Papers.

36. Account of Coates delivered to Cornman for Ninigret, John Allen to J. Winthrop Jr., November 23, 1675, Winthrop Family Papers; Thomas Stanton to Fitz-John Winthrop, November 4, 1675, Winthrop Family Papers

37. Thomas Stanton to John Winthrop Jr., September 22, 1675, Winthrop Family Papers.

38. Petition of Thomas Stanton, October 2, 1677, Colonial War Series, doc. 133, Connecticut State Archives, Hartford.

39. Ibid.

40. John Stanton to Fitzjohn Winthrop, May 12, 1685, MHSC, 5th ser., 9 (1885): 140–41.

41. Richard S. Dunn, *Puritans and Yankees: The Winthrop Dynasty of New England, 1630–1717* (Princeton, N.J., 1962), 220–26.

42. Testimony from Sarah Pickering and Confession by William Smith, September 29, 1675, Massachusetts Archives Series, 30:177, Massachusetts State Archives, Boston; Leach, *Flintlock and Tomahawk*, 115.

43. *United Colonies Records*, 2:360–61.

44. Hubbard, *Narrative of the Troubles*, Postcript, 59–60.

45. *United Colonies Records*, 2:360–61; *Plymouth Records*, 10:357; Governor Leverett to Sir Joseph Williamson, December 18, 1675, CSP, CO 1/35, Nos. 61, 61 I; Yale Indian Papers, 1675.11.19.00; Leach, *Flintlock and Tomahawk*, 115–21.

46. Stanton to Fitz-John Winthrop, November 4, 1675, Winthrop Family Papers, reel 12, unbound manuscripts.

47. Hubbard, *Narrative of the Troubles*, 164–65, 178–81, 194–95.

48. Sherburne F. Cook, "Interracial Warfare and Population Decline among the New England Indians," *Ethnohistory* 20 (1973): 1–24; Russell

Bourne, *The Red King's Rebellion: Racial Politics in New England, 1675–1678* (New York, 1990), 12, 36, 242–43; Michael J. Pulgisi, *Puritans Besieged: The Legacies of King Philip's War in the Massachusetts Bay Colony* (Lanham, Md., 1991), ch. 4; Neal Salisbury, "Introduction: Mary Rowlandson and Her Removes," in Salisbury, ed., *The Sovereignty and Goodness of God, Together with the Faithfulness of His Promises Displayed: Being a Narrative of the Captivity and Restoration of Mrs. Mary Rowlandson and Related Documents* (Boston, 1997), 1.

49. Franklin B. Hough, ed., *Narrative of the Causes which Led to Philip's Indian War, of 1675 and 1676, by John Easton of Rhode Island* (Albany, N.Y., 1858), 145; Gookin, "Historical Account of the Doings and Sufferings of the Christian Indians," 488; Examination and Relation of James Quannapaquait, January 24, 1675, in Salisbury, ed., *Sovereignty and Goodness of God,* 124; Samuel Symonds to Sir Joseph Williamson, April 6, 1676, CSP, CO 1/36, no. 43; *Williams Correspondence,* 712; Mather, *Brief History,* 110. Generally, see Emerson Woods Baker II, "New Evidence on the French Involvement in King Philip's War," *Maine Historical Society Quarterly* 28 (1988): 85–91.

50. *Connecticut Records,* 2:397, 404, 478; Mather, *Brief History,* 113–14, 134; Samuel Symonds to Sir Joseph Williamson, April 6, 1676, CSP, CO 1/36, no. 43; Hough, ed., *Narrative of the Causes which Led to Philip's Indian War,* 178–79; Answer of Edward Randolph to Several Heads of Query concerning the Present State of New England, October 12, 1676, CSP, CO 1/37, no. 70, and CO 5/903, 114–16; Examination and Relation of James Quannapaquait, in Salisbury, ed., *Sovereignty and Goodness of God,* 124.

51. Leach, *Flintlock and Tomahawk,* 142.

52. Ibid., 200–203.

53. To see how community divisions could serve dual purposes during wartime, see Colin G. Calloway, *The American Revolution in Indian Country: Crisis and Diversity in Native American Communities* (New York, 1995), 65–84; and Karim M. Tiro, "A 'Civil' War? Rethinking Iroquois Participation in the American Revolution," *Explorations in Early American Culture* 4 (January 2000): 148–65.

54. *Williams Correspondence,* 2:712–14.

55. Harris, *A Rhode Islander Reports,* 67.

56. Richard Johnson, "The Search for a Usable Indian: An Aspect of the Defense of Colonial New England," *Journal of American History* 64 (1977): 622–51.

57. As cited in Leach, *Flintlock and Tomahawk,* 146.

58. *Connecticut Records,* 2:420–21, 427; Mather, *Brief History,* 115.

59. Thomas Stanton to John Allyn, May 10, 1676, Yale Indian Papers 1676.05.10.00.

60. Noyes's History, MHSC, 3rd ser., 6 (1837): 186–87.

61. Ibid.

62. Mather, *Brief History*, 115; Hubbard, *History of the Indian Wars*, 60.

63. Nathaniel Saltonstall, *A New and Further Narrative of the State of New England* [1676] in Charles H. Lincoln, ed., *Narratives of the Indian Wars, 1675–1699* (New York, 1913), 91.

64. Kathleen Bragdon, *Native People of Southern New England, 1500–1650* (Norman, Okla., 1996), 235.

65. Examination of Pessicus's Messenger Wuttawawaigkessuek Sucqunch, April 29, 1676, Yale Indian Papers, 1676.04.29.01.

66. William Harris to Sir Joseph Williamson, August 12, 1676, *Collections of the Rhode Island Historical Society*, vol. 10 (Providence, R.I., 1902), 177; Hubbard, *Narrative of the Troubles*, 205–7.

67. Leach, *Flintlock and Tomahawk*, 211, 221–22, 233, 233–36. Generally, see 199–241.

68. *Connecticut Records*, 2:441; Thomas Stanton Sr. to John Allyn, May 10, 1676, Yale Indian Papers 1676.05.10.00.

69. *Connecticut Records*, 2:441.

70. Petition of Nowwanquanu, Ninigret's Brother-in-Law, to the Connecticut General Court, October 7, 1676, Yale Indian Papers, 1676.10.07.00.

71. *Connecticut Records*, 2:427; Mather, *Brief History*, 115.

Epilogue

1. Winthrop, *Journal*, 1: 191–93. Generally on issues surrounding Indians, colonists, and livestock, see Virginia DeJohn Anderson, *Creatures of Empire: How Domestic Animals Transformed Early America* (New York, 2004).

2. Poquium is identified as Ninigret's brother-in-law in *United Colonies Records*, 1:208. Howard W. Chapin, *Sachems of the Narragansetts* (Providence, R.I., 1931), 92, and Lafantasie, ed., *Williams Correspondence*, 177, n4, identify him as Ninigret's brother.

3. *Connecticut Records*, 1:27.

4. *United Colonies Records*, 1:208. On the price of horses, see Katherine Alysia Grandjean, "Reckoning: The Communications Frontier in Early New England" (Ph.D., diss., Harvard University, 2008), 175–76.

5. Mason, *Brief History of the Pequot War*, in Charles Orr, ed., *History of the Pequot War: The Cotemporary Accounts of Mason, Underhill, Vincent, and Gardener* (Cleveland, Ohio, 1897), 80.

6. The Articles of Agreement are reprinted in Alden T. Vaughan, *New England Frontier: Puritans and Indians 1620–1675*, 3rd ed. (Norman, Okla., 1995), 340–41.

7. *United Colonies Records*, 1:169.

8. *Connecticut Records*, 1:227.

9. See the entry for Filer in James Savage, *Genealogical Dictionary of the First Settlers of New England*, 4 vols. (Boston, 1860–62), 158; and for Fyler in the New England Historic Genealogical Society database.

10. *United Colonies Records*, 2:224; *Connecticut Records*, 1:362, 370, 2:119.

11. On this aftermath, see Paul R. Campbell and Glenn W. LaFantasie, "Scattered to the Winds of Heaven: Narragansett Indians, 1676–1880," *Rhode Island History* 37 (1979): 69–70; Michael J. Pulgisi, *Puritans Besieged: The Legacies of King Philip's War in the Massachusetts Bay Colony* (Lanham, Md., 1991); Colin G. Calloway, *The Western Abenakis of Vermont, 1600–1800: War, Migration, and the Survival of an Indian People* (Norman, Okla., 1990), 79–89; Evan Haefeli and Kevin Sweeney, "Wattanummon's World: Personal and Tribal Identity in the Algonquian Diaspora, c. 1660–1712," in William Cowan, ed., *Proceedings of the 25th Algonquian Conference* (Ottawa, 1993), 212–24; Margaret Ellen Newell, "The Changing Nature of Indian Slavery in New England, 1670–1720," in Colin G. Calloway and Neal Salisbury, eds., *Reinterpreting New England Indians and the Colonial Experience* (Boston, 2003), 106–36; James Drake, *King Philip's War: Civil War in New England, 1675–1676* (Amherst, Mass., 1999), 168–96; Jill Lepore, *The Name of War: King Philip's War and the Origins of American Identity* (New York, 1998), 150–70.

12. Campbell and Lafantasie, "Scattered to the Winds of Heaven"; John Wood Sweet, *Bodies Politic: Negotiating Race in the American North, 1730–1830* (Baltimore, 2003), 15–57; Daniel R. Mandell, *Tribe, Race, History: Native American in Southern New England, 1780–1880* (Baltimore, 2008); David J. Silverman, *Red Brethren: The Brothertown and Stockbridge Indians and the Problem of Race in Early America* (Ithaca, N.Y., 2010); Brad Jarvis, *The Brothertown Nation of Indians: Land Ownership and Nationalism in Early America, 1740–1840* (Lincoln, Neb., 2010); Linford Fisher, *The Indian Great Awakening: Religion and the Shaping of Native Cultures in Early America* (New York, 2012).

Glossary of Key People and Places

Adussah: Sachem of the Manisees of Block Island. Implicated in the 1636 murder of John Oldham.

Atherton, Humphrey: A military officer of Dorchester, Massachusetts. He led the United Colonies' 1650 expedition against the Narragansetts. In the late 1650s and 1660s he was leader the so-called Atherton Company in its purchases of Narragansett land.

Awashaw: Also known as Awashous. One of Ninigret's right-hand men.

Canonchet: Son of Miantonomi. Nephew of Pessacus. Prominent military leader among Narragansetts during King Philip's War.

Canonicus: Sachem of the Narragansetts until his death of old age in 1647. Uncle of Miantonomi. Father of Mixano.

Cassacinamon, Robin: Sachem of the Western Pequots of Nameag, Noank, and Mashantucket, from the 1640s until his death in 1692. A close ally of John Winthrop Jr.

Caushawashott: See Garrett, Harmon

Cocumscussoc: Site of a trading post manned by Roger Williams and then Richard Smith on the site of modern Wickford, Rhode Island.

Cojonoquant: Brother of Miantonomi and Pessacus. One of the grantees in a series of Narragansett land sales in the late 1650s.

Corchaugs: Community of Long Island Indians living on the North Fork just west of Southold.

Cowesit: Tribute-paying community of the Narragansetts on the northwest side of Narragansett Bay.

Dennison, George: Sometime interpreter and go-between to Indians around his home in New London, Connecticut.

Eliot, John: Missionary to Indians near Boston and minister in Roxbury, Massachusetts, from the 1640s until his death in 1690. A driving force behind the translation of the Bible into the Wampanoag language.

Gardiner, Lion: Military commander at Fort Saybrook, owner and sometime resident of Gardiner's Island off of Long Island, sometime resident of East Hampton, and a strong ally of the Montaukett sachem Wyandanch.

Garrett, Harmon: Also known as Cashawashet (also Caushawashott) and Wequashcook (II). Son of Wepitamock. Brother of Wequashcook (I)

Gookin, Daniel: Massachusetts Superintendent of Praying Indians during 1670s. Close associate of missionary John Eliot.

Jannemo: Ninigret's original name, which he dropped shortly after the death of Miantonomi.

Manisees: The Indians of Block Island. Tribute payers to the Narragansetts. Implicated in the murder of John Oldham in 1636.

Mason, John: Officer of Connecticut forces during the Pequot War. Longtime member of the Connecticut General Court (or legislature) and deputy governor from 1660 to 1668. Chosen several times as one of Connecticut's commissioners to the United Colonies. Uncas's primary English advocate. Died in 1672.

Massasoit: Also known as Ousamequin. Sachem of Pokanoket and paramount sachem of the Wampanoags. Father of Wamsutta (or Alexander) and Metacom (or Philip). Ally of Plymouth colony. Died in 1661.

Matantuck: See Quaiapen.

Mattakist: See Newcomb.

Metacom: See Philip.

Misquamicut: Landed area in what is now southwestern Rhode Island located between the Pawcatuck River on the west and Ninigret Pond on the east. Sold by Sosoa to Rhode Island land speculators in 1660. Becomes the town of Westerly.

Mixano. Also known as Meeksaw and Meyanno. Eldest son of Canonicus. Marries Matantuck (or Quaiapen), the sister of Ninigret, in the 1630s. Father of Scuttup, Quequaquenuit (or Gideon), and Quinimiquet (or Conimicut). Died in the winter of 1656–57.

Newcomb: Also known as Nucom, Newcome, Mattaeckis, Mattackcees, and Mattakist. Often served Ninigret as a deputy and manager. Lived for a time near the Hudson River. Known for his ability to repair firearms.

Nipmucks: Native people of what is now known as central Massachusetts. Particular communities paid tribute to the Mohegans, Narragansetts, or Wampanoags. The Narragansetts claimed authority over some Nipmuck communities in the Blackstone and Quinebaug River valleys.

Pawcatuck Pequots: A community of survivors from the Pequot War who organized under the leadership of the Pequot-Niantic sachem, Wequashcook, and then Harmon Garrett. Initially located around Weekapaug and Miasquamicut east of the Pawcatuck River, but shortly before King Philip's War had relocated to the west side amid tensions with Ninigret.

Pawtuxet: Native community that paid tribute to the Narragansetts. Located on the west side of Narragansett Bay between the English towns on Warwick and Providence. Under the authority of the sachem Socononoco.

Pessacus: Brother of Miantonomi. About twenty years old when he became primary Narragansett sachem in 1643 with the death of Miantonomi. Also known as Quissucquansh, Sucquans, Wemosit, Moosup, and Canonicus. Died in 1676.

Pettaquamscutt: Area around Point Judith on the southwest point of Narragansett Bay.

Philip: Also Metacom, Metacomet, and Pumetacom. Sachem of the Pokanoket Wampanoag community and the general Wampanoag tribe during the 1670s. Successor to his father, Massasoit, and his brother, Wamsutta or Alexander. Leader of the Indian war effort against the English in 1675–76. Died in 1676.

Podunks: Native people inhabiting what is now Windsor and East Hartford, Connecticut.

Pomham: Sachem of Shawomet (modern day Warwick, Rhode Island) and a tributary of the Narragansetts. Died in 1676.

Quaiapen: Also known as Matantuck, Magnus, and the "Old Queen." Sister of Ninigret. Wife of Mixano. Mother of Scuttup, Quequaquenuit (or Gideon), and Quinimiquet (or Conimicut). After the death of Mixano in the winter of 1656–57, she split the rule of his sachemship west of Cocumscossoc with her son, Scuttup. The United Colonies attacked her community in

December 1675 in the same campaign as the Great Swamp Fight. Killed by English-Indian forces on July 2, 1676.

Quantisset: A Nipmuck community of the Quinebaug River Valley.

Quinabaag: A Nipmuck community of the Quinebaug River Valley.

Sassacus: Primary sachem of the Pequots after the death of Tatobem and during the Pequot War.

Scuttup: A Narragansett sachem. Son of Mixano and Quaiapen.

Sequassen: Also known as Sequin. Sachem of the Wagunks near Hartford.

Setaukets: An Indian group on eastern Long Island near modern day Stony Brook.

Shawomet: Native community of what is now Warwick, Rhode Island. Tributary to the Narragansetts.

Socononoco: Sachem of Pawtuxet and a tributary to the Narragansetts.

Sosoa: A Pequot who later joined the Narragansetts and distinguished himself in war against his former people. Rewarded with land at Misquamicut, which he later sold to the English.

Stanton, Thomas: The primary interpreter to the Indians for Connecticut and the United Colonies.

Tatobem: Pequot sachem until his death in the early 1630s.

United Colonies: Military and foreign-policy alliance of Massachusetts, Plymouth, Connecticut, and New Haven founded in 1643. Governed by a body of eight commissioners, two from each member colony.

Unkechaugs: A Native people of eastern Long Island around what is now the community of Mastic.

Wabquisset: A Nipmuck community of the Quinebaug River Valley

Wagunks: A Native people of the Connecticut River Valley around Hartford.

Weekapaug: Niantic territory between Winnapaug and Quonochontaug ponds.

Wepitamock: Ninigret's brother. Father of Wequashcook.

Wequashcook (I): Son of Wepitamock, nephew of Ninigret, and brother of Caushawashott/Wequashcook (II)/Harmon Garrett. Leader of the Pawcatuck Pequots. Appears to have resided between Weekapaug Brook and

Pawcatuck River. Appears to have been killed by Long Island Indians in 1654.

Western Niantics: Native people living in the area of what is now Lyme, Connecticut. Closely affiliated with the Pequots at the time of the Pequot War. No relation to Ninigret's Niantics.

Weunquesh: Daughter of Ninigret and sunksquaw of the Niantics/Narragansetts shortly after her father's death in 1676.

Whitman, Valentine: An interpreter to the Indians for Connecticut and the United Colonies.

Williams, Roger: Founder of Rhode Island and an important figure in Narragansett-English relations as a trader, interpreter, scribe, and go-between. Died in 1683.

Winthrop, John, Jr.: Founder of New London, close ally of Robin Cassacimon, and prominent political figure in Connecticut as a commissioner to the United Colonies and governor of the colony. Died in 1676.

Winthrop, John, Sr.: Long-time governor of the Massachusetts Bay Colony during its early years. Died in 1649.

Wyandanch: Sachem of the Montauketts and a close ally of Lion Gardiner.

Index